Union Public Library

O9-BTN-589

SCREEN DOORS
AND SWEET TEA

SCREEN DOORS AND SWEET TEA

Recipes and Tales from a Southern Cook

Martha Hall Foose

Union Public Library

CLARKSON POTTER/PUBLISHERS

NEW YORK

Copyright © 2008
by Martha Foose
Photographs copyright © 2008
by Ben Fink

All rights reserved.
Published in the United States
by Clarkson Potter/Publishers,
an imprint of the
Crown Publishing Group,
a division of Random House,
Inc., New York.
www.crownpublishing.com
www.clarksonpotter.com

Clarkson N. Potter
is a trademark and Potter
and colophon are
registered trademarks of
Random House, Inc.

LIBRARY OF CONGRESS
CATALOGING-IN-PUBLICATION DATA
Foose, Martha Hall.
Screen doors and sweet tea :
recipes and tales from a Southern
cook /
Martha Hall Foose. — 1st ed.
p.   cm.
Includes index.
1. Cookery, American—Southern
style.   II. Title.
TX715.2.S68F65   2008
641.5975—dc22   2007031646

ISBN 978-0-307-35140-1

Printed in China

Design by Maggie Hinders

10 9 8 7 6 5 4 3 2 1

First Edition

This book is dedicated
to my dear son, Joseph Haque Bender,
my family, and my friends

Contents

Introduction

SOME PEOPLE MIGHT SAY I GOT WHAT I DESERVE, ENDING UP RIGHT BACK WHERE I STARTED, HERE IN MISSISSIPPI'S DELTA. Growing up in and around Yazoo City, Mississippi, I spent a lot of time daydreaming about how to get out of here. Oh, we had fun, mind you. But there was the whole wide world out there, and not much of it seemed to pass down Highway 49. Food always offered a ticket to adventure for me all my life. Some of those first experiences were visits to New Orleans, a city that still fascinates me with its unique flavors and mysterious tales. I remember sneaking into Tipitina's kitchen back door with my uncle to hear the Neville Brothers. I ate my way through the food tents with alligator po' boys and other exotic fare at Jazz Fest each spring break and had my first dress-up white-linen-tableclothed dinner at Antoine's. Other revelations about the world came by way of the occasional appearance of recipes brought back home as souvenirs by traveling relatives. Friends with family ties to faraway homelands informed and intrigued me with exotic spices.

Books offered alternative adventures to me as I grew up amid the kudzu. Mrs. Wilburn would read aloud to our fourth-grade class each morning from Willie Morris's books. We hung on every word, sending up a sorrowful "awww" when she would leave us hanging until the next day. For the first time I realized that a book could be about where you were from. Until then they had been about fairy-tale kingdoms or tales of old or distant places covered by *National Geographic*. Later the lovely Bea Donnelly, Dean of Girls at my high school, introduced me to Faulkner's story "The Bear," and my love of books about the South became firmly rooted.

I went to work right out of high school in Oxford, Mississippi, upstairs in the café at Square Books, which sparked a love of cookbooks. Legendary local cookbooks *Bayou Cuisine* and *Gourmet of the Delta* never left my kitchen and were referenced until dog-eared. As I grew up a bit more, food service offered employment to a girl looking for her first taste of independence.

Jobs from Austin to Aspen, Burlington to Los Angeles, and New Orleans to Minneapolis allowed me to take the ride on the ticket.

When I went off to cooking school in France, I quickly found out that to some people, being from the Mississippi Delta was exotic—as different as my fellow students' provenances were to me. It slowly came to light that when most of these folks thought of America, they thought of the South. To many of my new acquaintances it appeared that American music meant rhythm 'n' blues and jazz; tales of America were learned from Miss Eudora Welty; and when it came to food, fried chicken was for dinner. This sentiment seemed to echo throughout all my travels—anywhere from Africa to South America—and was even expressed by my *tuk-tuk* driver in Thailand.

I moved back home to the Delta about five years ago to our family's place, Pluto Plantation, and into the home I inherited from my grandmother. Homesickness brought me back. But what has kept me here is a love and appreciation for the land and its people. The hardscrabble life of hill-country Mississippi rolls down to the genteel seas of loam in the Delta and spreads out to a straight-lined horizon. Bordered by bayous, this place, described by Richard Ford as "the South's south," is in a constant state of change. The maneuverings of rivers change its borders, and migrations of people change its population. Still, folks hold on, conceivably out of hardheadedness, or perhaps because there is a unique bond here between the people of the Mississippi Delta and the alluvian plain on which they live.

All in all, this book is about my home, and I know no better way to tell its stories than through food. Recipes for collard greens and black-eyed peas capture our superstitions, but trust passes them along. Recipes like crisp, golden-rimmed tea cakes scented with nutmeg conjure dimly lit homes of elderly relations. The smell of a skillet bread browning on the stovetop transports me back in time to when this land was cleared at the end of the century before last. The slow simmering of my gumbos mimics the pace of our speech down here. The unadorned perfection of home-grown tomatoes paired with delicate lady peas is just one way for me to explain this place—and I guess myself, too.

I hope this album of recipes and memories imbues you with a sense of this extraordinary place as it lays bare the deep, rich textures, colors, rhythms, and flavors of my home. My wish is that you feel inspired to re-create them in your own home for a little taste of what life is like down South.

MAILBOX HAPPY HOUR
and Pick-Up Party Food

McCarty Pottery Juleps
Cool Clay Marked with the River

• • •

Lee and Pup, Pup and Lee. I have never heard the McCartys referred to other than as a couple. I might have caught a glimpse or two of them separately over my lifetime, but I can't recall. Lee is a tall drink of water and Pup is just a drop. The McCartys' place over in Marigold has brought many pottery collectors on a pilgrimage to the former mule barn in search of clean-lined vessels, thoughtful objects, and whimsical figures. Since 1958, the two have fashioned a world enrobed in cypress and bamboo, with a style so true it could never be dreamt of by anyone else.

To see their local clay, kiln-fired tumblers sitting in rows on the rough-hewn boards of their studio is to see the colors of the soil. Instantly, when you cradle one in your hand, the cool clay says to you, "You are holding this earth." All of their timeless pieces are stained with a dark, deep, humus-colored vein cut over the rim, signifying the river that formed the land of their homestead and provided the raw ingredients of their craft.

Traditionally, a sterling or pewter cup is used to serve juleps. To me, these drinks seem to taste a little sweeter and stay cool a little longer when insulated in Pup and Lee's Mississippi clay cups. • **SERVES 4**

¹/₂ cup turbinado (raw) sugar
4 sprigs fresh spearmint plus
more for garnish

8 ounces good Bourbon
Crushed ice

In a small saucepan, combine the sugar, ¹/₂ cup water, and the mint. Bring to a boil. Simmer over low heat for 5 minutes, or until the mixture is reduced to a thin syrup. Remove the mint. Allow the sugar syrup to cool and then chill it.

Fill each cup with 1 tablespoon mint syrup and 2 ounces Bourbon. Add crushed ice and stir until the mixture is well chilled and the cup is frosty cold. Garnish each with a sprig of mint. Serve posthaste.

NOTES

• By mint, I mean spearmint, not peppermint, which is too medicinal. Go ahead and use peppermint if you have croup.

• Mint is notorious for running amok in the yard. Plant it in containers to keep it in check. Try pineapple mint or lemon mint for a flavor boost and variety of color.

• Use bruised leaves to steep in the simple syrup, and save the jaunty sprigs to garnish the juleps and tickle the nose.

• Visit McCarty Pottery in Marigold, Mississippi, or online at mccartypottery.com.

• I have always enjoyed the story of Mint. Pluto, god of the Underworld, and a wood nymph fall in love. A jealous girlfriend turned her into a plant.

"FAUGH," Doctor Louis used to grimace, "I'd as soon as try to enjoy a mint julep by sucking through a straw as to attempt necking a pin-up gal while wearing boxing gloves."
—NASH BUCKINGHAM, *HE THAT KINDLED THE FIRE,* 1939

Mailbox Cocktail

Fold Down Door, Set Down Drink

• • •

Bobby T. started it a few years back. Out on Rural Route 2, mailboxes are all on the same side of the road. Lined up and spaced about three feet apart, marking each community, miles stretched out between clutches. The mail run is around four o'clock. About five most afternoons, nearly everybody on Pluto comes down to check the mail. Propped or perched on a variety of seating (old tractor seat, stump, log, lawn chair, wheelchair, four-wheeler, and tailgate), they go through their daily post, trusty dogs at their sides, mailbox doors folded down, with a drink of some sort resting on each one. As our newspaper comes a day late, everyone waits for the tractors to come in to hear the latest news of the field, as that is the latest news. Bobby T. also keeps bets on what day of the year the sunset will line right up with the road. It's generally a wonderful time of day. • SERVES 1

Crushed ice
At least 2 ounces good
    Bourbon

2 ounces ginger ale
Lime wedge

Fill an insulated tumbler with crushed ice. Pour the Bourbon over the ice. Top with the ginger ale and a squeeze of fresh lime.

NOTES

• I particularly enjoy Maker's Mark Bourbon in this drink.

• Allow 1 pound of ice per guest.

• When showing out for company, you can rim the glasses with lime juice and dip them in a small saucer of raw sugar. A slice of candied ginger added for more formal occasions is stimulating.

• Tervis Tumbler insulated cups are made of the same plastic used for airplane windows and are virtually indestructible. These tumblers will keep ice from melting on the hottest of days.

• "Mississippians will vote dry as long as they can stagger to the polls."

—WILL ROGERS

WHEN Steve Henderson Garcia was a little pie-faced boy, about ten, with a pretty firm grasp on English, his second language, he became fascinated by an ad in the back of a comic book for a "Regulation-Size B.B. Gun Pistol." We drove into town and got a money order, and sent it out, and then waited and waited. Every day Steve checked the mail. Many late-afternoon mailbox meetings were spent speculating on the delay. At last the package arrived. He methodically opened the package and, with bilingual indignation, Steve declared, "This is a damn toy! It is an insult."

Bloodies

With Pickled Snap Beans

• • •

NOTES

• Pureed tomato juice from seeded fresh tomatoes (whirled in a blender) makes these especially delightful. I choose Red Gold brand, if using canned juice. Make frozen cubes of additional tomato base so they don't dilute your cocktail as they melt.

• If using celery as a garnish, string it: Snap each stalk until it bends about $1/2$ inch up from the color change between white and green. The strong strings will stay attached. With a quick downward jerk, pull the strings down the length of the stalk.

• Serve and store the vegetable garnishes in ice to keep crisp.

• Pickapeppa sauce from Shooter's Hill, Jamaica, West Indies, is made from tomatoes, cane vinegar, mangos, tamarind, raisins, onions, peppers, and spices. Since 1921 the Pickapeppa Company has stuck with their method of aging the sauce in oak barrels for a year. The popular sauce is sometimes called Jamaican ketchup.

People have strong beliefs about the preparation of this vegetative restorer. (I hate to call it just a drink, and **cocktail** *seems too formal.) They like what they like, and don't mind critiquing others' handiwork. Additions I have come to know and appreciate (in large part owing to the enthusiasm of the preparer) include, but are not limited to, beef stock, oyster liquor, clam juice, and anchovy paste. Some versions almost fit as a meal replacement.*

Even once you have settled on a tomato juice base and your seasonings of choice, there is still the question of garnishes: celery (and, please, string before service as no one looks cute flossing his teeth), carrot sticks, pickled okra, olives, garlic cloves, shrimp, avocado slices, citrus twists and wedges. Pickled snap beans are my personal favorite.

Now, making Bloody Marys individually is fun and somewhat competitive. So, for parties I usually set up a Bloody Mary station with all conceivable ingredients.

If you serve these alongside cheese straws spiked with cayenne (see Yazoo Cheese Straws, page 17), the vicious circle of trying to extinguish the fire created from one with the other eventually leads to laughter that will relieve any lingering pangs from the night before or will set the day ablaze. • SERVES 1

3 dashes hot pepper sauce	Grated zest and juice of 1 lime
2 dashes Worcestershire sauce	$1/4$ cup tomato juice
Pinch of celery seeds	2 teaspoons Pickapeppa sauce
1 teaspoon prepared horseradish, or 2 teaspoons grated fresh	2 ounces chilled soy vodka
	Ice cubes
	Pickled Snap Beans (recipe follows)

In a tall glass combine the pepper sauce, Worcestershire, celery seeds, horseradish, lime zest and juice, tomato juice, and Pickapeppa sauce. Stir well to combine. Add the vodka and stir well. Fill the glass with ice, garnish with a pickled snap bean, and serve.

PICKLED SNAP BEANS

<small>MAKES 2 PINTS</small>

$^1\!/_2$ **pound haricots verts,**
    Blue Lake, or runner
    green beans

1 cup white vinegar
1 tablespoon sugar
2 tablespoons pickling spice

Submerge the beans in boiling salted water for 3 minutes or until tender, then plunge the beans into a bath of icy water to stop them from cooking and set the color. Drain well.

    Combine the beans, vinegar, $^1\!/_4$ cup cold water, sugar, and pickling spice in a food storage bag. Refrigerate for 24 hours. Drain and serve.

Cantaloupe Daiquiris
A Courtyard Concoction

• • •

The hottest I have ever been in my life was at 5:45 P.M., on August 29, 1998, on the no. 923 St. Charles Avenue streetcar in New Orleans. I had been working down in the French Quarter as pastry chef for Susan Spicer's Bayona. Some days the unique commute felt like a scene in a movie. After rattling down the boulevards, and immediately upon entering our Uptown digs, I stripped down and stood in the shower with only cold water running. I could almost hear the sizzle on contact. I really felt as if I had been braised.

The courtyards of New Orleans offer a haven from the heat. Shaded and mossy, planted with sweet-smelling Confederate Jasmine, they're like Mrs. Venable's arboretum in Suddenly Last Summer. *She had her trusty secretary deliver a daiquiri every day at five. The musky sweetness of the melon, married to the brightness of the basil and mint, suspended in an icy slurry, will cool an afternoon down to the slow simmer of twilight.* • SERVES 6

1 cantaloupe, seeded, peeled, and finely diced	1 tablespoon chopped basil leaves
1/2 cup sugar	1 cup light rum
1 tablespoon fresh lemon juice	4 cups crushed ice
1 tablespoon chopped mint leaves	

In a large bowl or food storage bag, combine the cantaloupe, sugar, lemon juice, mint, and basil. Let the melon macerate in the refrigerator until very soft and juicy, about 2 hours.

Meanwhile, chill glasses in the freezer.

When ready to serve, puree the melon mixture in a blender or food processor. Add the rum and ice, and blend until slushy.

NOTES

• When picking out a cantaloupe, see that there is no stem attached, as a melon plucks right off its vine when ripe. A cantaloupe does not ripen after being picked. It will, however, soften and get juicier if left in the sun. As you look over the melons in the market, pick them up and give the belly button a good sniff. It should smell sweet and melony; it may not be the prettiest one, but it will be the tastiest. A true cantaloupe does not have a netted skin; their skins are smooth. Most melons we see for sale as cantaloupes are actually muskmelons.

• The cantaloupe base can be made in advance and stored in the refrigerator for two days or frozen for a while.

• The rum in a finished batch of daiquiris will keep the mixture from freezing solid, so you can make the recipe a day ahead and store it in the freezer.

Milk Punch

Please, Whatever You Do

• • •

NOTES

• An easy method for making larger batches is to blend vanilla ice cream with a little milk and Bourbon.

• Steeping a split vanilla bean for several hours, or days, in the Bourbon to be used for milk punch intensifies the vanilla notes.

• I prefer the taste of freshly grated nutmeg. Small grinders with a housing to store the whole nutmeg are widely available.

• The French island of Bourbon in the Indian Ocean, now named Réunion, is home to vanilla beans used extensively in the production of vanilla extract.

• Bourbon is a whisky distilled from a mixture of corn, rye, and malt. Bourbon County, Kentucky, is home to some of the finest whisky makers in the world.

• I made this recipe on the highly competitive TV show *Iron Chef America,* and think the drink won it for the team.

The annual Cotton Ball put on by an auxiliary of civic-minded ladies is one of the biggest social events of the year. The themed gala raises money for a worthy cause; a few years back, Egypt was the theme and the members decked out the County Civic Center with pyramids and scarabs.

By chance a photographer was visiting the area for National Geographic—*a nice guy who grew up on the East Coast. He received a phone call early the morning after the ball from an older attorney, inquiring if the photographer had ever had milk punch. The photographer replied that he had not and was promptly invited over for a cup.*

Upon arriving he found two gentlemen on the patio, frosty drinks in hand, dressed in bedraggled formal attire with the first rays of sunrise glinting off their pharaoh headdresses and collars. "Honey, National Geographic *is here," the esquire called up the stairs. A few moments later, down the staircase descended the wives, with hairdos and makeup from the prior evening and clad in gold lamé pumps and negligees. After the ladies had taken up their cups, they sat down for a visit on patio furniture still a bit chilly from the morning dew. The lady of the house squealed, and shared with the visiting photojournalist that she had hopped out of bed so quickly she had not remembered her panties. As the sun brightened the day, she leaned across the table and took the photographer by the hand, looking deep into his eyes. With a look described to me as complete desire, she said, "Please, whatever you do, try not to make us look foolish." The northern gentleman caller never removed his camera from its bag.* • SERVES 1

1½ ounces good Bourbon or brandy

3 ounces half-and-half

1 teaspoon superfine sugar

Drop of vanilla extract

Ice cubes

Freshly grated nutmeg

Combine the Bourbon, half-and-half, sugar, and vanilla in a cocktail shaker with ice. Shake thoroughly until the mixture is cold and frothy. Strain into a highball glass filled with ice. Top with a grating of nutmeg.

Sweet Tea

Voted Best in the Delta, with Crooked-Neck Spoons

• • •

Sweet tea or unsweet tea? That is the question waitresses across the southeastern United States pose as a greeting to diners. As Dolly Parton proclaimed in her role as Truvy in the movie based on the play Steel Magnolias, *it is the "house wine of the South."*

The summer Mockingbird Bakery opened, Delta *magazine, our regional* Vanity Fair, *bestowed upon us the honor of "Best Sweet Tea." We had ordered dozens and dozens of those crooked-neck spoons that can hang on the side of an iced tea glass. In the following eighteen months, the spoons had almost all disappeared. I could not imagine they were getting thrown away. I even installed a magnetized trash can cover to catch them. I had scoured the place looking for them. Then one day, in the middle of the lunch rush, I spied a woman deftly swipe her tea spoon into her expensive handbag. As she was a regular customer and well regarded in the community, I decided to let her get away with the petty theft. I was, at the very least, glad that the mystery of the disappearing spoons had been solved. Several days later she returned with her usual luncheon coterie. I'll have you know that when the table was bussed, there was not a single crooked-neck spoon to be found. The next time she lunched with us, the spoons were left behind when she departed. I do not think she had reformed her ways; I think she simply had acquired a service for eight. The rest of the spoons must have been absconded with by similar crooks.* • MAKES 3 QUARTS

4 pitcher-size cold-brew tea bags, or 6 tablespoons orange pekoe tea leaves in a diffuser	3/4 cup sugar Ice cubes 2 lemons, sliced Fresh mint sprig (optional)

Place the tea bags in a large pitcher. Add 3 quarts cold water, and steep for 30 minutes.

Meanwhile, in a small saucepan, combine 1 cup water and the sugar. Boil, stirring occasionally, until the sugar is dissolved.

Remove the tea bags. Add the sugar mixture and stir to combine. Serve over ice with lemon and fresh mint, if desired.

NOTES

• Lemon juice should be squeezed into tea and the lemon then discarded. The bitterness from the pith will infuse the tea if it is left to wallow in the glass.

• Tea was the most common nonalcoholic drink in the South through the 1800s. A drink steeped from a southern holly, yupon tea, was widely consumed.

• The first mechanical ice maker was produced in New Orleans in 1865. Before that, ice was harvested and brought down from the Great Lakes and stored in underground ice houses insulated with straw or sawdust.

Blackberry Limeade
Amethyst Elixir

• • •

An elixir is allegedly able to prolong life indefinitely. Ancient Greeks believed the violet jeweler's stone was a remedy for drunkenness and so this purple drink is fittingly nonalcoholic. Now, this drink may not possess the powers of Ponce de Leon's fountain of youth or relieve the Friends of Bill W., but on a long afternoon in August, when the sun has just about exhausted your will to live, the deep amethystine hue and exotic flavor may provide a respite and revive the scene. • SERVES 8

4 cups fresh blackberries, or unsweetened frozen blackberries, thawed, plus extra for garnish

1 cup turbinado (raw) sugar or grated palm sugar

1 kaffir lime leaf, crushed, or 1 tablespoon grated lime zest

1 green cardamom pod, lightly crushed

¹/₂ cup fresh Key lime juice (about 8 small limes)

Thin lime slices, for garnish

2 cups ginger ale

Ice cubes

Lay a doubled piece of cheesecloth on a nonporous work area. (As the berries will stain a wide array of cutting surfaces and clothes, this may be best done outside or over newspaper and wearing an apron or smock.) Place the blackberries on top of the cheesecloth and gather into a bundle like a hobo sack. Hold the sack of berries over a glass, stainless steel, plastic, or ceramic bowl. Twist the top of the sack to squeeze the juice from the berries into the receptacle. (This will yield about 1 cup very strong, tart, dark juice.) Refrigerate the juice until needed; discard the purple mash.

In a small saucepan, combine the sugar, 1 cup water, the lime leaf, and the cardamom pod. Bring to a boil. Simmer over low heat for 10 minutes, or until the mixture is reduced to a thin syrup. Remove the lime leaf and cardamom. Allow the sugar syrup to cool and then chill it.

In a 1-quart pitcher, combine the blackberry juice, sugar syrup, and lime juice. Stir to combine and then refrigerate until cold.

To serve, stir the ginger ale into the pitcher, fill glasses with ice, and pour in the blackberry limeade. Garnish with slices of lime.

NOTES

• Berries can be pulsed briefly in a food processor and strained. Be careful not to crush the seeds, as this lends a dirty taste to the blackberries.

• Freeze blackberries in ice cubes for a nice accessory to the drink.

• The sugar syrup can be transferred to a metal mixing bowl set in a bowl of ice to cool it down quickly.

• For a wonderful frozen cocktail, puree ice and a jigger of gin with the blackberry-lime mixture in a blender.

Cherry-Vanilla Cream Soda
Fizzing Drink

• • •

For some reason—most likely, because it drew kids to it like moths to a flame—the cream soda pop bottled down on the Mississippi gulf coast was a bright ruby red. Although it was a color that might have denoted strawberry- or cherry-flavored pop to cousins from north of Memphis, it was actually vanilla flavored. This dazzling drink came in bottles that were faceted on the sides like cut gems, with blue and white painted script that glowed when the bottles were turned up and their contents gulped down in the sunshine. An ice chest was transformed into a treasure chest when it was filled with those effervescent garnet soda bottles. A shot of cherry juice adds the color to this rendition of my summertime childhood favorite. • SERVES 8

2 cups sugar
1 vanilla bean, split
   lengthwise
2 tablespoons vanilla extract

$1/4$ teaspoon almond extract
$1/4$ cup cherry juice
1 quart soda water

In a small saucepan, combine 1 cup water and the sugar. Add the vanilla bean. Boil over medium heat for 2 minutes or until the mixture has reduced to a thin syrup.

Remove the vanilla bean. Rinse in hot water. Set aside to air-dry and reserve for another use.

Allow the syrup to cool. Stir in the vanilla and almond extracts and the cherry juice.

Pour 2 tablespoons of the cherry-vanilla syrup over ice cubes in a tall glass and fill with soda water. Stir to combine. Serve with a silly straw.

NOTES

• Look for cherry juice in the natural foods section of the market if it is not in the juice aisle. If you can't find cherry juice in your market, substitute a few tablespoons of grenadine.

• This syrup will keep in the refrigerator for 1 week.

• Look in home-brewing supply stores for all you need to bottle your own pop. This process makes a nifty science fair project.

Roasted Pecans
Deeply Darkened

• • •

Silhouetted against winter skies, the brittle black branches of the pecan grove surrounding our house look like arthritic hands reaching up toward the heavens. Backlit by the pinks, oranges, and blues of sunset, they look more like hands folded in prayer on a gospel album cover or funeral-home fan. It seems at times they might have given up the ghost, but such is the nature of alternate-bearing trees. Though unlucky for the past few years, with the winds of the fall storm season claiming the green pecans early one year and a drought the next, they will recover in time and should be prolific once again. Amen. • MAKES 4 CUPS

1 pound pecan halves
4 tablespoons (^{1}/$_2$ stick)
  unsalted butter, melted

1 tablespoon Worcestershire
  sauce
Fine sea salt

Preheat the oven to 300°F.

Put the pecan halves in a colander in the sink. Pour 2 quarts boiling water over the pecans and drain well.

Spread the pecans in a single layer in a baking pan. Sprinkle with the butter, Worcestershire, and salt. Tumble around in the pan until well coated.

Bake for 15 minutes. Stir the pecans, and turn off the oven. Allow the pecans to stay in the oven for 1^1/$_2$ to 2 hours with the door closed.

Remove from the oven and allow them to cool completely. Store in an airtight container.

NOTES

• To roast pecans in the microwave, combine the pecans and seasonings in a large bowl. Working in batches, place pecans in a single layer on a micro-wavable plate. Cook on high power for 2 minutes, stir, and continue to cook in 1-minute intervals until they reach the desired shade.

• Store raw or roasted pecans in the freezer to protect them from becoming rancid. To crisp thawed pecans, place them uncovered in a microwave on high power for 1 minute.

• Pecans trees are a variety of hickory. For the most success in pollination, two types of cultivars are needed. So, if you are planting a grove of your own, plant more than one variety.

• The world's largest pecan nursery is in Lumberton, Mississippi.

See photograph page ii.

Buttermilk Bacon Pralines
Sweet, Salty, Ridiculous

• • •

These salty–sweet electuaries are brilliant paired with drinks before dinner. The out-landish combination of smoky bacon and pecans, scented with orange, in a brown sugar disk, is an amusing, tongue-teasing conversation starter—a true amuse-bouche.

• MAKES 24 SMALL PRALINES

1 cup granulated sugar
$1/2$ cup packed light brown sugar
$1/2$ cup buttermilk
1 tablespoon light corn syrup
$1/2$ teaspoon baking soda
$1/4$ teaspoon kosher salt

4 tablespoons ($1/2$ stick) unsalted butter
$1/2$ teaspoon vanilla extract
1 cup chopped pecans
$1/2$ teaspoon grated orange zest
4 slices bacon, cooked crisp and crumbled

In a heavy-bottomed, deep saucepan, combine the granulated and brown sugars, the buttermilk, corn syrup, baking soda, and salt. Cook slowly over medium heat for about 20 minutes, until the mixture reaches 235°F on a candy thermometer (see Notes).

Remove from the heat and add the butter, vanilla, pecans, orange zest, and bacon. Being mindful of exposed skin as the mixture is very hot, beat like the dickens with a wooden spoon until smooth and creamy. Drop by teaspoonfuls onto a silicone mat or buttered parchment paper. Let stand for 30 minutes, or until cool and firm. Store in an airtight container.

ACTIVIST Robert King Wilkerson made pralines in his jail cell at Louisiana's Angola Prison. During his 29 years in solitary confinement, he was able to procure ingredients from inmates on his cell block, and with a makeshift stove made of soda cans, he cooked his candy based on a recipe he learned from a fellow prisoner named Cap Pistol. After he was exonerated on the charges that led to his imprisonment, he started a candy-making business. On his first day of freedom he made pralines; now he calls his candy Freelines. Mail-order Freelines can be purchased at kingsfreelines@gmail.com.

NOTES

• If you don't have a candy thermometer, drop a spoonful of the mixture into a cup of cool water. If the test drop can be formed into a pliable ball, then it is ready for the additional ingredients. If not, let the mixture cook a little longer and try again. Change water between tests for more accurate results.

• Although I usually frown on the practice, cooking bacon in the microwave in this instance helps render it extra-crispy.

• Silicone mats are available in cookware stores and can be used time and again. Granite and marble are excellent surfaces for candy and fudge making. I once bought a mismarked marble tombstone at a very low price. The inscription was only on one side, so the reverse side worked well for my confectionery needs.

• Withholding the bacon makes a classic praline. These really aren't too much of a production and make a great hostess or teacher's gift that can be ready in 45 minutes. Quicker than brownies or cookies.

See photograph page 9.

Yazoo Cheese Straws
Aged and Sharp

• • •

Cheese-straw doyenne Mary Margaret Yerger began her business right before retiring from work in the Yazoo City public school system. Now at 79 years of age, the white-haired lady with a spirited glint in her steely blue eyes—kind of a plucky Mrs. Claus—can be found with walking cane in hand at the helm of the Mississippi Cheese Straw Factory. With ingenuity and sheer determination, Mrs. Yerger transformed an old family recipe into a thriving family business producing 3,000 pounds of cheese straws a day, 280 days a year. With the support of her children, her little factory on Mound Street, much like the feisty dame, shows no sign of slowing down. • MAKES 48 STRAWS*

1 pound extra-sharp Cheddar cheese, grated, at room temperature (about 4 cups)
1 cup (2 sticks) unsalted butter, softened
1 teaspoon kosher salt
$^1/_2$ teaspoon cayenne pepper
Dash of hot pepper sauce
3 cups unbleached all-purpose flour, sifted

In a food processor fitted with the metal blade, combine the cheese, butter, salt, cayenne, and hot sauce by pulsing several times until well blended. Add the flour and pulse until the dough forms a ball.

Preheat the oven to 375°F. Fit a cookie press with the ribbon or star template.

Press long, continuous strips of the dough 2 inches apart onto ungreased cookie sheets. Using a sharp knife, score the strips every 3 inches. Bake for 10 to 12 minutes, or until the edges just begin to brown ever so slightly.

Remove the cheese straws from the oven and cut or break on the scored lines. Place them on a rack to cool completely. Store in an airtight container.

NOTES

• Letting the grated cheese come to room temperature before combining it with the butter yields a smoother, more homogenous dough.

• If a cookie press is unavailable, form the dough into 2-inch round logs. Chill the dough until firm and slice into $^1/_8$-inch-thick disks.

• It is almost impossible to make too many cheese straws for the holiday season. Plan on making two batches of these if there is anybody around while you are making them, as many will be eaten before there is even a chance to store them away.

• To catch up on all that is happening with Mrs. Yerger and her family, visit mississippicheesestraw factory.com.

See photograph page ii.

Sold My Soul to the Devil-ed Eggs
Cooking to the Blues

• • •

The tales of Robert Johnson and other mystic blues men meeting Papa Legba, the trick-ster god, at the crossroads, and trading their eternal soul for fame and fortune, are the mythologies of this land, echoing across the open spaces like the moan of a freight train in winter. Legend and evidence have it that Robert Johnson was buried three times before his bones had a final resting place, just outside of town out on Money Road, at the small white clapboard Little Zion Church.

These deviled eggs are featured in a cooking class I teach, accompanied by a blues man by the name of Terry "Harmonica" Bean. It is an amusing tribute to our local flavors and rhythms. Mr. Bean's business card informs the recipient that "his band or himself" is available for gigs. He plays the guitar, drums, and obviously the harmonica all at the same time, a one-man blues band. I think this self-sufficient musical talent may have cut into the need to book a whole band. It also gives me confidence that he never cut a deal with that old trickster, Papa Legba. • SERVES 12

NOTES

• I am very ticky about hard-boiled eggs. That unsightly green ring around yolks can be avoided by following these simple steps: Place the eggs (it is best if they are close to the expiration date so they'll peel well later) in a medium saucepan. Cover by 1 to 2 inches with cold water. Add 1 tablespoon salt. Bring to a boil over high heat. Cover the pot, reduce the heat, and simmer for 30 seconds. Remove from the heat and let sit undisturbed for 13 minutes. Rinse the eggs under cold running water for 5 minutes to cool. Gently crack each egg and place in cold water for 5 more minutes before peeling.

• I always give a deviled-egg plate as a wedding gift.

• For a canapé, deviled quail eggs are a unique choice. The eggs need to be at least a week old to peel easily. Simmer in water for 5 minutes only. Cool under running water and crack the shells. Let stand in the cold water for 15 minutes before peeling.

12 large eggs, hard-boiled, peeled, and split lengthwise
1 teaspoon fine sea salt
2 green onions, white and green parts, finely chopped

2 tablespoons unsalted butter, softened
1 tablespoon dill pickle relish
1 teaspoon yellow mustard
2 tablespoons mayonnaise
Paprika, for garnish

In a small bowl, mash the egg yolks with a fork until smooth. Stir in the salt, onions, butter, relish, mustard, and mayonnaise. Spoon or pipe the mixture into egg-white halves. Sprinkle with paprika.

TO pay homage at the great blues man Robert Johnson's final graveside, get in touch with Mr. Sylvester Hoover at Hoover's Grocery and the Old Times Museum in Baptist Town, Green-wood, Mississippi.

Scotch Eggs
Homeroom Projects and Girl Cousins

• • •

• To fry Scotch eggs, heat oil to 350°F and deep-fry for 4 minutes or until brown, turning as needed.

• Serve Scotch eggs hot, or cold, split lengthwise, with sliced tomatoes.

• Just this past year, a new girl cousin came into my life. Charlotte Bosenquet is my second cousin on my mother's side. At twenty-five she came to Mississippi from Scotland to meet her American cousins for the first time. Charlie had just finished at the Glasgow School of Art and wanted to take some time off to travel. It was fun to meet the woman we now call our "bonus" cousin. She looks just like the rest of us and is quite the scene-booster. Her creative bent and whole-souled nature have led to many hijinks since her arrival. One of her "bril-liant" plans is to turn the Delta into the "Leisure Sports Capital of the World." All over the world, people are trying to make flat spaces to play lawn games, whereas here we naturally have the perfect landscape for lawn bowl-ing, croquet, badminton, bocce, polo, horseshoes, and cricket. She may never leave.

My best girl cousin, Lenore Anne, and I are just four months apart in age. When we were in elementary school, we each had to do a class project tracing our family trees. My mother taught Mississippi history for several years, and made me do research like crazy for the project. Visiting cemeteries and the church-going cousins who kept up with the family Bible, I assembled information for my poster-board-and-tempera presentation.

On the big day, I stood in front of the class and expounded on our Scotch-Irish ancestry and their settlement of the area soon after it was opened in the 1830s. When my dear cousin stepped forward for her presentation, she said innocently enough, "Well, if she's Scotch-Irish, I guess that makes my side of the family Bourbon and water."

Whenever I prepare these hard-boiled eggs encased in sausage, that elementary-school afternoon comes to mind; and if served to either side of the family, the tale is undoubtedly retold by someone. • SERVES 6

1 pound ground pork
   breakfast sausage
2 large eggs
1/2 teaspoon dried savory
1/2 teaspoon dried sage

1 teaspoon whole-grain
   mustard
6 large eggs, hard-boiled
   and peeled
2 tablespoons all-purpose flour
1 cup fresh bread crumbs

Preheat the oven to 400°F. Line a baking sheet with parchment paper.

In a bowl, mix the sausage, one of the eggs, the savory, sage, and mustard. With slightly damp hands, envelope each boiled egg in one-sixth of the sausage mixture.

Put the flour in a small dish and beat the remaining egg in a small bowl with 1 teaspoon water. Put the bread crumbs in a sepa-rate small dish. Roll each sausage-coated egg in flour, then in egg wash, and then in bread crumbs. Set the crumb-coated eggs on the prepared baking sheet.

Bake for 20 minutes, rotating the sheet once, until evenly browned.

Smoked Tomato Canapés
In the Glow of Citronella

· · ·

"You are cordially invited to a black tie barbecue," the invitations read. My girlfriends and I pulled out the white twinkle lights and slung them up in the trees. We didn't go crazy or anything with the food; we just dressed up some of our late-summer favorites and served them on the good china. We slathered ourselves in the mosquito-repellent body lotion sold door to door and put on high-heeled, strappy sandals. Everyone looked lovely in the glow of the citronella candles. • MAKES 24 CANAPÉS

2 pints grape or cherry
   tomatoes
2 tablespoons corn oil
2 tablespoons plus 1 teaspoon
   chopped fresh oregano
$^1/_2$ teaspoon cracked black
   peppercorns
24 slices party-size rye,
   pumpernickel, or batter
   bread, cut with a 2-inch
   round cutter

1 cup mayonnaise, preferably
   Homemade (page 66)
I teaspoon chopped fresh
   chives
1 teaspoon chopped fresh
   basil
Salt

Set up a stovetop or outdoor smoker. In a medium bowl, combine the tomatoes, oil, 2 tablespoons oregano, and pepper. Place in the smoker for 15 minutes. Remove from the smoker and allow to cool.

Spread the top of each bread slice with mayonnaise. Top with some smoked tomato and a sprinkling of the remaining 1 teaspoon oregano, the chives, basil, and salt.

NOTES

• I prefer hickory chips with tomatoes. Convenient oven-smoker bags are widely available with wood chips built right in. The bags work perfectly with this recipe and there is hardly any cleanup at all.

• Go ahead and smoke tomatoes any time you fire up your smoker. They freeze well or can be stored in the refrigerator for about three days, and add a great depth of flavor to pasta sauces and salads.

Watermelon Salsa

Sandia y Jalapeño *and the Story of Miguel*

. . .

Olga and Miguel's son Steve appeared at our door one day, stuck out his hand, and said, "I'm Steve Henderson and I've come for a visit." Miguel and Olga had raised a charming boy. Through the years the Hendersons, their children, and their grand-children have grown to be dear friends and seem more like cousins than neighbors. Back at their family home in Tampico, Mexico, Miguel raised watermelons and canta-loupes with great success. Here in Mississippi, he has raised cotton and Steve has grown to be a handsome young man. Miguel is good at raising things. Hats off to him.

- SERVES 8 TO 10

4 cups diced, seeded
  watermelon cubes
1 cup diced, seeded cantaloupe
  cubes
2 green onions, white and
  green parts, thinly sliced
  on the diagonal
1 jalapeño, seeded and finely
  chopped

2 teaspoons salt
1 teaspoon turbinado (raw)
  sugar
1 teaspoon ancho chile powder
1 tablespoon chopped cilantro
1 tablespoon chopped basil
Grated zest and juice of
  1 lime

In a large bowl, combine the watermelon, cantaloupe, onions, jalapeño, salt, sugar, chile powder, cilantro, basil, and lime zest and juice. Chill for 30 minutes before serving.

NOTES

- Ripe watermelons will scratch easily with a finger-nail and have a sharp, full sound when thumped. The stem will also come off easily.

- Cutting herbs with scis-sors right into the salsa is quick and direct.

- Spoon this salsa over grilled catfish and serve with black beans and rice for a fresh summer dinner. Nice with tortilla chips, too.

- Served side by side with chunky guacamole, this vibrant salsa makes a colorful addition to a party spread. Or add some diced avocado right into the salsa and call it a day.

- If you are interested in taking this on a picnic, put it in a 2-gallon freezer ziptop bag and lay it across the top of the stuff in the ice chest so it doesn't get all mushed.

> " WE know it was not a southern watermelon that Eve took; we know it because she repented."
>
> —MARK TWAIN

The Painter's Black-Eyed Pea Cakes
Artist's Favorite First Course

• • •

M. Taylor Bowen Ricketts has been a dear friend for years and years. We have watusied in cottonfields under full moons until morning in celebration, and have sat real still and quiet with each other in mourning. I have always admired the passion she brings to all she does. Her paintings of women and children adorn the walls of collectors' homes and galleries throughout the South. She is a fine cook, whose understanding of flavor and texture is rivaled only by her innate sense of color and form. The dishes that grace her table honor humble, local ingredients with the same respect and admiration she gives the citizen subjects of her paintings.

Taylor's pea cakes served with Comeback Sauce and greens have kicked off many dinner parties at her home and in her restaurants. • MAKES 12 CAKES

1 slice bacon, cut into 1-inch pieces
4 whole garlic cloves, plus 2 cloves, minced
1 pound fresh black-eyed peas
1/2 cup minced white onion
1/2 cup finely chopped green bell pepper
1/2 cup finely chopped red bell pepper
1 tablespoon finely chopped parsley
1 teaspoon finely chopped basil

1/2 teaspoon cayenne pepper
1 1/2 teaspoons salt
1/2 cup heavy cream
1 cup unbleached all-purpose flour
1 large egg
1/2 cup buttermilk
2 cups panko or fresh French bread crumbs
4 tablespoons (1/2 stick) unsalted butter
4 tablespoons olive oil
Comeback Sauce (page 69)

In a large pot over medium heat, cook the bacon until crisp. Add the whole garlic cloves and cook for 1 minute more. Add the peas and enough water to cover by 2 inches. Simmer for 30 minutes, or until tender. Drain the peas and discard the garlic. Transfer half of the peas to a large bowl, and with a potato masher or the back of a spoon, mash until a chunky puree.

Add the remaining tender cooked peas, the minced garlic, onion, green and red bell peppers, parsley, basil, cayenne, salt, and cream. Mix well. Refrigerate for 1 hour.

NOTES

• If fresh black-eyed peas are not readily available, substitute frozen or soaked and cooked dried black–eyed peas. Pictsweet black-eyed peas are my choice from the market freezer section. Canned black-eyed peas can be used in a pinch, but they are a little on the mushy side; rinse and drain them well before you add them. You will need about 3 cups of any of these.

• Pea cakes can be assembled a day ahead and stored on a baking sheet covered in plastic in the refrigerator for a day. Allow them to come to room temperature before frying.

• Cooked cakes can be held on a cooling rack set in a 200°F. oven, uncovered, or in a warming drawer for an hour. The rack keeps them from sweating on the bottom.

• For a nice vegetarian option at a cookout, larger cakes minus the bacon can be served in place of burger patties.

With damp hands, form the pea mixture into 12 patties, each about 3/4-inch thick. Set aside.

Set up an assembly line to coat the pea cakes. Put the flour into a shallow dish. Next to that dish, get out a small bowl, add the egg and buttermilk, and beat with a fork to combine. Next to the egg mixture, set a shallow dish of bread crumbs. Coat each cake on all sides lightly with flour. Next, dip each cake in egg mixture, allowing the excess to drip off. Then, pat the coated cake in bread crumbs. Coat all of the cakes and set them aside.

Set a wire rack over a baking sheet lined with newspaper or paper towels.

In a skillet over medium heat, heat 2 tablespoons of the butter with 2 tablespoons of the olive oil. Working in batches, fry the cakes for 3 minutes per side or until toasty brown. Place on the rack to drain and cool. (If the oil becomes dark, pour it out of the skillet and wipe the skillet with a paper towel; add additional butter and oil before frying the remaining cakes.)

Serve the cakes with Comeback Sauce.

• Taylor can be found in the kitchen at Delta Fresh Market, 301 Park Avenue, Greenwood, Mississippi, with her children tugging at her apron strings.

Fried Okra

Morgan Freeman and Ground Zero Blues Club

• • •

The Mississippi Delta is known the world over as the home of the blues. The fertile imaginations of legendary blues men such as B. B. King, Robert Johnson, Howling Wolf, John Lee Hooker, and Muddy Waters all came of age on its soil. All of these musicians influence bands today, like the North Mississippi All Stars, the White Stripes, and Widespread Panic, and they continue to inspire Eric Clapton.

Clarksdale is one of the largest cities in the area, located smack-dab in the heart of Delta Blues country. Some people consider the town "ground zero" for the blues because blues legend Muddy Waters called it home. At a time when local joints were being squeezed out by soulless chains and small-town downtowns were being boarded up, Morgan Freeman and Bill Luckett opened up Ground Zero Blues Club, giving folks a place to revel in and get over their blues.

At Ground Zero, fried okra is eaten right out of hand like popcorn while people sway to the music of guys like Kenny Brown, Terry "Harmonica" Bean, and Big T. Super Chicken. At home, have some paper lunch sacks handy to prepare and even serve the crisp okra. And listen to Muddy Waters' "Long Distance Call" playing in the background. • SERVES 4

NOTES

• Tiny okra no larger than a lady's little finger can be fried whole.

• If the oil begins to smoke in the least bit, reduce the heat and let cool slightly. Conversely, make sure the oil comes back up to temperature between batches to avoid soggy okra.

• If you let the hot okra just sit on paper towels, it will get soggy. Cooling and draining on a rack keeps the cooked okra crisp. I like to line the pan under the cooling rack with old newspaper to catch drips (much cheaper than paper towels).

• Serve the okra in paper sacks, with ketchup or hot pepper sauce alongside for dousing.

• Visit Ground Zero in Clarksdale, Mississippi, or find out who's playing at groundzerobluesclub.com.

---

1 pound okra, cut into
$^{1}/_{4}$-inch-thick rounds
2 cups yellow cornmeal
Fine sea salt

Freshly ground black pepper
Vegetable oil, for frying
(about 1$^{1}/_{2}$ cups)

Put the okra in a large plastic bag. Add 1 tablespoon water. Close the bag and shake several times to coat each segment with water. In a separate large bag or paper sack, combine the cornmeal, 1 teaspoon salt, and 1 teaspoon pepper. Add the okra about a cup at a time to the cornmeal mixture and shake to coat. Set the coated okra aside and repeat until all is coated.

In a large, heavy, deep-sided skillet or shallow pot, heat the oil over medium heat until hot, around 325°F. Prepare an area for the cooked okra to drain and cool by placing a wire cooling rack over a tray lined with newspaper or paper towels.

Using slightly spread fingers or a slotted spoon or skimmer, lift the coated okra from the cornmeal and shake it slightly to dislodge any excess cornmeal. Add a single layer of okra to the hot oil in the pot. Fry for 5 to 6 minutes, turning to crisp and brown evenly. Remove the okra to the cooling rack. Sprinkle with additional salt and pepper. Repeat the process with the remaining okra. Serve hot.

HOT TAMALE

HOLE CATFISH
SANDWICH 3.50
2.50
DINNER 6.50
JUMBO SHRIMP
POPCORN
SHRIMP
BUTTERFLY
SHRIMP

BUFFALO FISH
Rib DINNER 5.50
Reg. DINNER

Chicken Strip
Plate $5.50
Chicken Strip
Sandwich $2.75

Delta Hot Tamale
Save Those Coffee Cans

• • •

Sam the Tamale Man had a vision 22 years ago while recovering from a stroke. He was moved by these apparitions to build a truly movable feast. From his well-appointed truck he has found his way to a contented spot on the shoulder of Highway 49. He sells catfish and buffalo fish and some shrimp, too, but as the bold hand-printed sign advertises, hot tamales are the main attraction. He stays open until sunset every day, then cranks up his restaurant and heads home.

Every little honky-tonking town throughout the Delta has at least one hot tamale stand. You'll see these first cousins of Mexican tamales individually wrapped in traditional corn husks, as well as an assortment of other wrappers like coffee filters and waxed paper. They are most often bundled in threes, tied with butcher's twine and swaddled in newspaper for eating right then, or packed in lard buckets or #10 cans recycled out of necessity for travel. Dozens and dozens of tamale transactions take place every day from outfitted trucks, roadside stands, and out-the-back screen doors of neighbors' kitchens, creating a thriving tamale economy. Delta tamale theory holds that African American farmworkers met migrant Mexican workers in the field. These two disparate groups of workers both brought lunches featuring cornmeal from home, and the tamale assimilated into this area of the country. Whoever brought a love of hot tamales to the Delta, the Signas began meeting the demand.

Like many Delta dining establishments, Doe's Eat Place began in 1903 as a grocery store. Carmel Signa sailed from Sicily, Italy, and somehow made his way to the Mississippi River town of Greenville. With the family's living quarters in the back, the store—called "Papa's Store" by the Signa family—flourished until the flood of 1927. To help the family recover from their loss, Carmel's son Dominic, or Big Doe, started bootlegging whisky. Several years later, he sold his still for $300 and a Model-T Ford. Big Doe worked in the cafeteria at the Air Force base in Greenville, and was given a hot tamale recipe by one of the enlisted men. Mamie, Big Doe's wife, improved on the initial recipe and began selling them from her kitchen. The tamales were popular, and soon the Signa women and children were rolling tamales together, frequently to sell to the families who showed up with coffee cans and pots to get some of their spicy, saucy red hot tamales for their dinner. Doe's is still going strong, and still sells hot tamales at the table or by the coffee can. The Signa family was recently honored with a James Beard Award. To understand the economic and social history of the Mississippi Delta from the 1920s up to today, all you need to do is follow the tamale. • **Makes 3 DOZEN TAMALES**

NOTES

• Tamale making is an event, an all-day affair. Fill the kitchen with friends and family, and keep their hands busy. Perhaps a little bit of family history will be passed on while gathered 'round the table set about this communal task. There will be plenty of tamales to divvy up at the end of the day.

• This recipe is inspired by Greenville native Joe Sherman's recipe. Again the Delta's history is reflected in the tamale. Joe's family is of Lebanese descent and settled in the area as merchants.

• Soaking corn husks: Place the corn husks in a large container and cover with warm water. Soak until soft and pliable, about 3 hours. If necessary, weight down with an inverted plate and a heavy can. Before rolling the tamales, drain the water from the corn husks. Rinse each husk, and remove any corn silk. Stand the husks upright in a colander to drain before applying the cornmeal dough.

• Cook the pork for the filling up to two days before making the filling. Or, cook the filling up to two days before making the tamales.

- Choose a pot that is just the right size for all of the tamales to remain standing upright. If the pot is too big, the tamales will fall over or come unrolled. If necessary, place a heat-proof mug or bowl in the center of the pot to fill up space.

- The completed tamales can be made up to two days in advance and refrigerated. Or, they freeze very well both cooked and raw. If cooked then frozen, thaw in the refrigerator overnight, and steam to heat through, 15 to 20 minutes.

- Delta Hot Tamales can be served wet or dry. Dry tamales are served right out of the husk (sometimes with chopped green onions). Wet tamales are served with a few spoonfuls of the tamale simmering liquid poured over the top. No matter whether you like them wet or dry, most people from the Delta like to add a few dashes of hot sauce and eat them along with saltine crackers and a cold beer.

TAMALE FILLING

4 pounds boneless pork shoulder

$3/4$ cup canola oil

$4^1/2$ tablespoons chili powder

$1^1/2$ tablespoons garlic powder

$1^1/2$ tablespoons ground cumin

$1^1/2$ tablespoons paprika

$1^1/2$ tablespoons salt

$1^1/2$ teaspoons freshly ground black pepper

$3/4$ teaspoon cayenne pepper, or to taste

CORNMEAL DOUGH

$1^1/2$ cups lard or shortening, chilled

$1^1/2$ tablespoons chili powder

1 teaspoon ground cumin

1 tablespoon garlic powder

1 tablespoon paprika

2 teaspoons salt

$1/2$ teaspoon cayenne pepper, or to taste

1 teaspoon baking powder

4 cups yellow cornmeal

2 (8-ounce) packages dried corn husks, soaked in water until soft (see Notes, page 29)

TAMALE SIMMERING LIQUID

$1/2$ cup canola oil

1 tablespoon chili powder

1 tablespoon garlic powder

1 tablespoon paprika

1 tablespoon salt

1 teaspoon ground cumin

$1/2$ teaspoon cayenne pepper, or to taste

MAKE THE FILLING. Put the pork in a medium pot or Dutch oven and add just enough cold water to cover. Whisk together $1/2$ cup of the canola oil, 3 tablespoons of the chili powder, 1 tablespoon of the garlic powder, 1 tablespoon of the cumin, 1 tablespoon of the paprika, 1 tablespoon of the salt, 1 teaspoon of the black pepper, and $1/2$ teaspoon of the cayenne pepper. Add the spice mixture to the pot and bring to a boil over high heat. As soon as the water boils, reduce the heat and cover the pot. Simmer until the pork is very tender, 2 to 3 hours.

Transfer the pork to a large bowl to cool. Strain the cooking liquid, and reserve for making the cornmeal dough. Cut the pork into chunks, and using the small holes of the meat grinder attachment on an electric stand mixer or by pulsing in a food processor, grind the pork.

Combine the remaining $1/4$ cup oil with the remaining $1^1/2$ tablespoons chili powder, $1/2$ tablespoon garlic powder, $1/2$ tablespoon cumin, $1/2$ tablespoon paprika, $1/2$ tablespoon salt, $1/2$ teaspoon black pepper, and $1/4$ teaspoon cayenne pepper in a large sauté pan over medium heat. Cook until just warm, about 2 minutes. Stir in the ground cooked pork and mix with the spice mixture until well combined, 2 to 3 minutes. Transfer the filling to a shallow dish and set aside to cool completely.

MAKE THE CORNMEAL DOUGH. In an electric stand mixer fitted with the paddle attachment, beat the lard, chili powder, cumin, garlic powder, paprika, salt, cayenne pepper, and baking powder on high speed until fluffy. Add the cornmeal, and beat at low speed until well combined. Mix in 1 cup of the reserved cooking liquid and then add more, up to 1 more cup, a little at a time, until the mixture is quite moist and has the consistency of soft cookie dough.

MAKE THE TAMALES. Spread each soaked corn husk flat on a counter or cutting board with the pointed end away from you. With a small spatula or butter knife, spread about 2 tablespoons of cornmeal dough over two-thirds of the husk, leaving about one-third of the husk on the right side uncovered and at least a $1/2$-inch border at the top of the tamale.

Place about 2 generous tablespoonfuls of the filling on the dough about 1 inch from the left edge. Fold the sides over to cover the filling. Continue rolling, then fold up the bottom part of the husk to seal. As each tamale is completed, place, folded-side down, on a baking sheet in a single, even layer until all of the dough and filling are used. Using butcher's twine, tie the tamales into bundles of three. It is best to tie the tamales in two places: about 1 inch from the bottom and 1 inch from the top. You may need someone to help hold the bundles while you tie the tamales together.

MAKE THE TAMALE SIMMERING LIQUID. Mix together any remaining broth from cooking the meat with enough cold water to make 2 quarts. Add the oil, chili powder, garlic powder, paprika, salt, cumin, and cayenne.

COOK THE TAMALES. Stand the tamales upright (folded-side down) in a large pot with a tight-fitting lid. Add the tamale simmering liquid to the pot, pouring it around the tamales and not directly over them. Then, carefully fill the pot with enough water to come just to the top of the tamales. Bring to a boil over high heat, then immediately reduce the heat, cover the pot, and simmer until the dough is firm and easily pulls away from the husk, about 1 hour. Serve wet or dry (see Notes).

Ain't No Thing, Chicken Wing
Itta Bena, Home of the Fighting Delta Devils

• • •

Retired Mississippi Valley State University head football coach Archie "The Gun-slinger" Cooley said on more than one occasion, while wearing a ten-gallon hat and a rumored pistol slung on his hip, "Jerry could catch a BB in the dark of night." He was talking about Jerry Rice, possibly the greatest wide receiver ever to play the game of football, who was also a star on the TV show **Dancing with the Stars.** *He surely knows a thing or two about fancy footwork. In the 1984 South Western Athletic Conference season, Rice teamed with quarterback Willie Totten, and "The Satellite Express" averaged 59 points a game. The Delta Devils rounded out the season with an unprecedented 628 points.*

The Devils introduced college football to the "no huddle" offense and ushered in an era of showmanship. The tiny town of Itta Bena blazed with excitement, and the tail-gating was legendary. Today the Alcorn State vs. Valley game brings the fans to a fevered pitch, and the wings are still hot as the devil. • SERVES 6

NOTES

• This marinade works well on shrimp, chicken, and pork kabobs.

• For a pronounced cumin kick, heat the cumin seeds briefly in a dry skillet to bring out the flavor and then let cool. Grind seeds in a spice mill, or with a mortar and pestle.

• Sometimes, in a less casual setting where sticky fingers and tons of paper napkins might be frowned upon, little skewers of boned chicken are a better option.

• For tailgating or outdoor grilling, I have found it best to follow the recipe up until the wings are to be brushed with the sauce. Remove the wings and allow them to cool; cool the sauce and store both in a cooler or refrigerator until ready to grill.

• To grill, place the wings over the indirect heat of medium coals or over a medium gas flame. Cook, brushing occasionally with the sauce, until browned, glazed, and heated through.

2 garlic cloves, minced
1 cup chili sauce
1 teaspoon ground cumin
1 teaspoon ground ginger
1 teaspoon salt
2 tablespoons apple cider vinegar
3 tablespoon hot pepper sauce
1 tablespoon honey
12 chicken wings

In a large bowl, combine the garlic, chili sauce, cumin, ginger, salt, vinegar, hot pepper sauce, and honey. Add the chicken wings and let marinate for 1 hour in the refrigerator.

When ready to cook, preheat the oven to 375°F.

Line a large, rimmed baking sheet with aluminum foil. Remove the wings from the marinade (reserving marinade) and arrange them in a single layer on the foil.

Bake for 30 minutes. Turn the wings for even browning and cook an additional 20 minutes.

Meanwhile, in a small saucepan over high heat, bring the reserved marinade to a boil. Cook for 3 minutes, or until thick. Brush the thickened sauce over the wings and bake for 5 to 8 minutes, or until the wings are well glazed and no longer pink next to the bone.

Inland Prawn Toast
Grown in Leland

• • •

Each fall, as the water temperatures begin to drop, Steve and Doris Fratesi of Lauren Farms in Leland gear up for the big Saturday Pond Bank Sale of their signature freshwater prawns. This past year over 1,600 pounds were sold to people lining the banks. That just about emptied out two ponds. One lady, admiring the lapis lazuli–colored shells, looked wistfully at the crustaceans and said to Doris, "If only I had a ring that color."

Golden crisp sesame–sprinkled prawn toasts are beautiful served as passed hors d'oeuvres. • **Makes 48 pieces**

1 pound peeled and deveined freshwater prawns
1 (1 x 4-inch) piece salt pork, very cold, cut into 1-inch pieces
1 tablespoon cornstarch
2 green onions, green and white parts, thinly sliced
1 teaspoon sesame oil

1 teaspoon fish sauce (*nuoc nam* or *nam pla*)
1 tablespoon rice wine or sherry
1 large egg white
24 (2-inch square) slices crustless white bread
2 tablespoons sesame seeds
Vegetable oil, for frying
Jezebel Sauce (page 68)

In a food processor fitted with the metal blade, chop the prawns and salt pork by pulsing three or four times. Add the cornstarch, onions, sesame oil, fish sauce, rice wine, and egg white. Pulse until the mixture resembles a chunky paste.

Using a small offset spatula or a spoon, divide the paste among the slices of bread, spreading it all the way to the edges and sealing around the sides. Pat the sesame seeds on top. With a sharp knife, cut each square in half diagonally, to form two triangles.

Prepare an area for the cooked shrimp toasts to drain and cool by placing a wire cooling rack over a tray lined with newspaper or paper towels. Heat 1^1/$_2$ inches of oil in a heavy-bottomed 3-quart saucepan, a wok, or a deep-fryer to 350°F.

Place a few shrimp toast triangles, coated side down, in the hot oil and fry for 1 minute or until golden brown. Flip the toasts over using a slotted spoon or skimmer. When golden underneath, after about 1 minute, transfer to the wire rack to drain and cool slightly. Fry the remaining toasts.

Serve warm with jezebel sauce for dipping.

NOTES

• Contact Steve and Doris Fratesi at Lauren Farms, 655 Napanee Road, Leland, Mississippi 38756; phone 662-686-2894/ 662-390-3528; or visit laurenfarms.com.

• Jim Henson's Kermit the Frog first appeared on the banks of Deer Creek in Leland.

• U.S. Department of Agriculture's Jamie Whitten Delta States Agriculture Research Station at Stoneville, Mississippi, is doing groundbreaking research in all aspects of agriculture and aquaculture affecting the mid-South region. It is one of the largest Ag research stations in the world.

Refuge Crawfish Pies
For Shade Seekers

• • •

The original bell out at the commissary on the Jones's place was cast in bronze. It was said to have such a beautiful tone to its peal because old man Jones had thrown 100 silver dollars into the molten mixture of copper and tin when it was forged. It hung on a bell rack 60 feet from the ground, right out front of the commissary. Large black block letters spell out REFUGE PLANTATION *above the shade-dappled porch next to the site where the bell once hung. The waters of Little Eagle Lake, just a piece further down the road, teem with crappie, perch, and brim and the muddy banks are home to scores of crawfish. A well-baited crawfish trap set out while fishing is an insurance policy for dinner if the fish aren't biting.* • MAKES 8 INDIVIDUAL PIES

$^1/_2$ **cup (1 stick) unsalted butter**
1 cup finely diced red onion
$^1/_2$ **cup finely chopped celery**
$^1/_4$ **cup finely chopped green bell pepper**
$^1/_4$ **cup finely chopped red bell pepper**
2 garlic cloves, minced
$^1/_2$ **teaspoon dried thyme**
2 tablespoons tomato paste

$^1/_2$ **cup cake flour**
2 cups shrimp stock (see page 78) or clam juice
1 pound peeled crawfish tails
Salt
Freshly ground black pepper
Hot sauce
2 large eggs
$^1/_4$ **cup whole milk**
Versatile Pie Crust Dough (page 192)

In a large sauté pan, melt the butter over medium heat. Add the onion, celery, and green and red bell peppers. Cook and stir for 2 minutes, or until slightly tender. Add the garlic, thyme, and tomato paste and cook and stir for 1 minute more.

Sprinkle the flour over the vegetable mixture and cook, stirring with a wire whisk, until it just begins to give a toasty smell, 2 to 3 minutes. Slowly add the stock a little at a time, whisking well to

ANOTHER bell of silver coin can be found at St. John's Episcopal Church in Aberdeen, Mississippi. The inscription on the bell says it was presented by "A.D. Bowman and 35 New York merchants, 1853."

NOTES

• Even if the package has a crawfish standing there in a straw hat and overalls on the front, and calls itself something like "Boudreaux's Best Bayou Crawfish," check the fine print and make sure the crawfish are from Louisiana—or are at least a product of the United States. Small producers down there can use our help after that dreadful storm, Katrina.

• If fresh crawfish are unavailable, or you don't feel like fooling with them, look for frozen crawfish tails in 1-pound packages labeled "crawfish tails and fat." Also, check to see if the label says "partially cooked." (This is part of the packaging process for some brands.) Subtract a minute or two from the cooking time if they are.

• Small fried pies can be made with egg roll wrappers and fried instead of baked.

combine between additions. Bring the mixture to a boil, then reduce the heat and let simmer for 20 minutes.

Add the crawfish tails. Cook until the crawfish begin to curl slightly, 1 to 2 minutes more. Season with salt, pepper, and hot sauce.

Transfer the crawfish filling to a shallow pan and allow to cool. When completely cool, whisk in one of the eggs and the milk.

Preheat the oven to 375°F. Line a baking pan with parchment paper or a silicone baking mat.

Roll the dough out on a lightly floured work surface until it is $1/4$-inch thick. Cut out eight 6-inch rounds. Spoon about $1/4$ cup cooled crawfish filling in the center of each round.

In a small bowl, whisk the remaining egg and 1 tablespoon water. Brush the edges of each pie with a little of the egg wash. Crimp the edges closed with the tines of a fork or a pastry crimper. With a sharp knife, cut a small steam vent in the top of each pie. Brush the pies with the remaining egg wash.

Arrange the pies 2 inches apart on the lined baking sheet. Bake the pies for 20 minutes or until golden brown.

N.O.B.B.Q. Shrimp
New Orleans Misnomer

• • •

Since these tangy, buttery shrimp are neither cooked on a barbecue grill nor with bar-becue sauce, the name may mislead the uninitiated. It's the same way New Orleans natives call the median of a boulevard "neutral ground."

The shrimp fat from the head and the flavor from the shells add to this signature Crescent City dish. Eating the shrimp is a funky proposition involving removing the heads with a pinch and sucking out the buttery sauce. This technique is best accomplished accompanied by the haunting tunes of Dr. John and his Medicine Show, with your sleeves rolled up above the elbow and with lots of French bread for sopping.

• SERVES 4

1 cup (2 sticks) unsalted
  butter
1/2 cup olive oil
1/4 cup Worcestershire sauce
4 garlic cloves, minced
1 teaspoon salt
1 teaspoon freshly ground
  black pepper
1/4 teaspoon cayenne pepper,
  or to taste

1 bay leaf
1/2 teaspoon dried thyme
1/2 teaspoon dried rosemary
1/2 teaspoon dried oregano
Dash of hot pepper sauce
1 lemon, thinly sliced
3 pounds large shrimp with
  heads on

Preheat the oven to 400°F.

In a large ovenproof skillet over low heat, melt the butter with the olive oil. Add the Worcestershire sauce, garlic, salt, black and cayenne peppers, bay leaf, thyme, rosemary, oregano, hot sauce, and lemon slices. Add the shrimp and stir to coat well with the sauce.

Place in the oven and bake, basting with the sauce occasionally, for 20 minutes, or until the shrimp are pink and the tails just slightly curved.

Remove the skillet from the oven. Remove the bay leaf from the sauce, then spoon the shrimp and sauce into bowls, and serve.

NOTES

• Shrimp are sold by the count; this number indicates the approximate number it takes to make a pound. The smaller the number, the larger the shrimp. Look for 21–25 count or larger to use in this recipe.

• If you or your guests are the least bit squeamish, peeled and deveined shrimp may be used, but flavor and ritual will be sacrificed.

• Peeled large shrimp cooked in this sauce are wonderful on a po' boy sandwich dressed with lettuce and tomato.

Red Drum Starter
Fresh from the Gulf

• • •

The red drum fish gets his name from his bronze-tinged red markings and his rhythmic thumping during mating season, like the sound of licked fingers drawn across the tight skin of a bongo drum. The grassy beds and flats along the Gulf of Mexico offer surf casters and pirogue fishermen a chance to land this most sporting of fish.

If you are not just in from the marshes with one of these beauties in your cooler, a whole yellowtail snapper or other favorite whole fish from the market will suffice for this shared dish, which is a wonderful replacement for the often-seen smoked side of salmon. Allow about 10 minutes of cooking time per pound of cleaned fish.

• SERVES 12

1 whole, small (4-pound) red drum, cleaned and scaled, head and tail attached
2 lemons
Salt and freshly ground black pepper
4 tablespoons ($^1/_2$ stick) unsalted butter, melted

Homemade Mayonnaise (page 66), to cover fish (approximately $1^1/_2$ cups)
1 shallot, finely chopped
1 cup finely chopped parsley and/or other herbs

NOTE

• Although somewhat tacky, I know, I keep a packet of very large rhinestones, or Swarovski crystals, on hand to poke down in the cooked fish's eyeball holes. This garnish is cool, I think. Get them at a craft store.

• Serve with toast points and cucumber slices.

Preheat the oven to 350°F.

Place the fish on a parchment-lined rimmed baking sheet.

Grate the lemon zest over the fish, both inside and out. Drizzle the fish inside and out with the lemon juice.

Sprinkle with salt and pepper everywhere, then slather the seasoned fish inside and out with the melted butter.

Bake for 40 minutes or until the flesh is opaque inside and begins to flake with a fork. Remove from the oven.

While the fish is still hot, remove the skin. With a thin fish spatula, carefully remove the top fillet and discard the backbone. Pat the fillet back into the shape of a whole, undisturbed fish. Pour the pan juices over the fish. Let cool in the pan, then cover and refrigerate for 4 hours, or until ready to serve.

When ready to serve, slide the fish onto a serving dish and neaten up a little, if needed. Spread the mayonnaise over the fish. Sprinkle the shallot and then the parsley over the mayonnaise.

Broiled Apalachicolas
A Tribute

. . .

Joe York, a young Mississippi filmmaker with an unassuming charm and the handsome looks of a 1940s matinee idol, never appears in his films. One of his superb documentaries, Working the Miles, *is about the few remaining oystermen who work the beds of Apalachicola, Florida.*

Tommy Ward and his family, who are featured in Working the Miles, *have been in the harvesting business for generations with their 13 Mile Oyster Company. Tommy and his wife, Patty, are some of the last holdouts in a backbreaking business with spectacular views. I got to hang around the bed of their pickup once as Tommy popped some of his sweet briny oysters open, shooting the breeze and tossing spent shells in the gravel. Tommy was being honored that night with the Ruth Fertel Keeper of the Flame Award. His modest, thoughtful nature would allow him only to accept the honor on behalf of the hardworking people he grew up around and works with.*

Each time I nestle the oysters into the bed of rock salt when I broil them, the smoky, tart-tinged flavors remind me that to enjoy oysters fully you have to attribute the flavor to the work of the oystermen. • SERVES 4

1 dozen fresh oysters,
   shucked, liquor reserved
2 cups rock salt
1 tablespoon fresh lemon
   juice
1 tablespoon tarragon vinegar
$^1\!/_2$ teaspoon dry mustard

$^1\!/_4$ teaspoon celery seeds
$^1\!/_4$ teaspoon freshly ground
   black pepper
2 tablespoons unsalted butter
3 strips of bacon, cut into
   1-inch pieces

Return the drained oysters to the bottom shells. Place the filled shells on a bed of rock salt in a large, shallow metallic baking dish.

Preheat the broiler.

In a small saucepan, combine the oyster liquor, lemon juice, vinegar, mustard, celery seeds, pepper, and butter. Warm the sauce over low heat, stirring until the butter is melted and the ingredients are combined.

Spoon the sauce over the oysters in the shells. Top each oyster with a piece of bacon.

Broil 6 to 8 inches from the heat for 10 to 15 minutes, or until the bacon is crisp and the oysters begin to ruffle around the edges.

NOTES

• Black pepper–coated bacon may be used, and the ground pepper eliminated from the recipe.

• Tarragon vinegar adds acidity and a slightly licorice flavor reminiscent of the Pernod or anisette added to Oysters Rockefeller.

• Serve with hot pepper sauce.

• The Apalachicola oyster's unique flavor is derived from the combination of fresh river water inflow and salinity regulated by the wind patterns along the estuaries bordering St. Vincent's Island.

• For more information on the Ruth Fertel Keeper of the Flame Awards and an interview with Tommy Ward by Southern Foodways Alliance Oral History Project, visit southernfoodways.com.

• Some of Joe York's other films, including *Whole Hog* and *Saving Seeds,* document the work of a wide variety of disappearing foodways. These films may be viewed or purchased by visiting the University of Mississippi's Center for Media Production at olemiss.edu.

Catfish Ceviche
Two Rock

• • •

My great-uncle, Robert L. Thompson, was a strong, silent man. Every day he dressed his long, lean frame in khaki shirts and khaki pants. He had an uncanny gift of knowing what was going on at any time, anywhere on his land. While some planters survey their acreage from trucks with loud motors and big wheels, Uncle Bobby preferred the purr of sleek Galaxy 500s and Ford Crown Victorias. If you were up to something and in the midst of thinking you were going to get away with it, suddenly out of nowhere he appeared. Some fellows from Mexico working out on Pluto started to call him "Dos Penascos," or "Two Rocks," because all you heard were two rocks hitting together before you turned around and he had you in his sights. Never a look of intimidation or anger, and never coupled with a raised voice, his stealthy arrival was all that was needed to remind you what you should and should not be doing on his land.

Uncle Bobby started catfish farming around 1958. Every day he drove the levees he conceived and constructed for what must have totaled in the thousands of miles. He knew not only what was on the surface of his half-floating land, but also how the artesian water flowed beneath it and where the runoff of each spring's high water wanted to go. His understanding of lands in the South was not confined by the Yazoo River and Bee Lake, the two bodies of water that bordered his homestead. He had owned a farm down in Tampico, Mexico, called El Coyote and had traveled throughout South America extensively. Buck, as he was known to his friends, had an esteemed propensity for siestas and all things picante. *The 350 water acres of Thompson Fisheries provided him an endless supply of fresh fish for making ceviche.* • SERVES 6

1 pound U.S. farm-raised catfish fillets, cut into $^{1}/_{2}$-inch pieces
1 teaspoon grated lemon zest
$^{1}/_{2}$ cup fresh lemon juice
1 teaspoon grated lime zest
$^{1}/_{2}$ cup fresh lime juice
2 tablespoons extra-virgin olive oil
1 cup seeded and diced ripe tomato

$^{1}/_{2}$ cup finely diced red onion
2 garlic cloves, thinly sliced
2 tablespoons cilantro leaves
1 tablespoon oregano leaves
1 jalapeño, seeded, deveined, and minced
1 teaspoon salt
$^{1}/_{2}$ teaspoon sugar
1 avocado, pitted, peeled, and diced

NOTES

• Catfish works well with this preparation because of its mild flavor and texture. To learn more about catfish, visit thecatfishinstitute.com.

• Allowing the catfish to marinate in the acidic citrus juices turns the fish opaque and produces a texture similar to poached fish.

• One-half cup of chopped green olives may be added for a briny kick.

• Serve this dish with some spicy popcorn, corn tortilla chips, or on a bed of greens.

In a large resealable food-storage bag, combine the fish with the lemon and lime zests and juices. Allow to marinate in the fridge for a minimum of 4 and a maximum of 18 hours, turning every once and a while to mix.

Thirty minutes before serving, drain the fish and discard the liquid. Put the fish in a large mixing bowl and add the olive oil, tomato, red onion, garlic, cilantro, oregano, jalapeño, salt, sugar, and avocado. Mix gently, cover, and chill until ready to serve.

CATFISH spawn when the water temperatures warm to 70°F., in late spring. The male catfish seeks out a secluded spot for his nest. Out at Pluto, surplus World War II ammunition cans are used. The frisky male swims round and round to clean out his new home. He then lures a willing female into his nest. She enthusiastically lays eggs, which the male fertilizes. He runs her out of there and stays with the eggs to protect his progeny. The male fish will swim around the clutch of up to 10,000 eggs, lightly pumping them occasionally and rolling them about to keep them oxygenated.

During hatching season, the cans are checked every three days and the eggs are transported to the hatchery. A simple system of troughs and paddle wheels simulates the action of the male fish. After just a few days, the eggs hatch. Small wire baskets allow the small fish to fall through while catching the egg shells and membranes. These baskets are then tossed into tanks of tilapia, and in a matter of seconds they are picked clean by the fish and ready to be put back in circulation. For the first few days the small fish feed on the yolk sac attached to them when they hatch. As this food source is depleted, the fish are fed a fine-ground floating grain feed. This pure diet and method of feeding, and the clear waters of the Delta's alluvial aquifers, have eliminated the muddy taste associated with wild-caught catfish.

At the end of the season the tilapia are released into the catfish ponds. Tilapia are native to South America and do not winter over this far north. In late fall, as the water temperature lowers, the tilapia become sluggish and are eaten by the brooder catfish, providing them an excellent source of protein for the winter as they begin forming eggs for the next hatching season.

Grass-eating carp are used as worker fish, too. These fish eat aquatic grasses and keep the banks free of unwanted growth. Large Canada geese roam the levees between the ponds, eating unwanted weeds and grasses.

LUNCHEONS, SALADS, AND DRESSINGS

West Indies Salad

For the Bridesmaids' Luncheon

• • •

This all-white crab salad is frequently served at bridesmaids' luncheons on good china and damask tablecloths, presented on lettuce leaves with fresh tomato and avocado. About half of a making disappears within the allotted marinating time right out of the mixing bowl, scooped out with plain saltine crackers.

This recipe is based on the salad served since 1947 at the famous Mobile, Alabama, seafood institution Bill Bailey's Restaurant. • SERVES 4

1 pound (3 cups) fresh lump crabmeat
1 small white onion, finely chopped
1/2 cup soybean oil
1/3 cup cider vinegar

1/2 teaspoon salt, or more to taste
1/4 teaspoon finely ground black pepper
Pinch of cayenne pepper, or more to taste

Layer the crabmeat and onion in a glass bowl. Drizzle with the oil, vinegar, and 1/4 cup cold water. Season with the salt, pepper, and cayenne. Cover and refrigerate for at least 24 hours.

Toss lightly and adjust the seasonings, if needed, before serving.

NOTES

• Check fresh or processed crabmeat for translucent cartilage that might have been overlooked before it was packed.

• If fresh crabmeat is not available, canned or pasteurized may be substituted. If using canned, taste it to check for any metallic taste; if any is present, rinse the crab several times with very cold water and drain well in a colander.

• My good girlfriends—sisters Kay "Cudibug" Mills and Marylee "Precious Magnolia" Baker—always use a cocktail shaker when assembling the dressing for this salad. The ounce markings on the side ease measuring and ice can be added right to the marinade, shaken to chill, and easily strained like a martini right over the layered crab and onion.

See photograph page 42.

Pimiento Cheese
Not Store-Bought, Please

• • •

Pimiento cheese can be a unitive, or divisive, sandwich spread. I do not think that is too drastic a statement. I have seen people have such heated discussions on what constitutes proper pimiento cheese that faces have turned red and someone has stomped off in a huff. I have read works by my peers who seem to have taken up the mantle of ambassador for pimiento cheese, extolling its virtues throughout the country. I have heard pimiento cheese apologists seek absolution from gourmands. There don't seem to be many on the fence when it comes to the issue of pimiento cheese. Folks like it or don't, and folks will eat store-bought or they won't. I like it—and I won't. If you feel the same, I recommend this recipe. • MAKES APPROXIMATELY 2 CUPS

1 cup mayonnaise, preferably Homemade (page 66)
1 teaspoon finely chopped sage
1 teaspoon fresh lemon juice
1 teaspoon dry mustard
$1/4$ teaspoon cayenne pepper
$1/2$ teaspoon Worcestershire sauce

8 ounces Colby cheese, grated (2 cups)
8 ounces sharp Cheddar cheese, grated (2 cups)
1 (4-ounce) jar chopped pimientos, drained
Salt and freshly ground black pepper
Hot pepper sauce

In a medium bowl, with a rubber spatula, combine the mayonnaise, sage, lemon juice, mustard, cayenne, and Worcestershire sauce.

Add the two cheeses and pimientos, blending thoroughly to combine. Season with salt, pepper, and hot sauce. Refrigerate until ready to use.

NOTES

• Substitute $1/4$ cup chopped roasted red bell pepper for the pimiento, if you like.

• For extra kick, add 1 teaspoon diced pickled jalapeño or green chiles.

• I prefer my pimiento cheese on lightly toasted wheat bread. It is also good with bagel chips and stuffed into celery stalks.

• Elvis is said to have liked pimiento cheese cheeseburgers. Zingerman's Roadhouse in Ann Arbor, Michigan, features one on their menu. Zingerman's prides itself on being the pimiento cheese capital of the Midwest.

Chicken Salad

Cool in Broth for Tenderness

• • •

This is the chicken salad I like for sandwiches or for stuffing big tomatoes, or serving on a bed of lettuce. A friend described it as being one of the triumvirate of white salads (the other two being tuna and potato, of course). It is a somewhat involved process, but worth it for the tender results and bonus fortified chicken broth. Start early in the morning if you are intending to serve it for lunch, or better yet, make it the day before so the flavors have time to mingle. • SERVES 6

NOTES

• Cooling the chicken in the broth makes the meat extra-tender and gives you a great base for gumbo or soup. Cooled broth can be refrigerated for one week or frozen for up to six months.

• Variations on the basic recipe can be made by adding diced apple, toasted pecan pieces, or fresh herbs to the salad.

CHICKEN

4 cups chicken broth
2 carrots, peeled and chopped
1 white root end of a bunch of celery, chopped
1 yellow onion, skin and all, chopped
5 black peppercorns
2 garlic cloves, smashed
1 teaspoon salt
1 lemon, halved
5 sprigs fresh thyme
2 tablespoons chopped parsley stems

5 (5-ounce) chicken breast halves, bones and skin attached

SALAD

1 cup finely chopped celery
1/2 cup diced sweet pickle relish
3 large eggs, hard-boiled, peeled, and chopped
1 cup mayonnaise, preferably Homemade (page 66)
Salt and freshly ground black pepper

COOK THE CHICKEN. In a large stockpot over medium heat, bring the broth, carrots, celery, onion, peppercorns, garlic, salt, lemon, thyme, and parsley to a boil. Cook for 20 minutes or until the vegetables are tender.

Reduce the heat to low and add the chicken; add water if needed to cover. Simmer for 30 minutes, stirring occasionally.

Remove the pot from the heat and let the chicken cool in the broth. Separate the meat from the skin and bones. Return the bones to the broth and simmer, covered, over low heat for 20 minutes. Strain and cool the broth, reserving for another use.

Shred the cooked chicken by pulling it into small pieces with your fingers. Refrigerate until ready to use.

MAKE THE SALAD. In a large bowl, combine the chicken with the celery, relish, eggs, mayonnaise, and salt and pepper to taste.

Lunch Counter Egg Salad Sandwich
Ode to Waxed Paper

• • •

The egg salad sandwiches at two of my favorite soda fountains, Brent's Drugs and (Miss Eudora Welty's favorite) Parkin's Pharmacy, come neatly wrapped in waxed paper, which seems a little retro these days, what with press-and-seals and zips and locks. Truth is, waxed paper is quite handy. It has myriad uses and is pretty cheap. I like unwrapping a sandwich that's been carefully folded in waxed paper. It has a nostalgic quality and it keeps the sandwiches ever so fresh. • SERVES 4

4 large eggs, hard-boiled, peeled, and coarsely chopped
1 cup finely chopped celery
1 tablespoon finely chopped pimiento-stuffed olives
1/2 cup mayonnaise, preferably Homemade (page 66)

8 slices Good Sandwich Loaf (page 175), lightly toasted
4 iceberg lettuce leaves
Salt and freshly ground black pepper

In a medium bowl, with a rubber spatula, combine the eggs, celery, olives, and mayonnaise.

Divide the salad among four slices of toast. Top each with a lettuce leaf and some salt and pepper. Cover with an additional slice of toast. Wrap in waxed paper and refrigerate until ready to eat, for up to 4 hours.

NOTES

• For instruction on hard-boiling eggs, see Notes on page 18.

• Some of the handy uses for crumpled waxed paper, compiled by cooking-tip expert Sharon Tyler Herbst, include rubbing the lip of honey jars to prevent drips and rubbing wooden salad bowls after cleaning to seal the surface.

ANOTHER use for waxed paper I learned from my great-aunt Mary is to sit on sheets of it for a few trips down the slide on the playground. It buffs it right up and really improves the ride!

Mother of the Church Ambrosia
A Labor of Love

• • •

Charlotte Miles came to work for our family one day right after we got home from my father's medical residency in Ohio, the summer I learned to write cursive. She walked up the driveway in a white nurse's uniform, and she informed my mother she had taken care of Doc when he was a baby and was here to take care of us now. She lived in a red house on Cherry Street. She was a Mother of the Church. When asked exactly what that meant, she said it meant you were "not compelled."

Upon further inquiry, it became apparent that it meant you were not compelled to do anything. Not compelled to feed the preacher, not compelled to have folks over after a funeral, not compelled to do pretty much anything you didn't feel like doing anymore, as you had done enough through the years. And you get to sit in the back row, so you can leave early without everybody seeing, or right up front in the first row. I hope to live long enough and do enough good works to be "not compelled."

Making proper ambrosia requires a good deal of labor and is offered lovingly by many mothers of the church. This dish gives you a lot of time to think while cutting the oranges and grating the coconut. I think about Miss Charlotte and her little red house on Cherry Street, and her years of kind works. • **SERVES 8**

8 navel oranges	**1 pineapple, cleaned, cored,**
1 coconut, cracked and	**and finely chopped (about**
shredded (see Notes, page	**3 cups)**
224), or 1$^1/_2$ cups	**2 cups maraschino cherries**
unsweetened flaked coconut	**(see Notes)**

Using a sharp knife, cut a small slice from each end of the oranges just large enough to expose the flesh and provide a flat base. Set the oranges on a cutting board. With steady strokes, follow the contour of the oranges, removing rinds, spongy piths, and stringy membranes. Carefully hold the fruit over a bowl to catch the juice, and cut between the membranes to free the segments from the oranges, giving a good squeeze to the remaining membranes once the sections have been removed to get every drop of juice.

Combine the orange segments and their reserved juice with the coconut, pineapple, and cherries. Let mellow in the refrigerator for 2 hours before serving chilled.

NOTES

• Drop hard-to-peel citrus in boiling water for a few minutes and then in ice water to loosen the pith and peel.

• To make maraschino cherries, soak 1 pound pitted fresh Queen Anne cherries (2 cups) or frozen tart red cherries in 2 cups maraschino liqueur and $^1/_2$ cup sugar overnight. Drain before adding to the ambrosia.

• This dish is pretty served in a cut-glass punch bowl.

• Ms. Lucy Gladness (above) is a Mother of the Church at the East Percy Street Christian Church. She has done many good works and makes a fine ambrosia herself.

Strawberry Missionary Society Salad

Do Have Some More Congealed Salad

• • •

When my great-aunt Carrye began her slide into dementia, she often repeated the phrase, "Do have some more congealed salad."

For many years I have considered it an honor when she passed to inherit her recipe clippings, the majority of which were headed, "Methodist Tested Recipes." The collection contained the Perfection Salad, Asheville Salad, Apricot Delight Salad, and the Amazing Coca-Cola Salad. Of course, I eventually découpaged them on the tabletop of a 1950s dinette set.

The specter of congealed salads looms large over many gatherings. Just the other day, when I was at the funeral of an elderly cousin, a contemporary of mine came from the kitchen of the Parish Hall and said "I can't believe I was actually assigned Congealed Salad, like that was a committee." It was and it is. They are good. There is a place in life for congealed salads (even in the American Heritage Dictionary*). So, go ahead, make room on the sideboard; there won't be any leftovers. And in times of bereavement, do assign someone to the congealed salads.* • SERVES 10 TO 12

NOTES

• Laura Shapiro's *Perfection Salad* explores the deeper meanings and cultural expectations for those women outfitted in hostess aprons, dishing up congealed salads in America.

• Never add fresh papaya, figs, honeydew, ginger, mango, or pineapple to a congealed salad; the enzymes will not let the gelatin congeal. Use jarred or canned fruit, which has been precooked, rendering the enzymes inactive.

2 (3-ounce) packages strawberry-flavored gelatin
2 (10-ounce) packages frozen strawberries
1 (3-ounce) package lemon-flavored gelatin
1 (8-ounce) can crushed pineapple, drained, juice reserved

1 (3-ounce) package cream cheese, softened
1 cup heavy cream
$1/3$ cup pecan pieces, chopped, plus extra for serving

Spray a 3-quart mold or 9 x 13-inch pan with nonstick cooking spray and line with plastic wrap. In a medium bowl, dissolve the strawberry gelatin in $2^{1}/_{2}$ cups boiling water. Add the strawberries and stir until berries are melted and the gelatin is completely dissolved. Pour the strawberry mixture into the prepared mold and refrigerate until set, about 2 hours.

Meanwhile, dissolve the lemon gelatin in 1 cup boiling water. Add $^{1}/_{2}$ cup of the reserved pineapple juice and let cool to room temperature. Add the softened cream cheese and crushed pineapple, stirring well with a rubber spatula. Refrigerate until slightly thickened, about 1 hour.

Whip the cream until it holds firm peaks. Fold it, along with the pecans, into the lemon mixture. Pour the lemon cream over the strawberry layer in the mold. Chill until firm, about 1 additional hour.

To serve, unmold by inverting the mold onto a serving platter. Remove the plastic wrap and garnish with additional toasted pecans, if desired.

AUNT Carrye visited Westminster Abbey on a trip to England with my mother. (Aunt Carrye had agreed to go on the trip when she was 81 years old, if she did not have cancer or diabetes when the results came back from a battery of tests at her annual physical; she declared, "My condition is unchanged," and in Aunt Carrye speak that meant she was healthy as a horse.) She saw the effigy on the tomb of one of England's Plantagenet kings and said, "I wish I had thought to do that for Junior." Instead, her husband, Jessie Faulkner Heard, is memorialized by the AstroTurf-covered concrete J. F. Heard Memorial Steps at Blackjack Baptist Church.

Frozen Cucumber Salad

Tangy, Chilling

• • •

Homegrown cucumbers, whether from your garden or someone else's, are one of the delights of summer. Cooling this salad way, way down by leaving it in the freezer for a few hours gives it a unique icy texture. Served in pitted avocado halves or hollowed-out cucumber boats, with a nice piece of cold poached salmon or gravlax, and with thin slices of buttered pumpernickel, this salad is quite good for a luncheon. • SERVES 6

2 English cucumbers, skins scored, halved lengthwise, diced
$1^1/_2$ teaspoons fine sea salt
3 tablespoons sugar
1 cup sour cream

2 large egg whites, beaten to soft peaks
$^1/_4$ cup champagne vinegar
$^1/_4$ cup fresh lime juice
2 tablespoons chopped parsley
1 tablespoon snipped dill
Lime wedges, for garnish

In a colander, combine the cucumbers and 1 teaspoon of the salt. Set in the sink to drain for 30 minutes, tossing occasionally. Rinse the cucumbers and set to drain on paper towels.

In a large resealable freezer bag, combine the remaining $^1/_2$ teaspoon salt, the sugar, sour cream, beaten egg whites, vinegar, lime juice, 1 tablespoon water, the parsley, and dill. Add the prepared cucumber. Chill in the freezer for 1 hour.

Turn the salad into a large bowl and beat well. Return the mixture to the freezer bag and freeze for 2 hours, or until crystallized. Serve with lime wedges.

NOTES

• Long English cucumbers are rarely waxed and virtually seedless. I like to run a zester or channel knife down the sides of cucumbers to remove a little of the skin and create a corduroy look.

• To make cucumber boats, slice the cucumbers lengthwise and hollow out the seedy core with a spoon.

Lady Pea Salad

Delicate in Vinaigrette

• • •

The elegant little Lady Pea is its own specific variety. However, from time to time, truck farmers of poor repute will impugn the Lady's reputation by trying to pass off imposters like Elite, Zipper, White Acre, or Texas Cream 12 that have had a bad year or were picked late in the season. These larger kin are sometimes referred to as Rice Peas or by the quite unladylike name Turkey Toes in Georgia, owing to the size and shape of their small three-pronged peduncle (a quite unladylike-sounding word in itself for the stalk). The Lady Pea's diminutive dimensions make it vulnerable to these falsities. Much like their namesake, Lady Peas are hard to get, hard to pick, tender, expensive, fought over when in short supply, and turn white at maturity.

Lady Peas dressed with a light herb vinaigrette are a lovely filling for a ripe tomato.

• SERVES 4

2 cups shelled Lady Peas or favorite fresh field peas (from about 1¹⁄₂ pounds in the shell)	1 tablespoon finely chopped red onion
1 tablespoon unsalted butter	1 teaspoon finely chopped parsley
¹⁄₂ cup plus 1 tablespoon finely diced celery	1 teaspoon finely chopped basil
3 cups vegetable broth	2 teaspoons champagne vinegar
Salt and ground white pepper	2¹⁄₂ tablespoons extra-virgin olive oil
4 large ripe tomatoes	

Soak the peas in cold water to cull any trash and remove floaters. Set the peas aside to drain in a sieve or colander.

In a large saucepan, melt the butter over medium heat. Add the peas and ¹⁄₂ cup celery; stir to coat. Once the peas are thoroughly coated with butter, add the broth. Cook, stirring occasionally, over medium heat for 15 minutes.

Season the peas with salt and white pepper, and continue to simmer for an 10 additional minutes, or until the peas are just tender. Drain well.

With a serrated knife, cut off the top third of each tomato. Working over a strainer set over a bowl, gently squeeze each tomato to remove the seeds, letting the juice drain into the bowl. Use the

NOTES

• When choosing fresh shelled field peas, give them a good sniff. There should be no sour odor or hint of fermentation. If fresh peas are not available, look for cream peas in the grocer's frozen vegetable section.

• Store shelled field peas in the refrigerator no longer than three days, or freeze. If freezing peas, blanch for 2 minutes, then plunge in an ice bath to ensure they do not overcook; then drain and place in freezer storage bags.

point of a small knife to cut open any bits that have seeds trapped. Discard the seeds. Scoop out the tomato flesh, being careful to keep the tomatoes in good shape for filling.

Dice the tomato flesh into small pieces and add to the tomato juice. Add the cooked peas, onion, remaining 1 tablespoon celery, the parsley, basil, vinegar, and oil. Season with salt to taste. Refrigerate for at least 20 minutes or overnight. (Refrigerate the tomato shells, too, if not serving right away.)

When ready to serve, fill each tomato with the pea salad.

Apricot Rice Salad
Mrs. Ethel Wright Mohamed

• • •

A sign above the door to the lovingly preserved home reads "Mama's Dream World." By appointment, visitors are escorted through the house by Miss Ivy to admire Mrs. Ethel's stitchery.

Born in the rural hill community of Fame, in Webster County, Mississippi, Ethel Wright moved as a teenager with her family to the Delta town of Shaw. While working after school at a bakeshop counter, she met a handsome Syrian peddler named Hassan Mohamed, who began to pay regular visits to the bakery. Remarking on how he must really like the cookies sold there, he told her it was she he liked instead. He began to call on the family at their home, often spending the entire visit talking to her father.

He eventually asked for Ethel's hand in marriage. Her deeply religious father, Elijah, asked why he should grant his approval for his daughter to marry a Muslim man who could neither read nor write English. Hassan replied, "I may not be able to read or write, but I can count all the money in the world." And in 1924 this remarkable couple married.

In 1927, the couple moved to Belzoni, the busy Humphreys County seat. There, with a partner, Hassan opened the D. Homad & H. Mohamed General Store, where Ethel worked side by side with her husband until his death in 1965.

Insomnia brought on by her grief kept Ethel up nights. She longed to be able to relive the joyous days she shared with her husband, raising their eight children. As a child, her mother had taught her embroidery as a way to keep her and her sister busy and quiet. With the notions available from the family business, Ethel began to stitch in an effort to quiet her mind. Always working in the evening, she recorded reminiscences of special events and moments of daily life on bedsheets and tea towels.

Ethel never sold any of the hundreds of pictures she created. Instead she donated her talents, and through her generous stitching, raised thousands of dollars for charitable causes. As for her memory pieces, she said, "These are my memories; I can't part with them. I have dresses and shoes and hats and other items to sell in my store, but not my pictures." In 1974, Mrs. Mohamed's work was featured in the Smithsonian Institution's Festival of American Folklife and a commissioned piece graced the cover of the exhibit's catalog. Some of her work is held in the Smithsonian's permanent collection. Over a hundred pictures, each comprising thousands and thousands of stitches lovingly sewn in shades as vibrant as her memories, fill Mama's Dream World today.

The bright colors and exotic spices of this salad remind me of Mrs. Mohamed's life and work. • SERVES 6

NOTES

• If squeezing the orange juice yourself, grate the zest first and save it to sprinkle on top of the salad.

• Spray your knife with cooking spray or wipe it with a little oil to prevent dried fruits like apricots from sticking, if you chop them yourself.

• Letting the salad cool, covered by a towel, keeps it moist without overcooking the bottom, at the same time allowing steam to escape.

• If the rice in the salad seems a little tough after being refrigerated, place it in a steamer basket over boiling water for 5 minutes to soften and rehydrate.

• This salad is nice served with a slice of honeydew melon.

1/2 teaspoon cumin seeds
1/2 teaspoon coriander seeds
1 green cardamom pod, crushed
3 tablespoons olive oil
2 tablespoons chopped red onion
1 1/2 cups Basmati rice, rinsed thoroughly
1-inch piece cinnamon stick
1 bay leaf

1/2 cup chopped dates
1/2 cup diced dried apricots
1/4 cup golden raisins
1/4 cup dried cherries or cranberries
1 cup plus 1 tablespoon fresh orange juice
1/4 teaspoon salt
2 green onions, white and green parts, thinly sliced on the diagonal

In a 10-inch ovenproof pan with a tight-fitting lid, briefly heat the cumin, coriander, and cardamom over medium heat to toast, shaking the pan to prevent scorching. When the spices are fragrant, remove them from the pan and let cool. Grind the cumin and coriander finely with a mortar and pestle or in a spice grinder.

Add 1 tablespoon olive oil to the same pan and heat over medium-high heat; add the onion, cooking and stirring occasionally for 4 to 6 minutes or until the onion is tender. Reduce the heat and add the rice, spices, cinnamon stick, and bay leaf. Cook and stir until the rice is light golden and each grain is coated with oil. Remove the bay leaf and cinnamon stick and mix in the dates, apricots, raisins, and cherries.

Add 1 cup of the orange juice, 1 1/2 cups water, and the salt, stirring briefly just to combine. Bring the mixture to a boil over high heat; reduce the heat to low, cover, and simmer for 15 minutes, or until the rice is tender and has absorbed the liquid.

Using a large fork to fluff up the rice and fruit mixture, turn it into a serving dish, drizzle with the remaining 2 tablespoons oil and 1 tablespoon orange juice, and combine using the fork. Allow to cool, covered by a clean dish towel, then serve at room temperature or chilled, sprinkled with green onion across the top.

AN inscription on Mrs. Mohamed's headstone reads SHE SHALL BE BROUGHT BEFORE THE KING IN RAIMENT OF NEEDLEWORK. Psalm 45:14.

Tabbouleh
Ripe with History

• • •

When the American South is discussed, it is most often done so in terms of black and white. This limiting view, however, does not reflect the salad of humanity found throughout a region that has offered immigrants unclaimed economic frontiers from the turn of the century well into the 1950s and continues today. Middle Easterners established a flourishing mercantile society as the burgeoning agricultural economy grew. Vestiges of some of these Lebanese settlers are found in the common surnames Malouf, Shamoon, Moses, Antoon, and Abraham. Some Americanized the Tamous to Thomas and Alias to Ellis. Traces of these pioneering Mediterranean families are also still tasted, with the common addition of minted tomato and bulgur salad to community potlucks, right alongside fried chicken and sweet potato pie. • SERVES 6

1 cup medium bulgur wheat
2 large ripe tomatoes, seeded and diced
1 small cucumber, seeded and diced
3 green onions, white and green parts, chopped
$^1/_2$ cup chopped parsley leaves
$^1/_2$ cup chopped mint leaves

$^1/_2$ cup purslane leaves
Grated zest and juice of 1 lemon
1 tablespoon extra-virgin olive oil
Pinch of ground allspice
Fine sea salt
Freshly ground black pepper

Soak the bulgur for 1 hour in warm water to cover by at least 2 inches. Drain well by dumping the bulgur into a strainer and pressing.

In a large bowl, combine the tomatoes, cucumber, onions, parsley, mint, purslane, lemon zest and juice, and oil. Add the bulgur and season with allspice, salt, and pepper. Toss well to mix.

> JIMMY THOMAS, longtime friend and managing editor of the *New Encyclopedia of Southern Culture* for the Center for Southern Culture, is of Lebanese descent. He speaks warm-heartedly about the traditional Thanksgiving dinners at his family's home in Leland, Mississippi, where turkey, cornbread dressing, and sweet potato casserole sat side by side with kibbe, grape leaves, and tabbouleh.

NOTES

• Bulgur is cracked wheat that has been parboiled and coarsely ground. Look for it in Middle Eastern markets. I like to use size 4 in this recipe.

• Very ripe tomatoes should be used for this salad.

• Purslane, or "poor man's spinach," has a slightly bitter lemon flavor, with succulent crunchy leaves shaped a little like fat watercress. This salad is successful without the purslane, but it does add much in the way of authenticity and texture.

• Tabbouleh tends to get watery if it sits too long; therefore, it should be eaten the same day it is made or carefully drained in a fine sieve before serving.

Three Bean Salad

Washboards and Accordions

• • •

Zydeco music—that heart-pounding, fast-tempo, syncopated music of Louisiana and East Texas—shakes dance halls with the accent on the second and fourth beats. The name itself applies not only to the genre but also to the style of dance. It is thought to have come from a Creole title for a popular dance tune, "Les Haricots Sont Pas Salés" (The Snapbeans Are Not Salted). A diverse blend of melodies and instruments, zydeco mingles Caribbean, French West Indian, and African sounds with German polka, French waltz, and Polish mazurka, and then funnels them through rhythm and blues.

Everyone from little children to old folks can be found dancing together at a **fais-do-do,** *much like a covered-dish supper with nonstop dancing. Folding tables covered with all types of dishes rattle as two-steppers promenade. This substantial salad is always a nice addition to a gathering of any kind where stamina is needed, such as a family reunion.* • SERVES 8

NOTES

• One (14.5-ounce) jar of artichoke hearts, rinsed and drained, is a nice addition to the recipe.

• After marinating for several hours, the beans may soak up much of the dressing. Allow the salad to come to room temperature, and adjust the seasonings, adding a touch more oil and vinegar, if needed.

1 (14.5-ounce) can red kidney beans, rinsed and drained
1 (14.5-ounce) can wax beans, rinsed and drained
1 (14.5-ounce) can French-cut green beans, rinsed and drained
1 green bell pepper, thinly sliced

1 small onion, thinly sliced
$^2/_3$ cup garlic vinegar, or
$^2/_3$ cup sherry vinegar and 1 teaspoon minced garlic
$^1/_3$ cup sugar
1 teaspoon salt
$^1/_2$ teaspoon coarsely ground black pepper
$^1/_4$ cup extra-virgin olive oil

In a large bowl, combine the beans, bell pepper, and onion.

In a small bowl, whisk together the vinegar, sugar, salt, black pepper, and oil. Pour over the bean salad and refrigerate for 6 hours or overnight.

Three-Day Slaw
House Party Weekend

· · ·

The first week of August, in the east-central red-clay hill country of Mississippi, the Neshoba County Fair kicks off. It's known far and wide as the "Giant House Party," and the fairgrounds are transformed into a bustling, albeit temporary, city complete with a post office and even its own zip code. Hundreds of two-story cabins consisting mostly of bunkhouse-style sleeping quarters, a kitchen, and a porch encircle a racetrack where camptown harness races are hotly contested. The pavilion in the square provides a platform for political rivals to give forth with florid oratory. Children and old-timers alike visit from house to house, from sunup to way past sundown during Fair Week, stopping in for a bite here and a drink there.

This slaw will keep well for three or more days. It is great to have on hand through-out a weekend of houseguests. • SERVES 8

1 cup cider vinegar
¹/₄ cup sugar
1 teaspoon dry mustard
1 teaspoon celery seeds
1¹/₂ teaspoons salt
1 cup corn or vegetable oil

1 small head green cabbage, shredded
1 small white onion, halved and thinly sliced
1 red bell pepper, sliced thinly
1 cup shredded, peeled carrot

In a small saucepan over medium heat, combine the vinegar, sugar, mustard, celery seeds, and salt. Bring to a boil, stirring until the sugar is dissolved. Remove from the heat and add the oil. Cool until just warm to the touch, about 30 minutes.

In a large bowl or resealable food bag storage, combine the cabbage, onion, bell pepper, and carrot. Pour the warm dressing over the cabbage mixture. Cover and marinate for 8 hours, refrigerated, or up to three days.

NOTES

• Celery seeds are harvested from smallage, a marsh plant that produces the seed during the second year of its growth, not from the more familiar celery found in the produce department.

• Dry mustard has little aroma, but when the enzyme myrosinase that's in it comes in contact with liquid, a sharp aroma is released. So, although it may not smell like much, it grants a pungent bite once moistened.

• To freshen the flavor of this slaw or change it during its long run, stir in an apple cut into matchsticks or thinly sliced fennel bulb and orange segments.

Homemade Mayonnaise
Aunt Marynaise and Baby Jane

• • •

NOTES

• Have your eggs at room temperature or run them under warm water. Cold eggs will not incorporate into the emulsion as easily as warmed eggs.

• As with any time raw eggs are used, the possibility of salmonella is present. If you are concerned that the mayonnaise may be consumed by someone with a compromised immune system, or the very old or very young, use pasteurized eggs or replace the egg and yolk with ¼ cup egg substitute.

• Although contrary to first thoughts and household lore, Alton Brown advises that homemade mayonnaise be left covered at room temperature 8 to 12 hours, to enable the acid in the mixture to coagulate the proteins and kill any suspect bacteria in the eggs, then refrigerated for no longer than a week.

• Assorted fresh herbs or spices, such as curry or cumin, can add interesting flavor to what could become your signature mayonnaise.

The Wesson Oil Company produced a home mayonnaise-making mechanism back in the 1930s—an ingenious device consisting of a heavy quart jar embossed with a recipe and a resealable screw-top lid (that could be replaced with a standard lid), which housed a long plunger that terminated in a netted disk. The center of the lid sloped toward the hole for the plunger at an angle, allowing the perfect amount of oil to be trickled into the container while being pumped like mad to create an emulsification with velvety smoothness.

When the Culinary Institute of America's Worlds of Flavor Travel Program paid me a visit last summer out at the farm, I fashioned an entire afternoon of festivities in homage to the colloid emulsion.

After a soul-stirring performance by the Double Quick Gospel Choir, comprising Double Quick convenience-store managers from the greater Arkansas and Mississippi Deltas, we held the first in what, we hoped, would become an annual event, The Aunt Marynaise and Baby Jane Burdine Invitational Mayonnaise Making Contest. After a demonstration of the wondrous device by Jane Rule Burdine, daughter of late mayonnaise afficionada Baby Jane Burdine, and myself, contestants were paired into teams, each provided with an antique Wesson Oil Mayonnaise Maker, eggs, salt and pepper, and an assortment of oils, acids, and herbs. As our special celebrity judge, my great-aunt Mary Stigler Thompson, author of the homemade mayonnaise recipe (pronounced hō-mĕd máneez) *found in the beloved* Tchula Garden Club Cookbook, *judged on criteria of her own discretion.*

The teams were set to task. While one member assembled the flavorings, the other separated the eggs. Then when the mayonnaise apparatus was assembled, one pumped the plunger with furious speed up and down as the other teammate haltingly poured in the oil. As the last droplets of oil were incorporated and the onlookers' cheers reached crescendo, time was called and judgment commenced.

After tasting each entrant, Aunt Mary, in her octogenarian wisdom, declared none to be as good as her own and all not salty enough; but pressed to choose, she eventually granted the title of inaugural winner to one. A lunch followed, with the winning mayonnaise served in a place of distinction alongside freshly baked white slicing bread and ripe beefsteak tomatoes for sandwiches. The runners-up were relegated to minted fresh pea salad and pimiento cheese. • MAKES 2 PINTS

1 large egg
1 large egg yolk
1 tablespoon fresh lemon
 juice
1 tablespoon white vinegar

1 teaspoon dry mustard
1 teaspoon salt
1 teaspoon sugar
Dash of cayenne pepper
2 cups vegetable oil

In a food processor fitted with the metal blade, a blender, or the jar of mayonnaise maker, combine the whole egg, yolk, lemon juice, vinegar, mustard, salt, sugar, and cayenne. Pulse several times to blend.

With the processor running at high speed, or while quickly dashing the plunger of a mayonnaise maker, very slowly drizzle in the oil, allowing it to fully integrate as added until all the oil has been incorporated.

• For aïoli, the classic garlic-infused mayonnaise of France's Provence region, add 2 minced garlic cloves with the lemon juice and replace the vegetable oil with olive oil. Le Grand Aïoli is a luncheon spread of cold poached meats and vegetables.

• Extra-virgin olive oil should be avoided because it is unrefined and contains monoglycerides that may cause the emulsion to separate.

• A little plastic wrap pressed to the surface will prevent a translucent skin from forming on the surface of the sauce.

• Spread a thin layer of mayonnaise over fish fillets before baking; it puffs and browns nicely as it flavors the fish.

• Sometimes these mayonnaise makers can be found for sale on eBay or at antique stores or junk shops. If you are using one, it helps to place the maker on a damp cloth set in the sink, to prevent slips or spills. A tag-team approach, with one person pouring oil and the other plunging, works well.

Jezebel Sauce
Named for the Wanton Woman

• • •

In the movie trailer from the 1938 Academy Award—winning film Jezebel, *headlines flash across the silver screen: "Bette Davis as . . . Jezebel! The story of a woman who was loved when she should have been whipped! Pride of the South that loved her. . . . Shame of the Man she loved!" The saucy Ms. Davis as the title character dares to wear a red dress to the Olympus Ball. Coquettish with a sharp tongue, this sauce is aptly named. What sweet heat.* • MAKES 2⅓ CUPS

1 (5-ounce) jar pineapple
   preserves
1 (5-ounce) jar apple jelly
1 (5-ounce) jar prepared
   mustard

1 (4-ounce) jar prepared
   horseradish
1 teaspoon kosher salt

Combine the preserves, jelly, mustard, horseradish, and salt in a medium saucepan. Heat over medium heat until the mixture is hot and bubbly. Carefully pour the sauce into clean jars and allow to cool.

Place the lids on the jars and store in the refrigerator for up to two weeks.

NOTES

• This condiment is wonderful paired with smoked meats, and can dress up cream cheese as a spread.

• If giving as a gift, remember to place a note on the jar to remind the recipient to keep the sauce stored in the refrigerator. You may want to add an expiration date, too.

See photograph page 177.

Comeback Sauce
Put It on Anything

• • •

This is first-rate served over chilled boiled shrimp or as a dressing for vegetable salads. It's a crowning condiment for fried pickles, onion rings, and crackers. Chef and food writer Robert St. John calls Comeback Sauce "the Queen Mother of all Mississippi condiments." And it is.

Comeback Sauce (which is also spelled Kumback or Cumback, and will get you to all kinds of interesting sites if you Google these alternative spellings) originated in the Greek restaurants of Jackson, Mississippi. The Rotisserie opened in the late '20s or early '30s, and was Jackson's first Greek restaurant. Malcolm White, who is keeper of all information on Comeback, credits the genesis of Comeback Sauce to The Rotisserie and its owner, Alex Dennery. Comeback Sauce then spread to other Greek restaurants that opened in Jackson, such as The Mayflower, which has been serving Comeback Sauce in bottles left on each table with crackers since 1935.

Comeback, like kudzu, that miracle vine introduced to the South, couldn't be reined in. You'll find versions of the sauce at local hangouts like the Cherokee, C.S.'s, and Hal & Mal's. Some of the sauces use curry or extra garlic. You can find it at the Ajax Diner in Oxford or at Giardina's in Greenwood. It's often described to those from above the Mason—Dixon line as a spicy Thousand Island. But it is so much more than that. Comeback Sauce is heaven on a cracker, and it is home. • **MAKES 1 PINT**

1 cup mayonnaise, preferably
    Homemade (page 66)
$1/4$ cup salad oil
$1/4$ cup chili sauce
$1/4$ cup ketchup
1 tablespoon Worcestershire
    sauce

1 teaspoon yellow mustard
1 teaspoon freshly ground
    black pepper
1 teaspoon hot pepper sauce
$1/4$ teaspoon hot paprika
1 small white onion, grated
2 cloves garlic, minced

In a food processor or blender, combine the mayonnaise, oil, chili sauce, ketchup, Worcestershire, mustard, pepper, hot pepper sauce, paprika, onion, and garlic. Process until smooth. Store in the refrigerator for up to one week.

NOTE

• To lean this dressing more toward Thousand Island, add 2 chopped hard-boiled eggs and 1 tablespoon chopped capers or sweet-pickle relish.

Buttermilk Dressing
Head 'a Lettuce Salad

• • •

Back in the day of my grandparents, buttermilk *meant the liquid derived from churning cream into butter, mildly sour in flavor from the ripening of the cream. Today the cultured buttermilk we see in dairy cases is skim or low-fat milk that has been slightly fermented with the same cultures used in making butter and then heated to stop the fermentation process. Like so many things, all buttermilk is not created equal. Many are additionally thickened with stabilizers and gums. Pick buttermilk with a simple list of ingredients: whole milk and cultures.*

I like a simple iceberg wedge with a little of this dressing drizzled over the top and a nice crumble of blue cheese, maybe some diced tomato if they are good and in season, and crumbled bacon if there is some around. • MAKES $^3/_4$ CUP

$^1/_2$ **cup buttermilk**
2 tablespoons sour cream
2 tablespoons mayonnaise
$^1/_2$ **teaspoon chopped shallot**
$^1/_2$ **teaspoon chopped chives**
$^1/_2$ **teaspoon chopped parsley leaves**

$^1/_2$ **teaspoon thyme leaves**
$^1/_2$ **teaspoon cider vinegar**
$^1/_2$ **teaspoon sugar**
$^1/_4$ **teaspoon salt**
$^1/_8$ **teaspoon garlic powder**

In a medium bowl, whisk together the buttermilk, sour cream, mayonnaise, shallot, chives, parsley leaves, thyme leaves, cider vinegar, sugar, salt, and garlic powder.

Chill for 1 hour. Store in the refrigerator for up to one week.

NOTES

• When developing recipes with the opening team of Giardina's, the restaurant located in the Alluvian Hotel, we held a series of taste panels to review all of the dishes. We had sailed through 72 recipes, but that momentum came to a halt when we got to the ubiquitous ranch-style buttermilk dressing. "It's not ranchy enough," or "Oh, this one is a little too ranchy" was said with serious faces. What is "ranchy"? I gleaned through the 21 versions that the quality of "ranchy" was in direct proportion to the amount of buttermilk.

• A nice variation on this dressing to serve with crudités can be made by substituting yogurt for the buttermilk.

Cottonseed Oil and Vinegar
The Secret Ingredient

• • •

When you look out the passenger window of a car, the rows of cotton running along next to the highway give an illusion similar to the swiftly turning pages of a flip book. The tall green plants of summer are festooned with pink and yellow blossoms that flicker past like a fancy woman's fan being flicked open and shut. Those endless rows upon rows will become blue jeans and undershirts and sheets and rugs and rags. When the blossoms fade, bolls form. After the fields turn white, and the cotton is picked and ginned, removing the fibers from the seeds, the seeds are pressed at the oil mill. The oil is refined and finds its way into all manner of foods, from chocolates to fried chicken. The oil has a light, fresh, clean flavor, making it a good choice for salad dressings. Cottonseed oil is the secret ingredient in this simple vinaigrette. It's wonderfully tart tossed with greens and excellent sprinkled over fish to be broiled or grilled. • MAKES 1 1/2 CUPS*

1/2 cup white vinegar
1 tablespoon juice from a jar
  of pimiento-stuffed olives
1 1/2 teaspoons minced garlic
1/2 teaspoon salt

1/4 teaspoon celery salt
1/8 teaspoon onion powder
1/8 teaspoon sweet paprika
1 cup cottonseed oil

Combine the vinegar, pimiento juice, garlic, salt, celery salt, onion powder, paprika, and oil in a large jar. Tighten the lid and shake until well combined. Store in the refrigerator for up to a week.

NOTES

• Store cottonseed oil refrigerated and tightly sealed. It will go rancid quickly when exposed to air.

• If pure cottonseed oil is unavailable, use a vegetable oil that is a blend of canola and cottonseed or of soybean and cottonseed oil, which is more widely available. Grapeseed oil makes a nice substitution but can be a little pricey. (New varieties of cotton are being grown with completely edible protein-rich seeds.)

• This dressing is used to broil Greenwood Pompano (page 133).

THE dreaded boll weevil, scourge of cotton farmers, began its devastating campaign through the fields in 1892. The invasion spread at an astounding 70 miles a year. Efforts are still underway to eradicate this menace.

GUMBOS, SOUPS, DUMPLINGS, AND A BISQUE

Gumbo Z'Herbs

Thinking of Mrs. Leah

• • •

NOTES

• Filé is ground sassafras leaves. Introduced into Creole cooking by the Choctaws who lived around Lake Pontchartrain, filé has become a signature ingredient of the region. It derives its name from its improper use; when the powdered leaves are added to a boiling liquid, its mucilaginous qualities come out, forming threads, or *fils* in French. Never add filé until the end, when there is no chance of the liquid returning to a boil—filé will gently thicken the gumbo as it sits.

• The taste of filé powder is a little like mild marjoram. The sassafras powders available in some herb emporiums are made of the roots and bark and should not be confused with filé powder, which is made from the ground leaves.

• If you are intending to freeze or reheat this gumbo, add filé only to the portion about to be served. Add approximately 1½ teaspoons of filé to 4 cups of liquid.

Preparing this gumbo makes me think of Leah Chase, proprietress of Dooky Chase's Restaurant, on the corner of Claiborne and Orleans Avenues in New Orleans. Not much more than five feet tall, if even that, with a magisterial voice, Mrs. Leah Chase has commanded the cherished establishment for decades, receiving countless awards for her cooking and community commitment. In my eyes, she is the undisputed "Queen of Creole Cuisine."

This thick, verdant filé gumbo, like the one at Dooky Chase, is often served on Holy Thursday and Good Friday and throughout Lent, when it is prepared without meat, as it is here. The number of greens included in a batch may vary from cook to cook. Some use seven, as it is the "number of completion" throughout the Bible. Others choose seven types of greens to represent the seven African powers. Some use twelve, representing the number of apostles, while others choose as many as possible with the belief that with every green you add to your gumbo pot, you will make a new friend. Leah has added untold numbers of greens to her well-seasoned gumbo pot and has the friends to prove it. Remember, as the Grande Dame says, if more friends drop on in for gumbo than anticipated, you have to baptize the gumbo by stretching it out with a little water.

• SERVES 8 TO 10

Approximately 12 cups roughly chopped greens (no stems, please) of at least 5 of the following: spinach; collard; turnip, beet, or carrot tops; mustard; chicory; kale; watercress; pepper grass; poke sallet; cabbage; sorrel; or leaf lettuce

1 large onion, diced

3 garlic cloves, minced

¼ cup vegetable oil

¼ cup unbleached all-purpose flour

6 green onions, white and green parts, chopped

1 cup chopped parsley

2 bay leaves

2 sprigs thyme

1 teaspoon salt, or more to taste

1 teaspoon cayenne pepper

½ teaspoon sugar

¼ teaspoon ground allspice

1 tablespoon cider vinegar

1 tablespoon filé powder, plus extra for seasoning

4 to 5 cups cooked white rice

In a 2-gallon stockpot, simmer the greens, onion, and garlic with 1 gallon water for 2 hours, or until all types of greens are tender. Strain the greens, reserving the liquid, or fish out most of the greens with a sieve and set aside.

In a large Dutch oven over medium heat, heat the oil until it shimmers. Whisk the flour in slowly until no lumps remain. Continue to cook and stir for 2 minutes, or until about the color of a paper grocery sack.

Add the green onions, parsley, bay leaves, thyme, salt, cayenne, sugar, and allspice. Cook for 5 minutes. Add the greens and the vinegar, and simmer over low heat for 15 minutes. Add the reserved cooking liquid and cook for 1 hour over low heat. Remove from the heat, adjust the seasoning, and add the filé powder. Stir well. Remove the bay leaves.

Serve in bowls over a little rice with a sprinkling of filé powder over each.

Duck and Sausage Gumbo
From the Mississippi Flyway

• • •

Flyways are the long arterial air highways used by migrating birds. More than 3,000 miles long, the Mississippi Flyway is a major route used by geese and ducks. With barely a rise to interfere with the traffic flow from the Mackenzie River emptying out into the Arctic Ocean to the Mississippi River flowing into the Gulf of Mexico, this thoroughfare passes right over our farm.

For the last few mornings I have been awakened at dawn's first light by the report of shotguns from across the river. When row-crop fields are too muddy to work and the water is high in the new year, many sportsmen devote a good deal of time to duck hunting and other leisure activities. When the water recedes and the fields dry, they will be back to work before sunup. That means this gumbo is in season during duck season to warm the people on the chilly January evenings.

Either okra or filé can be used in this gumbo. But, please—one or the other. If you wish to use okra, add 1 cup sliced before you add the herbs. If you wish to use filé, add it to the gumbo when it has finished cooking. Turn off the burner and stir in 1 table-spoon. Allow the gumbo to sit undisturbed for a few minutes to thicken. • SERVES 6

NOTES

• Six quail, or 20 dove breasts, may be used in this recipe in place of the duck; reduce the cooking time to 1 hour.

• Venison sausage, found in many hunters' freezers, can be added in place of the andouille.

• If preparing this in late summer with ducks from the freezer, add 1 cup fresh corn kernels and two diced, seeded tomatoes, when you return the cooked duck and sausage to the gumbo; it brightens the flavors, especially when the gumbo is finished with a sprinkle of fresh herbs.

½ cup plus ⅓ cup peanut oil
2 wild ducks (such as mallards), dressed, skin removed, cut into pieces, bones and all
Salt and freshly ground black pepper
1 pound andouille sausage, cut in 1-inch rounds
⅓ cup unbleached all-purpose flour
1 medium onion, chopped

1 red bell pepper, chopped
1 celery stalk, leaves and all, chopped
½ cup chopped parsley
2 garlic cloves, minced
2 quarts vegetable broth
1 teaspoon dried thyme
1 teaspoon dried marjoram
¼ teaspoon dried sage
2 cups cooked wild rice
2 tablespoons chopped chives
Hot pepper sauce

Heat a large pot over medium heat. Add ½ cup peanut oil and heat until hot. Season the duck pieces with salt and pepper and add to the pot. Cook, turning and rearranging a few times, until browned on all sides, about 5 minutes. Remove the ducks from the pot and set aside. Discard the oil in the pot.

Add the remaining ⅓ cup oil to the pot and heat over medium heat until hot. Add the sausage and cook, stirring, until browned, about 2 minutes. Scoop out the sausage and set it aside with the duck.

Sprinkle the flour into the oil and sausage drippings in the pot. Whisk to combine. Cook, stirring, over very low heat for 5 to 7 minutes or until it makes a dark roux. Add the onion, bell pepper, celery, parsley, and garlic. Gradually stir in 1 to 2 cups of the broth to make a smooth sauce. Add the thyme, marjoram, and sage. Add the duck pieces and sausage, pouring in any of their drippings, too. Add the remaining broth. Bring to a boil, reduce the heat to low, and simmer for 2 hours, until the duck is fall-off-the-bone tender.

Serve over wild rice and sprinkle with chives and hot sauce to taste.

JUST as the Inuit people have many words for different types of snow, Delta people have many words for different kinds of mud. The most treacherous is the dreaded Gumbo Mud—black and sticky, created by eons of silt settling in the low areas.

Seafood Gumbo

From the Depths

• • •

Good seafood gumbo should be somewhat unsettling when presented. Submerged beneath the opaque, burnt-umber tide pool (and, for effect, reaching out from the bowl), a half-dismembered Gulf blue crab and various creatures from the deep must be almost obscured and mysteriously suspended.

Initially, seafood gumbo was prepared by people who made this dish from what they could catch, forage, and cultivate as a matter of subsistence. Today, for most people, a pot of seafood gumbo can be a pricey investment. Remember to take your time and enjoy the process as much as you will the final product. • SERVES 12

NOTES

• If your stockpot is not very thick bottomed, cook the roux in a heavy skillet and then transfer it to the stockpot. If the roux gets the slightest black specks, it has to be pitched and started again. The old saying goes that it should take about as long to make a dark roux as it does to drink two beers.

• Cooking the okra down keeps it from being slimy in the gumbo—what is known down here as "ropey." It will thicken the gumbo without making it stringy.

• Gumbo crabs are small, hard-shelled blue crabs with the top half removed and the claws and legs attached. They are sold frozen in some seafood markets or can be shipped overnight from 1-800-nu-awlins.

• Adding the shrimp, crab-meat, and oysters right at the end keeps them succulent.

SHRIMP STOCK
1 pound large shrimp, preferably shell on
1 medium onion, chopped
1 celery stalk, chopped
1 carrot, chopped
6 black peppercorns
2 garlic cloves
1 cup dry white wine
1/2 lemon
1 bay leaf

GUMBO
1 cup plus 2 tablespoons vegetable oil
1 1/2 cups unbleached all-purpose flour
1 large white onion, chopped
2 celery stalks, leaves and all, chopped
1 red bell pepper, chopped

3 garlic cloves, minced
1 teaspoon dried thyme
Salt
8 ounces okra, thinly sliced
1 large ripe tomato, seeded and diced
1 tablespoon light brown sugar
6 gumbo crabs, broken in half (see Notes)
4 green onions, white and green parts, chopped
8 ounces crabmeat
1 pint oysters, or 24 oysters, shucked, with liquor reserved
1 tablespoon fresh lemon juice
Freshly ground black pepper
Hot pepper sauce
6 cups cooked white rice

MAKE THE SHRIMP STOCK. Peel and devein the shrimp. Refrigerate the shrimp for later and toss the heads and shells into a large stockpot. Add the onion, celery, carrot, peppercorns, garlic, wine, lemon, and bay leaf. Add 3 1/2 quarts water and bring to a boil. Reduce the heat and simmer for 1 hour. Strain through a fine-mesh strainer, discard the solids, and transfer the stock to another smaller pot if you just have one large pot. Return the stock to a simmer.

MAKE THE GUMBO. Return the emptied stockpot to medium-high heat and add 1 cup of the oil. Whisking steadily, add the flour. Reduce the heat to very low and cook, whisking constantly, until the roux is a deep, deep pecan brown. This will take quite some time, up to 20 minutes or more (see Notes).

Add the onion, celery, bell pepper, and garlic. Cook and stir until vegetables are tender, 5 minutes. Add the thyme and season with salt. Slowly incorporate 3 quarts of the simmering shrimp stock, adding water if needed to make up any difference.

Meanwhile, in a medium saucepan, cook the okra in the remaining 2 tablespoons oil over low heat for 10 minutes, or until no longer ropey (see Notes). Add the tomato and brown sugar, and cook for 2 minutes. Add to the gumbo along with the gumbo crabs. Simmer the gumbo over very low heat for 30 minutes.

Add the green onions, the shrimp, the crabmeat, oysters and their liquor, and lemon juice. Simmer for 5 minutes, just until the shrimp are cooked through. Season with salt, pepper, and hot sauce to taste and serve over rice.

• Let your pocketbook decide what grade of crab-meat to use. Jumbo lump is spendy; lump or backfin special can be used and is very flavorful; inexpensive claw meat is very flavorful but can be quite stringy.

• The way you know what gumbo you like to make is to make it often. Let your personal taste dictate. There are as many recipes as there are cooks, and no two gumbos are ever the same.

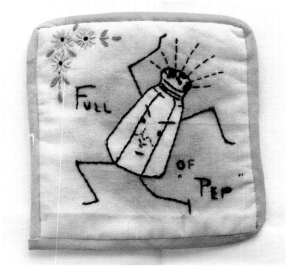

Oven Chicken and Okra Gumbo
I Got Work to Do Gumbo

• • •

Oh, if only I lived a life where my days could be spent minding a gumbo pot. This gumbo is slow-cooked in the oven for about 3 hours and only needs to be checked on a time or two. • SERVES 8 TO 10

2 pounds okra, sliced into
  $1/4$-inch-thick rounds
1 medium onion, chopped
1 celery stalk, chopped
1 red bell pepper, seeded and
  chopped
3 garlic cloves, minced
1 (14.5-ounce) can peeled
  whole tomatoes

1 (6-ounce) can tomato paste
3 cups diced cooked chicken
6 ounces tasso or smoked
  ham, diced
1 quart chicken broth
Salt and freshly ground black
  pepper
4 cups cooked white rice

Preheat the oven to 250°F.

Combine the okra, onion, celery, bell pepper, garlic, tomatoes, and tomato paste in a large roasting pan. Cover with foil and bake for 1 hour or until very tender.

Remove the foil and add the chicken, tasso, and broth. Return to the oven and bake for $1^1/2$ to 2 hours, or until desired thickness. Season with salt and pepper.

Ladle the gumbo into bowls and spoon a little rice into the center of each one.

NOTES

• Okra should not be slow-cooked in cast iron, as this will darken it.

• Tasso is made from slices of highly spiced smoked pork butt. Cappicola can be successfully substituted.

• Similar chicken gumbos made with many ingredients and andouille sausages are called Gumbo Ya Ya, from the Cajun saying for "everybody talking at one time."

• Texmati rice, a type of Basmati rice grown in Texas, is a nice choice for serving with gumbo.

Tomato Soup
Reminder of Summer Solstice

• • •

Around June 21, the longest day of the year marks the beginning of summer. It's at this time in my area that the first of the good tomatoes start coming in.

When local vine-ripened tomatoes are at a good price, or the homegrown ones have accumulated on the windowsill, investing less than an hour of those long afternoons in a batch of soup and depositing it in the freezer to withdraw in the dead of winter is a fine idea. • SERVES 4

3 pounds ripe tomatoes (about 9 globe or 24 plum), stemmed, halved, and seeded
2 tablespoons unsalted butter
1 medium white onion, chopped

$^1/_4$ teaspoon salt
$^1/_4$ teaspoon freshly ground black pepper
$^1/_2$ teaspoon sugar
2 tablespoons chopped basil
2 teaspoons chopped oregano

Preheat the broiler.

Place the tomatoes cut side down on a rimmed baking sheet and broil for 10 minutes, or until the skins begin to char and burst. Remove from the oven. When cool enough to handle, remove the charred skins.

Meanwhile, heat a large saucepan over medium heat. Add the butter and then the onion. Cook and stir for 3 to 5 minutes, or until tender but not brown. Add the tomatoes and simmer for 20 minutes, or until the tomatoes have cooked down. Season with the salt, pepper, and sugar and add the basil and oregano. Serve immediately, or remove from the heat and cool completely before storing in the refrigerator or freezer.

NOTES

• Use several varieties of tomatoes to get the full tomato spectrum of flavors, or all yellow or orange for a color variation. Simultaneously ladling two different colors of this soup, such as if you've made one batch with red tomatoes and another with yellow, into the same bowl makes for a beautiful presentation and interesting flavor juxtaposition; see photo below. Make a batch of soup from each color of tomato.

• For a creamy soup, add $^1/_3$ cup heavy cream at the end, or garnish with whipped cream seasoned with a little salt.

Curried Sweet Potato Soup
Pork Rind Crouton

• • •

I love the way a crisp puffed pork rind (or a scattering of pomegranate seeds) crowns this soup, which elevates the lowly sweet potato. A little heat from curry and sweetness from coconut milk make this dish worthy of the fine china. • SERVES 6

3 pounds dark orange sweet
    potatoes, peeled and diced
3 tablespoons unsalted butter
2 leeks, white and tender
    green parts only, chopped
1 tablespoon grated peeled
    fresh ginger
2 (2-inch) pieces lemongrass

2 garlic cloves, minced
1 tablespoon lemon curry
    powder blend
1 quart vegetable broth
1 (14.5-ounce) can coconut
    milk
Fried pork rinds, for garnish

In a large pot, cook the sweet potatoes in the butter for 5 minutes over medium heat. Add the leeks, ginger, and lemongrass. Cook for 3 minutes over low heat or until the leeks are tender. Add the garlic and curry, and cook for 1 minute. Stir in the broth and simmer until the sweet potatoes are very tender, about 20 minutes.

With an immersion blender, or carefully with a blender, puree the soup. Stir in the coconut milk and warm through over very low heat.

Ladle into bowls and top with a pork rind.

NOTES

• Do not cut sweet potatoes with a carbon steel knife; this will turn the cut edges black. Use a stainless steel or ceramic knife instead.

• Any of the autumn squashes, like kabocha, acorn, or butternut, can be substituted for the sweet potatoes with fine results.

• Ginger is easily peeled by just running a teaspoon across the thin skin. Grate the ginger against the grain of the fibers to keep it from clogging up the grater.

Belzoni Crawfish Rice and Corn Bisque
From the Side of the Road

• • •

Spread out across the low horizon of the Yazoo River Delta, the rice fields are beautiful with unpredictable curves patterning both sides of the roads for miles. Periodic shards shoot up at first, then around harvest, flashing silver blades are whipped by the wind, bowed heads heavy with grains. The fields are a perfect place for crawfish to make a home. Resourceful farmers grow rice in the warm months and crawfish in the cool ones.

On a good day someone will be selling the main ingredients of this simple bisque—crawfish and corn (depending on the price of cotton, more or less corn is grown in these parts)—from the back of a pickup on the side of the roads bordered by rice fields in Belzoni (which remarkably rhymes with bologna when not pronounced baloney), Mississippi. • **Serves 6**

NOTES

• Grilled corn on the cob can be used, adding a smoky flavor to this soup.

• If using whole boiled crawfish, peel them and reserve the tail meat and heads. Add the shells to the corn cooking liquid when you return the cobs to the pot. Stuff the heads to serve along with the bisque.

• In late March and early April, agricultural aviators, like Mr. Benny Stokes, swoop to within 50 feet of the ground at speeds of up to 150 miles per hour, broadcasting pre-germinated rice seeds onto flooded rice fields from their airplanes.

4 ears of corn, shucked, silks removed
3 slices bacon, finely diced
4 green onions, white and green parts, sliced on the diagonal
1/2 cup finely diced red bell pepper

1 cup half-and-half
1/2 teaspoon thyme leaves
Salt and freshly ground black pepper
1/2 cup cooked white rice
1 pound peeled crawfish tails and fat (see Notes, page 34)

In a large saucepan over medium-high heat, combine the corn with water to cover. Bring to a boil. Reduce the heat and simmer for 6 minutes. Remove the corn from the water (reserve the water for later) and let cool enough to handle. Slit each row of corn lengthwise down the center of the kernels with a serrated knife. Using the dull back of the knife, scrape down the cob to remove the corn from the kernels, leaving the hulls attached. Save the corn to add later. Return the cobs to the pot of water and cook for 20 minutes. Strain, reserving the liquid. Discard the cobs.

Meanwhile, in a medium saucepan, cook the bacon over medium heat until crisp, about 4 minutes. Scoop out the crisp bacon with a slotted spoon and drain on paper towels. Reserve the drippings in the pan. Set the bacon aside.

Add the green onions, bell pepper, and the corn pulp to the bacon drippings in the pan. Cook and stir for 5 minutes or until tender. Add 2 cups of the corn cooking liquid and the half-and-half and thyme. Season with salt and pepper, and bring to a simmer.

Add the rice and cook for 5 minutes. Add the crawfish and simmer for 5 minutes more, until the crawfish are cooked through and the soup is flavorful.

Ladle the soup into bowls and garnish each serving with the reserved bacon.

• To make stuffed heads, in a skillet cook 1 finely chopped medium onion in 2 tablespoons oil until tender, about 5 minutes. Add 2 whole chopped green onions, 1 minced garlic clove, and 2 table-spoons chopped parsley leaves. Cook and stir for 2 minutes. Transfer to a mixing bowl and stir in 1 cup French bread crumbs or cornbread crumbs, and some of the crisp bacon pieces. Season with Creole seasoning blend to taste. Stuff into hollows of the crawfish heads. (Check that antennae and eyes are removed.) Beat 1 large egg with a little milk; dip each stuffed head into the mixture. Fry the heads in 2 inches of hot oil, or a deep fryer, turning care-fully once until they are golden brown, about 2 minutes for each side. Drain and serve with the bisque.

Monday Red Beans and Rice
Back to Work with Hambone

• • •

The Reverend L. V. "Hambone" Howard, 68, walks all the streets of his town each day. His calling card is a copy of yesterday's newspaper. A bit of a celebrity, he dresses for his people—one day all vibrant royal blue, from patent leather shoes and socks, matching royal blue suit shirt and tie, to his head crowned with a royal blue fedora. The next day might find him circumnavigating town in a zebra-striped ten-gallon hat with matching tie cutting a sharp, thin line in a black three-piece suit. Occasionally, he dresses in a casual ensemble involving something like a salmon-colored cap and kelly-green pants, but always put together.

The Reverend has hosted his weekly radio prayer and community announcement show, "This Morning with God," on WMLA (AM 1380) since 1968 and turned it in in 2007. He is also an invariable figure at the Cotton Row Club on Ram Cat Alley, where he shines shoes and takes care of the assorted business needs of the cotton factors and businessmen of the district. Hambone reports that his last vacation was in 1963, when he went to Huntsville and worked in a barber shop for three weeks. This is a man on the move; he has a quick, clipped gait punctuated by a flat-palmed wave and brilliant mustachioed smile for his numerous admirers who honk from passing cars and shout hellos from across the block.

Monday is red beans and rice day, the ham bone left from Sunday dinner a foundation on which to build and a blessed dinner for the hurried pace of a workweek.

• **SERVES 10**

1 pound dried red kidney beans	3 garlic cloves, minced
1 pound smoked sausage links, cut into 1-inch-thick rounds	1 ham bone, with most of the meat removed and reserved, or 2 smoked ham hocks
1 bay leaf	Salt and freshly ground black pepper
1 large onion, chopped	2 cups cooked white rice
1 green bell pepper, chopped	1/4 cup chopped parsley
2 celery stalks, leaves and all, chopped	

Soak the kidney beans in 6 cups of water overnight. Drain well.

Heat a large Dutch oven or stockpot over medium-high heat. Add the sausage and cook, stirring, for 3 to 5 minutes or until the

NOTES

• Pick through the dried beans, removing any horribly shriveled ones. If you see any pinprick holes in them, the beans were bug infested; discard them. Beans will swell up to about double in size. A 5-quart container is good for soaking beans. Place a plate on top of the beans when you start to soak them to make sure they stay under the water. Do not refrigerate because it slows the tenderizing.

• If you wake up and find the skins have completely slipped off the beans, that means they were too old to begin with. Throw them out and pick up two (14.5-ounce) cans of kidney beans. Rinse and drain the canned beans well, and use them instead to keep you on schedule; reduce the water to 4 cups and the cooking time to 1 hour. Or start with new fresh dried beans and have this dish the next day.

• If you are very sensitive to beans, change the soaking water after the first and third hours to reduce the effects.

sausage is nicely browned. Remove the sausage and reserve to put back later.

Add the bay leaf, onion, bell pepper, and celery to the pot. Cook for 3 to 5 minutes, stirring occasionally, until tender. Add the garlic and cook for 1 minute more.

Add the ham bone, drained beans, and enough water to cover by 2 inches. Bring just to a boil, then reduce to a low simmer. Simmer for 2 hours, or until the beans are very tender. Stir occasionally, making sure to scrape any beans from the bottom of the pot that may have stuck. Add more water if the mixture is too thick. For a creamy consistency, mash some of the beans against the side of the pot with the back of a spoon.

Add the browned sausage and any bits of ham, and simmer for 10 minutes more. Remove the bay leaf. Season with salt and pepper. Serve over rice, garnished with the parsley

• Let the beans cook until tender before seasoning with salt; the skins will be tenderer. Also, keep the heat low and the mixture at a slow, steady simmer (not boiling) so the jackets stay on the beans instead of becoming little rolled-up pieces.

• Add oil, or in this case the rendered fat from the sausage, to the cooking beans to help reduce foaming and boil-overs. Skim that funky foam off the top.

• A unique, worry-free way to cook fluffy long-grain rice is to combine 2 cups water with 2 cups washed rice and 2 teaspoons salt in a double boiler. Cook over boiling water for 1 hour. Serve the rice with a fork to fluff it while serving.

Cornbread-Crusted White Chili
Green Chilies and Hominy

• • •

This is really no exaggeration: Just about any leftovers can be put in a skillet, topped with cornbread, and baked to make everybody full and happy. This cornbread crust is assembled before the filling ingredients, and used on the top and bottom. A 12-inch cast-iron skillet with 4-inch sides works well for this one-dish meal. A 2-quart casserole or baking dish can also be used.

Hominy is corn kernels that have been treated with an alkali like wood ash, slaked lime, or lye to remove the hulls. Grits are made from ground dried hominy. Yellow and white hominy are available canned, sometimes labeled with their Spanish name, posole. • SERVES 8

NOTES

• Tomatillos are a Mexican fruit resembling a small green tomato wrapped in a green tissue-paperish husk. Store tomatillos in the refrigerator with the husks attached. Remove the husks before using. Tomatillos begin to turn yellow as they ripen; they are preferably used when still green. Choose green tomatillos with dry husks attached that are not overly sticky.

• To roast chilies, place them whole under the broiler and broil until charred on each side. Cool and slip off charred skin, then remove seeds and stem.

• If using a baking dish, grease it lightly to ease cleanup.

• Pellagra is a disease often associated with diets high in corn, such as those of Southerners in the early 1900s. It is caused by a diet deficient in niacin, an important B vitamin. Corn is low in niacin; by treating it with the alkali, the niacin is made more readily available.

1 cup unbleached all-purpose flour

1 cup yellow cornmeal

1 teaspoon sugar

1 tablespoon baking powder

Salt

1 (8-ounce) can creamed corn

1/2 cup whole milk

1 large egg, beaten

3 cups diced cooked chicken

1 small white onion, chopped

2 (11-ounce) cans tomatillos, rinsed, drained, and chopped, or 1 1/2 cups diced hulled fresh tomatillos

2 (4.5-ounce) cans green chilies, rinsed, drained, and chopped, or 2 fresh green chilies, roasted (see Notes), seeded, and diced

1/2 teaspoon ground cumin

2 garlic cloves, minced

1 (15-ounce) can hominy, rinsed and drained

1 cup sour cream, plus extra for serving

1 cup shredded jalapeño jack cheese

Cilantro, for garnish

Preheat the oven to 375°F.

In a medium bowl, whisk together the flour, cornmeal, sugar, baking powder, and 1/2 teaspoon salt. Make a well in the center of the dry ingredients and add the creamed corn, milk, and egg. Whisk together just until moistened. Set aside.

In a medium bowl, combine the chicken, onion, tomatillos, green chilies, cumin, garlic, hominy, sour cream, and 1/2 teaspoon salt.

Spoon half of the cornbread mixture into the skillet or baking dish, and spread to an even, thin layer. Sprinkle with half of the cheese. Spoon the chicken mixture over the cornbread layer in the skillet. Sprinkle with the remaining $1/2$ cup cheese. Spoon the remaining cornbread mixture over the top and spread to an even layer.

Bake for 40 minutes, or until the crust is deep golden brown. Allow to cool and settle for 5 minutes before serving. Garnish with additional sour cream and the cilantro, if desired.

Turtle Soup
Won't Let Go Until It Thunders

• • •

Although some might find the thought of eating turtle somewhat upsetting, it is a long-cherished dining custom in the bayou lands. The large alligator snapping turtles, which can grow as wide as a pickup truck bed and weigh upwards of 200 pounds, are used in what is considered by many, oxymoronically, a delicacy. The common snapping turtle is more often seen in a tureen. In brackish wetlands of south Louisiana, the diamondback terrapin was once trapped and added to rich stocks.

This recipe makes a classic soup often elegantly served in New Orleans, with a small pitcher of sherry at each place setting for diners to add to their liking. Mock turtle soup may be made by substituting 1 1/2 pounds of diced veal. (Traditionally a calf's head is used for this, but if you won't deal with a turtle, a calf's head most likely is not up your alley, either.) • SERVES 6

NOTES

• Check with your State Department of Wildlife and Fisheries for regulations on trapping turtles in your area. Turtle meat is available for sale online at several exotic-meat companies and comes from farm-raised turtles.

• Hard-boiled eggs are used in place of turtle eggs, which were often used in this soup.

• The 1962 edition of *The Joy of Cooking* gives much advice on the subject of turtles.

• Many people I know swear a snapping turtle won't let go once he's snapped onto something until it thunders.

1/2 cup (1 stick) unsalted butter
1/2 cup unbleached all-purpose flour
2 quarts veal or chicken broth
1 large white onion, diced
2 celery stalks, leaves and all, diced
1/4 cup diced green bell pepper
1/4 cup diced red bell pepper
2 garlic cloves, minced
4 ripe plum tomatoes, seeded and diced
1 1/2 pounds boneless turtle meat or 1 1/2 pounds boneless veal shouder, cut into 1/2-inch pieces

1/2 cup diced smoked ham
2 bay leaves
1/2 teaspoon dried thyme
1 teaspoon freshly ground black pepper
1/4 teaspoon cayenne pepper
1/4 teaspoon ground cloves
1/4 teaspoon ground allspice
1/4 teaspoon freshly grated nutmeg
1 tablespoon Worcestershire sauce
1 lemon, thinly sliced
1/4 cup chopped parsley
3 large eggs, hard-boiled, peeled, and thinly sliced
6 tablespoons sherry

In a large stockpot over medium-low heat, melt the butter. Whisk in the flour and cook over low heat, stirring constantly, until the roux is golden brown, about 7 minutes. In a separate pot, bring the broth to a simmer.

Add the onion, celery, green and red bell pepper, garlic, and tomatoes to the roux. Cook and stir over medium heat for

5 minutes, or until the vegetables are tender. Add the turtle and ham. Stir to combine and heat through a minute or two. Add the bay leaves, thyme, black pepper, cayenne, cloves, allspice, nutmeg, and Worcestershire.

Add the broth and bring to a boil. Lower the heat so that the mixture simmers, and cook for $2^{1}/_{2}$ hours, or until the turtle is tender. Add the lemon slices, parsley, and eggs. Remove the bay leaves.

Spoon 1 tablespoon sherry into each serving bowl, or place a small pitcher of sherry at each setting. Ladle the soup into bowls.

I ASKED my dear friend, Uncle Hank Burdine, about his turtle-cleaning methods. Hank allowed, "It is the hardest thing in the world to do. Best advice I can give is to put it in the trunk of your car and drive over to Louisiana and get one of them to do it."

Sweet Potato Dumplings
With Browned Butter and Sage

• • •

Louisiana sweet potato producers in the 1930s, in an effort to distinguish their far sweeter, superior tubers from those of the dry, mealy Yankee sweet potatoes grown in places like New Jersey, started a campaign promoting them as yams. This has helped propagate the confusion between yams and sweet potatoes. True yams are a starchy, tuberous root of West Africa—not even a cousin of the sweet potatoes we know today. Many cookbooks throughout the South still refer to sweet potatoes erroneously as yams, though for the most part that is not what they mean a'tall.

Like cousins of gnocchi, these tender dumplings are bathed in butter that has been cooked until the milk solids begin to turn a nutty brown, and are dressed with fresh sage and a sprinkling of good Parmesan cheese. • SERVES 6

NOTES

• Store sweet potatoes in a cool, dark place for no more than a week.

• Baking the sweet potatoes instead of boiling them makes the dumplings lighter. Russet potatoes can be used in place of sweet potatoes.

• Dumplings can be made the day before and stored, covered tightly with plastic wrap, in a single layer on a lined baking pan. They can also be frozen in a single layer on a lined baking sheet until hard, then transferred to a resealable plastic bag and returned to the freezer. Add frozen dumplings directly to boiling water in small batches so the water can return to a simmer quickly.

• Add $^1/_2$ cup toasted pecan pieces at the end for a little crunch.

• These dumplings are good for breakfast, too, dressed with melted butter and maple syrup.

2 pounds sweet potatoes
1$^1/_2$ to 2 cups unbleached all-purpose flour
1$^1/_2$ teaspoons salt
$^1/_4$ teaspoon freshly grated nutmeg
1 cup (2 sticks) unsalted butter
$^1/_4$ teaspoon freshly ground black pepper
2 tablespoons chopped fresh sage
2 tablespoons grated Parmesan cheese

Preheat the oven to 375°F.

Place the sweet potatoes on the center rack of the oven and bake for 40 minutes or until tender in the center and pierced easily with the tip of a knife. Cool the sweet potatoes in their skins until easy to handle. Slice open the sweet potatoes and scoop out the flesh. Mash the flesh with a potato masher or put through a ricer or food mill. You'll need about 2$^2/_3$ cups mashed sweet potatoes.

Meanwhile, bring a large pot of salted water to a boil.

In a large bowl, combine the mashed sweet potatoes with 1$^1/_2$ cups flour, 1 teaspoon of the salt, and the nutmeg. Stir well to combine. Turn the dough out onto a lightly floured surface and knead briefly, adding additional flour until it is smooth and not too sticky.

Form the dough into a ball. Cut it into four equal wedges. Working with one wedge at a time, roll the dough into four ropes about $^3/_4$ inch in diameter. Cut each rope into $^3/_4$-inch-long segments. Roll each segment across the tines of a fork, pressing down slightly to form a depression in the middle of your fingerprint. Set each dumpling on a lightly floured surface while forming the others.

Line a baking sheet with a dish towel. Drop half of the dumplings into the boiling water, then reduce the heat and simmer for 4 minutes or until the dumplings rise to the surface. Remove with a slotted spoon to the prepared baking sheet to drain. Repeat with the remaining dumplings, allowing the water to return to a full boil between batches.

In a large skillet over medium heat, cook the butter, stirring occasionally, until light brown, about 3 minutes. Stir in the remaining $1/2$ teaspoon salt, the pepper, and sage. Add the dumplings, carefully stirring to coat with the butter, and slightly brown, about 3 minutes. Spoon the dumplings and sauce onto serving plates and top with the Parmesan cheese.

I adore Ian Hemphill's description of a sage leaf: "The underneath is deeply veined and filigreed like an opaque cicada's wing."

Chicken Thighs and Dumplings

Pillows Adrift in the Richest of Stews

• • •

Purists may cringe at the addition of herbs and mushrooms to this reassuring stalwart of Southern kitchens, but I believe it brings the dish up to date. • SERVES 4

CHICKEN

8 bone-in chicken thighs
Salt and freshly ground black
    pepper
6 tablespoons unbleached
    all-purpose flour
3 tablespoons clarified butter,
    canola oil, or schmaltz
2 shallots, finely chopped
4 ounces white mushrooms,
    sliced
1 quart chicken broth
2 tablespoons chopped parsley
    leaves

DUMPLINGS

1 cup cake flour
2 teaspoons baking powder
1/2 teaspoon salt
1/4 teaspoon coarsely ground
    black pepper
1 large egg
1/4 cup whole milk
1/2 teaspoon thyme leaves
1 teaspoon chopped chives

NOTES

• A speedy alternative is to replace the chicken thighs with one whole rotisserie chicken, cut up (bones and skin removed) and skip to the second half of the recipe.

• The meat from the thighs can be removed and added in the final step, and the bones discarded if you prefer. I think the bones add additional flavor.

• Jim Harrison's essay "Where Have All the Thighs Gone" inspired this recipe.

COOK THE CHICKEN. Season the chicken with salt and pepper. Combine 4 tablespoons of the flour with a little salt and pepper in a shallow bowl. Dredge the chicken in the flour. In a Dutch oven or large heavy-bottomed pot with a lid, heat the clarified butter until hot over medium-high heat. Brown the chicken in the hot butter, allowing each side to color before turning, 6 to 8 minutes. Remove the browned chicken from the pot and set aside for later.

Add the shallots and mushrooms to the pot. Cook and stir over medium heat for 5 minutes, or until the shallots are tender. Sprinkle the remaining 2 tablespoons flour over the mixture and cook, stirring continuously, for 1 minute. Whisk in the chicken broth a little at a time, fully incorporating each addition before adding more. Stir until smooth.

Return the chicken to the pot and add the parsley. Cover and simmer over low heat, skimming fat from the surface occasionally, for 45 minutes, or until the chicken is tender and no longer pink at the bone.

PREPARE THE DUMPLINGS. Sift the flour, baking powder, and salt together into a medium bowl. In a small bowl, whisk together the pepper, egg, milk, thyme, and chives. Using a fork, stir the egg mixture into the flour until just moistened. Pat the dough with your hands into a $^1/_2$-inch-thick square. With a sharp knife, cut the dough into 2-inch square pieces.

When the chicken is done, remove it to a plate and tent with foil while the dumplings cook.

Return the contents of the pot to a simmer. Drop the dumplings into the simmering mixture one at a time to keep the mixture simmering. Cover and cook for 5 minutes, or until the dumplings float to the top and are cooked through. Keep in the pot. Return the chicken to the pot, or pour the dumplings and sauce over the chicken. Serve immediately.

DISHES FROM THE BACKYARD AND KITCHEN

Backdoor Chicken
Split and Brick

• • •

Tales of chicken-snatching abound in song and story. The "yard pimp" or "gospel bird," depending on who you ask, is a major part of rural life. If you get yourself a good "free-range" bird, this is how I recommend cooking it—slathered with lemon zest and spices and pressed down over a hot grill. • SERVES 4

1 teaspoon grated lemon zest
3 tablespoons fresh lemon
   juice
1 garlic clove, minced
$^1/_2$ teaspoon salt
$^1/_2$ teaspoon freshly ground
   black pepper
$^1/_2$ teaspoon dill seeds
$^1/_2$ teaspoon ground cumin

$^1/_2$ teaspoon coriander seeds
$^1/_2$ teaspoon paprika
1 (3-pound) chicken,
   backbone removed, cut in
   half (see Notes)
3 tablespoons olive oil
2 bricks covered with foil or
   2 grill weights

In a small bowl, stir the lemon zest and juice, garlic, salt, pepper, dill, cumin, coriander, and paprika into a paste. Rub over the exposed surface of the chicken and under the skin. Then rub with the oil. Wrap in plastic and refrigerate for 2 hours.

Set a grill rack 6 to 8 inches above the coals or heat source and heat the grill to medium.

Remove the chicken from the refrigerator and allow to come to room temperature while the fire is getting ready, or 30 minutes ahead if using a gas grill.

The grill is ready when you can hold your palm over the coals for 2 seconds and the coals have a light coating of ash. Put the chicken skin side down on the hot grill rack. Weight the chicken down with the bricks and grill, covered, for 12 minutes. Remove the bricks, flip the chicken bone side down, and replace the bricks. Grill, covered, for 12 to 15 more minutes or until the joints move readily, the juices run clear when the meat is pierced, and the internal temperature taken at the thigh reads 165°F.

Remove the chicken to a cutting board and tent with foil. Let rest for 10 minutes before cutting into pieces and serving.

NOTES

• To prepare the chicken, cut down either side of the backbone from the tail to the neck with poultry shears. Remove the backbone and save for stock. Flip the chicken over so the breast side is up. Pull the ribs out a little and press down with a lot of force to flatten the bird. With shears, cut down the center of the breast to separate the chicken into two halves.

• Leg quarters can be prepared the same way as the chicken halves in this recipe.

• Do not let the chicken marinate for more than 6 hours. The acid in the lemon juice can make the meat seem mushy if it is exposed too long.

• A few handfuls of damp wood chips or pecan shells can be added to the coals for a smoky flavor.

Proper Fried Chicken
My Thoughts, at Least

• • •

Like country-fried steak, pimiento cheese, and fried catfish, fried chicken is a perilous subject. By even going here I am opening myself up to ridicule. But I have to say this: pan-fried chicken is the best.

Proper fried chicken takes a long time to master. If you want to make good fried chicken, you must make it often and learn the nuances. These are a few universals to guide the novice fry cook.

First, assemble all the tools and ingredients needed before setting out to fry. Pat the chicken dry with paper towels so the crust will adhere and the oil will not splatter. Have the pieces cut in reasonable, comfortable sizes (for instance, cut large chicken breasts in half crosswise to ensure even cooking and that no one gets to Bogart the breast). And finally, keep in mind that white meat cooks faster than dark meat.

The best choice for cooking pan-fried chicken is a 10 ¹/₂- to 12-inch cast-iron skillet at least 4 inches deep, with a lid or pan to use as cover in conjunction with a wire-mesh splatter guard. • SERVES 6

1 (3-pound) chicken, cut up
1¹/₂ cups buttermilk
2 tablespoons hot pepper
  sauce
2 cups unbleached all-purpose
  flour

Salt and freshly ground black
  pepper
1 to 2 cups vegetable
  shortening or lard

Soak the chicken in the buttermilk and hot sauce in the refrigerator anywhere from 2 to 8 hours. Drain the chicken in a colander and pat each piece dry with paper towels. Place on a wire rack set over something to catch drips.

When ready to fry, put the flour, 1 teaspoon salt, and ¹/₂ teaspoon pepper in a double paper bag or plastic sack. Working with one piece at a time, shake the chicken in the bag with the flour, turning over and over to coat evenly. Set the coated chicken on the wire rack while continuing to coat the remaining chicken. Let the chicken sit for 10 minutes before frying. Reserve 2 tablespoons of the coating flour if you are going to make gravy (see Notes) and discard the rest.

NOTES

• Cutting up the fryer yourself is best because the fried pulley bone (wishbone, to some) and back are special treats for the cook.

• To cut up a chicken, remove the wishbone and split down the back first. Turn breast side up and split down the middle of the breast to cut the chicken into halves. Take one side of the chicken bone side up and split between the breast and the thigh. On the upper portion, cut off the wing and remove the wing tips (save for stock). Separate the ribs from the breast (save them for stock with the wing tips); cut the breast in half crosswise if large. On the lower portion, cut off the back. Cut between the thigh and leg joint. You should now have six pieces of chicken plus the wishbone; repeat with other side of the chicken.

• Vegetable shortening is more highly refined and purified than lard. I prefer shortening to oil for frying chicken, but cottonseed or canola oil will work too. Look for vegetable shortenings free of trans fat; there are several on the market today, even Crisco.

Set a wire rack over a baking sheet lined with newspaper or paper towels. Heat 1 cup of the shortening in a deep cast-iron skillet to 365°F. The melted shortening needs to be $^1/_2$ inch deep, or enough to come halfway up the chicken pieces; add more if needed. Gently lower the chicken, skin side down, into the hot oil. Do not crowd the skillet and work in batches, if need be. (Once chicken is added, keep the temperature of the fat at 350°F.) Cover with the lid slightly ajar and cook for 6 minutes. Remove the lid and rearrange the pieces, but don't turn them yet. Cover again and let cook for 6 more minutes.

Turn the chicken over and season the cooked side with salt and pepper. Cook uncovered for about 8 minutes for white meat and 12 minutes for dark meat, rearranging halfway through until the crust is deep brown and the chicken is cooked through. Drain on the rack set over paper.

MRS. Ernestine Williams has never soaked a chicken in her life, and declares she will not start now. Her chicken is fine. If pinched for time, skip the soaking-in-buttermilk step.

• Arranging the chicken in the skillet is close to an art form. Working from the center outward, place the thighs, back, and legs in first. Next come the thicker breast parts pointing inward, and then finally the wings. One small cut-up chicken will fit nicely into a large skillet, but all parts do not cook at the same rate. Beginners may want to start with one cut of chicken at a time until they get the hang of it, all thighs or breasts, etc., or cook the dark and light meat in separate batches.

• Beginners may also want to fry chicken in an electric skillet. It is easier to keep the oil at a constant temperature.

• To make gravy, pour the fat off, leaving browned bits in the pan. Measure 2 tablespoons of drippings and return to the skillet and heat over low. Sprinkle 2 tablespoons of the coating flour over the hot drippings and cook, scraping up bits and stirring constantly from center to outer edge. Slowly add $1^1/_2$ cups chicken broth. Bring to a simmer and cook for 1 minute, or until desired thickness. Season with salt and pepper. Remember, gravy will thicken as it stands, so err on the side of thinness. I like a long-handled flat-bottomed wooden spoon for gravy making.

Chicken Pot Pie

With Leftovers or From the Top

• • •

Whether cooking chicken for this specific purpose or using leftovers, a pot pie is always welcome at dinnertime. This recipe makes two double-crust savory pies. Perfect for a movie-night dinner date at home. • SERVES 2

2 cups chicken broth
2 celery stalks, leaves and all, chopped
1 large carrot, diced
1 small waxy potato, diced
4 pearl onions, peeled and halved
2 (5-ounce) bone-in chicken breast halves, skin removed
1/4 cup small young peas, fresh or frozen
1/4 cup corn kernels, fresh or frozen
2 tablespoons unsalted butter
2 tablespoons unbleached all-purpose flour
1/8 teaspoon poultry seasoning
1/3 cup heavy cream, plus extra for brushing the crusts
Salt and freshly ground black pepper
Versatile Pie Crust Dough (page 192)

In a medium saucepan, bring the broth, celery, carrot, potato, and onions to a boil over medium heat. Reduce the heat to low and add the chicken. Simmer for 20 minutes, or until the chicken is no longer pink near the bone.

Remove the chicken to a dish to cool. Strain the broth, reserving the vegetables. Return the broth to the heat and simmer over medium heat to reduce to 1 cup, about 15 minutes.

Meanwhile, separate the chicken from the bones, shredding the chicken into bite-size pieces. Combine the chicken, reserved vegetables, peas, and corn.

In a medium saucepan, melt the butter over medium-low heat. Sprinkle in the flour and seasoning, and whisk to combine. Cook, whisking, for 2 minutes or until golden. Add the reduced broth slowly, whisking to combine. Whisk in 1/3 cup of the cream. Add the chicken and vegetables, and season with salt and pepper. Set aside to cool while preparing the crusts.

Preheat the oven to 400°F. Put two 10-ounce round ovenproof baking dishes on a baking sheet.

NOTES

• If using leftover chicken (a minimum of 1 cup diced), cook the vegetables in the broth and continue with the recipe, adding the chicken to the sauce after the cream is incorporated.

• Halved leftover biscuits can be used as top and bottom crusts, a time-tested shortcut for chicken pot pie. Brush the biscuit tops on the top of the pie with melted butter before baking. Tent the pies with foil and reduce the oven temperature a little if the biscuits begin to get too dark.

Roll out the pie dough until it is $1/8$-inch thick. Cut four circles from the dough slightly larger than the rims of the baking dishes. Press one circle into the bottom of each dish. Cut out shapes in the dough for the top crusts and set aside. Spoon the filling into the crust-lined dishes. Top with the remaining crusts, pressing the edges to seal. Brush the top crusts with a little cream. Cut a small slit in the center of each to allow steam to escape.

Bake the pies for 20 to 30 minutes, until golden brown and bubbly.

WHEN my son was a toddler, he would not hold still for a haircut. Our neighbor, Olga, came by and said give him to her and come over to get him in thirty minutes, and he will have his hair cut. She had already performed, what seemed to me as a new mother, the miraculous feats of curing cradle cap and thrush with homemade remedies. I gladly handed him over. Thirty minutes later, I walked over and found Joe standing perfectly still while Olga calmly trimmed his bangs. She had stood him on the top of the rooster cage. He was transfixed, as was the rooster. The next attempt at a home haircut without live poultry left him squirming and with bangs that looked like a picket fence. At his first barbershop haircut, Joe asked where the rooster was.

Smoked Turkey

Free Up the Oven

• • •

A whole turkey is a great option for feeding a crowd. Cooking it out of doors frees up the oven for other dishes. There are many configurations of grills and smokers out there on the market. Here, I have used a method for indirect grilling on a charcoal grill using hardwood charcoal with added wood chips.

Along with your grill instructions, consider different kinds of wood chips to tailor this recipe to your personal taste and needs. Oak and hickory chips are traditionally used in smoking because they have a high tannin content, which aids in preserving meat. Pecan, alder, and the wood of fruit trees are nice choices for a milder taste. Mesquite may be a little overpowering for the mild flavor of turkey. Brining the turkey ensures succulentness; even leftovers will still be juicy. • SERVES 8 TO 10

NOTES

• If the weather is cold outside, brine the turkey in an ice chest outside. Add bags of ice to the cooler, replenishing the ice bags as they melt to keep the bird nice and cold below 40°F.

• Do not brine a kosher or self-basting turkey; it will come out way too salty. Just use the poultry seasoning and butter, and continue on.

• Try to maintain a temperature of around 300°F. in your grill. Fresh hot coals can be added by heating pieces with lit newspaper in a coffee can or chimney starter and adding them to the grill once they have stopped flaming. Transfer the hot coals carefully with tongs and add them to the edges of the fire, then scoot them toward the center when they ash over.

• Big silicone mitts are very helpful in moving this bird around the grill.

• The turkey meat will take on a slightly reddish pink cast owing to the smoke. This is a good sign.

1/4 cup kosher salt
2 fresh bay leaves or a few small dried
1 medium onion, peeled and halved
2 celery stalks, chopped
4 garlic cloves, mashed
6 black peppercorns
1 tablespoon chopped sage
2 sprigs thyme

A few parsley stems
1 (8- to 10-pound) fresh turkey, giblets removed and rinsed
4 teaspoons poultry seasoning
1/2 cup (1 stick) unsalted butter, melted
4 cups wood chips, soaked in water or strong tea for 30 minutes and drained

In a 2-quart saucepan, combine the salt, 1 quart water, the bay leaves, onion, celery, garlic, and peppercorns. Bring to a boil and cook for 5 minutes, stirring to dissolve the salt. Remove from the heat and add the sage, thyme, and parsley. Pour into a pot big enough to hold the turkey comfortably. Add 8 cups ice and let cool.

When the brine is cool, submerge the turkey in it. Weight the turkey down with a couple of plastic-wrapped bricks or heavy pans. Keep cold (below 40°F.) in the brine for 4 to 12 hours.

Remove the turkey from the brine and rinse with cool water. Pat dry inside and out. Season inside and out with about half of the poultry seasoning, loosening the skin and working some of the seasoning between meat and skin, too. Tie the turkey legs together and make a triangle with the wings behind the neck by folding the wing tips behind the back. Coat all over with half of the melted butter. Add the remaining seasoning to the rest of the butter and set aside. Allow the turkey to come to room temperature, about 1 hour.

Make a pile of coals in one side of a charcoal grill. Place a drip pan beneath the area where turkey will cook opposite the coals. Light the coals, and when the coals have a light ash coating, add the soaked wood chips. Pour 2 cups of water or tea into the drip pan. Put the grill rack in place. Place the turkey in a disposable aluminum roasting pan on the grill over the drip pan, close the grill cover, and cook for 1 hour. Every hour, add 12 to 15 fresh coals, brush the turkey with the butter mixture, and rotate a quarter-turn. Continue cooking for 2 hours or until the thigh meat reaches 175°F. If the turkey starts to brown too much, tent it with foil.

Let the turkey rest on a cutting board for 15 minutes before carving. If cooking ahead, let the turkey cool all the way to the bone before refrigerating.

Mahogany-Glazed Game Birds
Bourbon and Molasses Lacquered

• • •

This is a beautiful treatment for any game bird. Here, I have used game hens because they fall about in the middle of the size range and can be found in most markets. If you are cooking dove or quail, the time will be shorter. The time for cooking grouse, pheasant, goose, and assorted ducks will be longer. • SERVES 6

6 Cornish game hens
Salt and freshly ground black
   pepper
2 satsumas or tangerines, cut
   into wedges, with peels
   attached
$^1/_4$ cup molasses

$^1/_4$ cup Bourbon, plus extra
   for the sauce
4 tablespoons ($^1/_2$ stick)
   unsalted butter
1 teaspoon grated fresh ginger
2 garlic cloves, minced
1 teaspoon thyme leaves
1 teaspoon sweet paprika

Preheat the oven to 375°F.

Rinse and pat the birds dry. Season inside and out with salt and pepper. Place a couple of fruit wedges in the cavity of each bird and tie the legs together. Turn the wing tips under the birds to make a triangle behind the necks.

In a saucepan, combine the molasses, Bourbon, butter, ginger, garlic, and thyme. Cook and stir over low heat until the butter is melted. Dip each bird in the sauce. Place the birds in a roasting pan. Sprinkle with the paprika.

Cover the pan with foil and bake for 30 minutes, basting occasionally with the glaze. Uncover, brush with the remaining glaze, and bake until browned, the juices run clear, and the internal temperature reaches 165°F., 20 to 25 minutes, more for larger birds.

When the birds are done, remove them to a platter and keep warm. Place the roasting pan over high heat and add $^1/_2$ cup water and a splash of Bourbon. Scrape up any browned bits and simmer the sauce until reduced to the desired consistency. Serve a pool of sauce beneath each hen.

NOTES

• Satsumas are tangerine-like citrus fruits that grow abundantly in southern Louisiana and are picked in early November. They were brought to the United States in the mid-1800s from Japan.

• Sorghum molasses or cane syrup may be used in this dish with equally good results.

• Sprinkle a little salt on the crushed garlic to help it stay together as you mince it.

• The birds may be stuffed additionally with a mixture of 1$^1/_2$ cups cooked white and wild rice, 1 tablespoon melted butter, and 2 tablespoons toasted almonds, when they are removed from the oven.

Chinese Grocery Roast Pork
Generations of Grocers

• • •

By the early twentieth century, the Mississippi Delta was home to a large community of Chinese Americans. As plantation commissaries began to close, more cash was circulated and the need grew for independent grocers. In 1920, the city of Greenville reportedly had 12 paved streets, 20 trains stopped there a day, and there were 50 Chinese grocery stores. Several families still run fourth- and fifth-generation groceries in tiny towns scattered across the Delta.

Many versions of this red-tinged pork have been cooked on stoves in the back of family-run groceries in the area for years and years. • SERVES 6

1 tablespoon vegetable oil
4 green onions, white and
   green parts, chopped
2 garlic cloves, minced
1 teaspoon grated peeled fresh
   ginger
1 cup dark soy sauce
$^1/_2$ cup dry sherry
$^1/_2$ cup rice vinegar, preferably
   red

1 tablespoon honey
2 tablespoons dark brown
   sugar
1 tablespoon hoisin sauce
1 star anise
2-inch piece cinnamon stick
$^1/_4$ teaspoon five-spice powder
1 (3-pound) picnic shoulder
   of pork or Boston butt

Preheat the oven to 325°F.

In a large Dutch oven or roasting pan, heat the oil over medium heat. Add the onions, garlic, and ginger and cook for 1 minute. Add the soy sauce, sherry, vinegar, honey, brown sugar, hoisin sauce, anise, cinnamon, and five-spice powder. Simmer for 1 minute. Add 1 cup water and bring to a boil. Reduce the heat under the pan so that the mixture simmers.

Loosen the skin from the meat in several places, but do not remove it. Place the meat in the liquid, turning several times to coat it with the sauce. Transfer the pan to the oven. Cook for 30 minutes undisturbed, then baste with the cooking liquid and continue to baste every 20 minutes until the internal temperature of the meat is 185°F., about 4 to 4$^1/_2$ hours.

Remove the pork to a cutting board or serving platter and let rest for 10 minutes. Slice thinly and pour the pan juices over the meat, removing the star anise and cinnamon.

NOTES

• Dark soy sauce is made from fermented soybeans, wheat, yeast, salt, and sugar. It is slightly thick and made sweet with the addition of bead molasses. Dark soy sauce is aged longer than other soy sauces.

• Bead molasses is a very dark, rich sugarcane molasses found in Asian markets. Unsulfered molasses may be used.

• Red rice vinegar is a tart, sweet vinegar found in Asian markets that gets its distinctive red color from red yeast rice.

• Open the oven door for as short a time as possible when basting. Leaving the door open increases the cooking time by lowering the heat of the oven.

• Serve this succulent roast pork over stir-fried cabbage.

Double-Cut Pork Chops
Apple Grilled

• • •

Have your butcher cut these pork chops if you don't see them in his case. Ask for 2-inch-thick center-cut pork loin chops. A slice of seasoned tart apple tucked in the center infuses them with sweetness. Right when the chops are pulled from the grill, a brush of apple butter finishes them off. • SERVES 4

4 double-cut pork loin chops
Salt and freshly ground black
   pepper
1 teaspoon unsalted butter
1/2 sweet onion (like Vidalia
   or Walla Walla), thinly
   sliced

1/2 teaspoon finely chopped
   rosemary
4 (1/4-inch-thick) slices tart,
   sweet apple (like Granny
   Smith or Winesap)
1 teaspoon light brown sugar
1/4 cup apple butter

With a sharp boning knife, cut a slit in the side of each chop, forming a pocket midway through the chop. Season each chop inside and out with salt and pepper.

Set a grill rack 6 to 8 inches above the coals or heat source and heat the grill to medium.

In a skillet set on the grates of the grill, melt the butter over low heat. Add the onion and rosemary. Cook, stirring occasionally, for 6 to 8 minutes or until the onion is very tender and caramelized; season with salt and pepper. Remove to a dish to cool slightly.

Rub the surface of the apple slices with the brown sugar. Insert one slice of apple into the pocket of each chop. Add one quarter of the cooked onion mixture to the pocket, too.

When ready to grill, you should be able to hold your palm over the grill for 3 seconds and there should be a light ash coating on the coals. Grill the chops for 6 minutes. Rotate the chops a quarter-turn and grill for 4 to 6 minutes more. Flip the chops and repeat. Cook until an internal temperature of 150°F. is reached. Remove the chops from the grill and brush with apple butter before serving.

NOTES

• Winesap apples are one of the last varieties to come to market in the fall. Look for them toward the end of October.

• Granny Smith apples, despite their Grand Ole Opry–sounding name, originated in New South Wales, Australia, on the farm of Maria Ann Smith around 1860. The apple does not grow true to seed. To produce true descendants, apples are grown from rooting a branch or grafting. Every Granny Smith apple in the world can be traced back to Granny Smith's tree.

OLD Johnny Appleseed, the folk figure depicted in cartoons with a saucepan hat, wasn't traveling about planting apple trees in hopes of keeping the doctor away. The eccentric John Chapman was distributing seeds as an investment in hard-cider stills. Unlike his animated doppelganger, the real Johnny was a sometime cross-dresser and bootlegger.

Barq's Root Beer–Glazed Ham
Amber Encasement

• • •

Edward A. Barq of Biloxi, Mississippi, developed his root beer in 1898. Soft drinks (as opposed to "hard" alcoholic drinks) gained popularity during the temperance movement of the later nineteenth century and claimed to have health-giving properties. Dr Pepper (1885), Coca-Cola (1886), and Pepsi-Cola (1896) were all developed in the South and are rooted in this movement.

Root beer is an effervescent blend of infusions and extracts either slightly fermented to produce carbon dioxide or mixed with carbonated water. Sassafras roots and bark, dandelion, wild cherry, burdock, spruce, wintergreen, ginger, nutmeg, cloves, and anise are flavorings found in root beers, and all make a wonderful enhancement to smoky ham. • SERVES 8 TO 10

NOTES

• A "city" ham is smoked and wet-cured. A country ham is dry-cured and smoked. Steer clear of hams that have been injected with saline or other additives. These hams are sometimes labeled "water added."

• Look for a ham that has the majority of its fat cap and rind intact.

• The ham bone from this recipe is an excellent addition to Monday Red Beans and Rice (page 86).

1 (3-pound) whole or butt end, bone-in, fully cooked "city" cured smoked ham
About ¹/₂ cup root beer

Root Beer Glaze (recipe follows)
Whole cloves

Preheat the oven to 250°F.

Line a large roasting pan with foil. Place the ham in the pan fat side up for shank end and whole hams, or position the meat cut side down for butt end hams. Add the root beer or enough to cover the bottom of the pan by ¹/₄ inch. Let sit awhile, at least 30 minutes, to come to room temperature.

Tent the ham loosely with foil. Bake undisturbed until a thermometer inserted in the center of the ham reads 110°F. (1 to 3 hours depending on size and cut of ham).

Remove the ham from the oven and increase the oven temperature to 325°F. Pour off any accumulated pan juices and reserve for the sauce. Cut away excess fat. Score the ham in a diamond pattern, cutting ¹/₄ inch into the meat. Brush a thin layer of Root Beer Glaze over the scored surface of the ham. Insert whole cloves at the intersections of the cuts.

Bake the ham until the internal temperature reaches 120°F., approximately 1 hour. Let the ham rest on a cutting board or platter for at least 15 minutes before carving.

Combine the reserved pan juices with the remaining glaze and simmer over medium heat until thickened, about 5 minutes. Skim the fat from the surface and serve the sauce with the ham.

ROOT BEER GLAZE

Makes 1¹/₂ cups

1 cup root beer
¹/₂ cup ketchup
¹/₂ cup dark brown sugar

Grated zest and juice of
1 lemon
2 tablespoons yellow mustard

Combine the root beer, ketchup, brown sugar, lemon zest and juice, and mustard in a saucepan. Simmer, stirring often, over low heat for about 10 minutes until a thin saucy consistency.

Slow, Low Oven Ribs
While Involved in Other Things

• • •

Cooking in a slow oven makes these ribs tender and nice. Country-style pork ribs are cut from the loin section, up near the shoulder, and are very meaty, with less bone than other types of ribs—sometimes they're even boneless. They are low-cost and a pretty good deal because you are paying for more meat than bone.

Most any style of ribs will work here, though. I think babybacks are a long road to a little house, so I would choose pork spareribs instead. • SERVES 4

• Golden cane syrup can be used in place of the maple syrup.

• The ribs can be baked inside the night before a backyard barbecue party and then warmed over indirect heat on the grill the next day.

• These ribs are good served with leftover take-out fried rice.

2 (14.5-ounce) cans diced tomatoes, with juice
¼ cup minced sweet onion (like Vidalia or Walla Walla)
2 garlic cloves, minced
½ teaspoon red pepper flakes
½ cup maple syrup
2 tablespoons soy sauce

2 tablespoons tomato relish, such as Mrs. Renfro's (optional)
4 bay leaves
4 pounds country-style pork ribs
Salt and freshly ground black pepper

In a small saucepan, combine the tomatoes, onion, garlic, and red pepper flakes. Simmer over low heat for about 15 minutes, until reduced by half. Stir in the maple syrup, soy sauce, and tomato relish (if desired).

Preheat the oven to 300°F.

Line a 9 x 13-inch baking dish with foil. Place the bay leaves in the bottom of the dish.

Season the ribs with salt and pepper, and arrange in the baking dish. Pour half of the sauce over the ribs. Turn them a few times to coat with the sauce. Cover tightly with foil. Refrigerate the remaining sauce.

Bake for 3 hours. Remove the foil and pour the remaining sauce over the ribs. Return to the oven and bake an additional hour, or until the sauce is a thick glaze and the meat is very tender.

Remove the ribs to a serving platter and let stand for 15 minutes. Ladle off the accumulated fat from the pan juices by tilting the pan carefully and spooning it off. Pour the pan sauce over the ribs, discarding the bay leaves, and serve as soon as you can.

Blue Cheese Porterhouse
The Gentleman's Cut

• • •

A porterhouse steak comes from the large end of the short loin of beef. Featuring a portion of both tenderloin and top loin divided by a T-shaped bone, this is the cut for people who enjoy the tenderness of a filet mignon and the flavor of a New York strip. This cut is good for date night. Meat from each side of the bone can be removed and sliced, then returned to their respective sides along the bone on a serving platter. A gentleman offers the tender filet to his date and enjoys the strip himself. • SERVES 2

1 ($1^1/_2$-pound) dry-aged
    porterhouse steak, 2 inches
    thick
1 garlic clove, halved
1 teaspoon olive oil
Salt
Coarsely ground black pepper
2 teaspoons minced shallot

1 teaspoon finely chopped
    parsley
$1/_2$ teaspoon finely grated
    lemon zest
4 tablespoons ($1/_2$ stick)
    unsalted butter, softened
2 ounces blue cheese,
    crumbled ($1/_2$ cup)

Put a rack in the oven so that it is 4 inches from the heat source. Put a broiler pan on the rack and preheat the broiler.

Rub the steak all over with the cut sides of the garlic clove. Brush the steak with the oil and season generously with salt and pepper on all sides.

Place the steak toward the back of the very hot broiler pan. Broil for 6 minutes. Carefully flip the steak, placing it toward the front of the broiler pan. Broil for 4 minutes for medium or until the desired doneness.

Remove the steak from the pan and place on a cutting board with a trench around the edge to catch the juices. Let the steak rest, tented with foil, while preparing the topping.

In a small bowl, combine the shallot, parsley, lemon zest, butter, blue cheese, and a sprinkling of salt.

Slice the steak and serve with a dollop of blue cheese topping.

NOTES

• Dry-aged beef is available from specialty butchers. To age steak at home, place the steak on a rack over a paper towel–lined pan. Drape a dish towel over the steak and keep refrigerated for two to four days.

• Artisanally produced American cheeses have become more widely available in recent years. Look for these cheeses at specialty and natural food stores. Clemson University produces an enjoyable blue cheese. E-mail bluecheese@clemson.edu to order this fine cheese, aged in an abandoned railroad tunnel in Stump House Mountain.

Mustard-Rubbed Ribs
Dry Rubbed and Vinegar Mopped

• • •

Personality flavors barbecue as much as anything else. Many chefs flambé with a look-at-me flourish, but a pit master or grill man tends his offerings with a more laid-back approach, as is appropriate to his craft. Character traits can be tasted.

• SERVES 4

MOPPING SAUCE
1½ cups cider vinegar
2 tablespoons ketchup
2 tablespoons prepared yellow
   mustard
1 tablespoon light brown sugar
1 teaspoon red pepper flakes

DRY RUB
2 tablespoons kosher salt
2 tablespoons chili powder
2 tablespoons hot or smoked
   paprika
1 tablespoon freshly ground
   black pepper

1 tablespoon dry mustard
1 tablespoon light brown sugar
1 tablespoon ground cumin
1 teaspoon garlic powder
1 teaspoon onion powder
1 teaspoon ground allspice

5 pounds beef short ribs,
   or 1 slab spareribs, rinsed,
   cleaned, and patted dry
   (see Notes)

MAKE THE SAUCE. Combine the vinegar, ketchup, mustard, brown sugar, and red pepper flakes in a lidded jar. Shake vigorously and refrigerate overnight.

MAKE THE DRY RUB. Mix the salt, chili powder, paprika, pepper, dry mustard, brown sugar, cumin, garlic powder, onion powder, and allspice in a small bowl.

Rub the spice blend firmly into the surface of the ribs. Wrap the ribs in plastic and refrigerate overnight.

Place coals on one side of a grill and set a drip pan on the other side. Set the rack 6 to 8 inches above the coals and light the coals.

When ready to grill, you should be able to hold your palm over the coals for about 2 seconds and there should be a light ash coating on the glowing coals.

NOTES

• To clean and prepare ribs for cooking, remove the membrane from the undersides of the bones. Start at one corner of the slab, and with a sharp knife, loosen the translucent membrane by running the tip of the knife between it and the bones and meat. Once you have got a little loosened, grab hold and snatch it down the length of the slab. It should come off in pretty good size pieces.

• Use a spoon to sprinkle the spice rub onto the meat so that you do not contaminate the rub with raw meat. (Leftover rub can be stored for future use. This is a nice blend to use on steaks, or it can be added to ground beef for hamburgers.)

• Likewise, pour a little of the sauce into a separate container and use that for mopping so as not to contaminate the remaining sauce with undercooked meat juices. Any extra sauce can be served along with ribs.

Place the ribs on the grill opposite from the coals and cover. Cook for 20 minutes, keeping the temperature at 200° to 225°F. (see Notes, page 104). Brush with the sauce, cover, and continue to cook, brushing with sauce every 30 minutes and covering between moppings, for 3 hours or until the bones move slightly when twisted.

Slice between the ribs and serve with any remaining sauce.

• Look for a barbecue mop. It looks just like its name—a long handle with a string mop head. After using, wash it thoroughly and scald it in boiling water. Allow the mop to air-dry thoroughly before storing. These mops work well for applying thin sauces; a traditional brush or silicone brush works best for thicker sauces.

Chile Lime Skirt Steak
Brought Up with the Pickers

• • •

The cotton pickers come up from Texas, working a circuit of farms for the harvest season. Along with their farm implements they bring a cook's trailer, a cook, and a cut rarely found in our local markets until recently—the skirt steak or fajita meat. Skirt steak is a lot like flank steak but a little narrower and leaner. It is very flavorful and benefits from an acidic marinade to help tenderize and season it. This cut, as well as flank steak and hanger steak, is best cooked no further than medium-rare. • SERVES 4

1 (1½-pound) beef skirt steak
    or flank steak
Grated zest and juice of
    3 limes
2 green onions, white and
    green parts, chopped
3 garlic cloves, minced
3 tablespoons chopped
    cilantro

2 teaspoons olive oil
¼ teaspoon ground coriander
¼ teaspoon ground cumin
¼ teaspoon ancho chile
    powder
Salt and freshly ground black
    pepper

NOTES

• Cilantro is the fresh herb; coriander is the dried seeds.

• The familiar chili powder found in most groceries is a blend of several spices and dried chilies. Ancho chile powder is made from the dried poblano chile. Often described as having a raisinlike flavor, the powder is a deep purple to reddish black.

• This steak can also be broiled on a hot grill pan 4 inches from the heat.

Place the meat in a resealable food-storage bag. Add the lime zest and juice, green onions, garlic, cilantro, olive oil, coriander, cumin, chile powder, and salt and pepper. Turn several times to coat the meat. Marinate in the refrigerator for 12 to 24 hours, turning every so often to coat the meat.

Set a grill 6 to 8 inches above the coals or heat source and heat to medium.

When ready to grill, you should be able to hold your palm over the coals for about 2 seconds and there should be a light ash coating on the glowing coals or gas grill.

Remove the steak from the marinade and discard the marinade. Place the meat presentation side down on the hot grill rack. Grill the steak briefly, 2 to 3 minutes per side, for medium-rare. Transfer the steak to a cutting board, tent with foil, and let rest for 5 minutes. For maximum tenderness, slice the steak very thinly at a slight angle against the grain.

Country-Fried Steak
The Brown Gravy/White Gravy Divide

• • •

I think the great brown gravy/white gravy divide might be around Texarkana, or perhaps right past Natchitoches. It happens in the same vicinity as the country-fried steak/chicken-fried steak border. I have not received a grant to collect data regarding this. And I will state right here and now that this is my own humble opinion and purely conjecture. The observation may not represent the gravy nor smothering tendencies of all people of a given geographic, sociopolitical, economic group; but the differences for brevity's sake can be cooked down to this: the farther west you go, the whiter the gravy turns. Just inside of East Texas, they stop country-frying round steak and start chicken-frying round steak.

This recipe is a way to make country-fried steak, and it is a good way. It may not be the one you grew up with; it is, perhaps, a compromise country-fried steak offering with a little something for everyone. It is skillet-fried, not deep-fried. The gravy is brown, but not too brown and milk is in the gravy. The meat is added back to the gravy for a bit of smothering. • SERVES 4

• Cake flour is very low in protein and blends easily into sauces and gravies. Look for instant flours such as Wondra to use as a thickener in pan sauces. Flour-thickened gravies must always be brought to a boil briefly to cook the starch.

• For those from the browner gravy camp, use beef stock in place of the milk.

• If the steak is returned to the gravy, as suggested here, serve it over rice; but if the steak and gravy are served separately, serve them with mashed potatoes.

• Tenderized venison steaks are enjoyed prepared this way at our house, with the meat and gravy spooned over fried cornbread or hoecakes.

1 ($1^{1}/_{2}$-pound) beef round steak, tenderized (see Note, page 120) and cut into 4-inch pieces about $1/_{4}$-inch thick	Pinch of cayenne pepper
	1 teaspoon baking powder
	1 large egg
	Vegetable oil, for frying
1 cup unbleached all-purpose flour	1 small onion, thinly sliced
	$1/_{4}$ cup cake flour
Salt and freshly ground black pepper	2 cups whole milk
	Hot pepper sauce

Pat the steak dry. In a bag, combine the all-purpose flour with 1 teaspoon salt, 1 teaspoon pepper, the cayenne, and baking powder. Add the steak pieces one at a time and shake in the flour to coat. Set the coated steak aside.

In a small dish, beat the egg with 2 tablespoons water. Dip each flour-coated steak piece in the egg wash and then shake in the bag with the flour again to coat well. Set the steak on a rack for about 15 minutes to dry slightly and to help the coating adhere.

Set a wire rack over a baking sheet lined with newspaper or paper towels. In a 10-inch skillet, heat $1/_{4}$ inch of oil over medium-high heat until it shimmers. Place the steak pieces in the skillet and cook until the sides begin to turn golden brown, 3 to 4 minutes per side. Carefully turn and rearrange the meat, cooking until no juices are running out and the crust is a deep brown, about 4 minutes. Set the steaks to drain on a wire rack.

Pour all but $1/4$ cup of drippings out of the skillet. If there is not enough oil left in the skillet, add enough to make $1/4$ cup. Add the onion. Heat the skillet over medium heat and scrape the brown bits from the bottom of the skillet. Sprinkle the cake flour evenly over the hot oil, stirring constantly. Cook for 1 to 2 minutes, until slightly brown. Slowly stir in the milk until smooth. Reduce the heat to low and simmer for 10 minutes, stirring occasionally, until thickened. Season with salt, pepper, and hot sauce.

Return the fried steak pieces to the skillet with the gravy and simmer for 5 minutes. Serve immediately.

Midnight Brisket
Feed the Band

• • •

Jackson, Mississippi, has seen legendary rhythm and blues artists pass through, such as Little Milton, Bobby "Blue" Bland, Johnny Taylor, Dorothy Moore, Z. Z. Hill, and Denise LaSalle, all of whom recorded at Malaco Records. Performing at clubs like the Hidden Agenda, Queen of Hearts, George Street Grocery, Freddie B's Hideaway, Hal and Mal's, and the basement club of a defunct hotel, the Subway Lounge, they kept the music scene thriving in the capital city.

The Tangents, known as the "House Band of the Delta," occasionally rolled into town to stir up trouble. My mother made this brisket for them once and had me deliver it over to "Blues Central," the nickname for a midtown flophouse frequented by musicians, back when I was in high school. She thought the guys in the band were looking a little peaked and thin. That gesture instilled in me the value of caring for and feeding musicians. This brisket is the perfect dish for anybody who works the night shift, such as bakers, firemen, and nurses.

Count backward 36 hours from the time you want to serve and this tells you the time to start preparation of this simple, soulful dish. • Serves 6

• Brisket is a cut of beef that contains a large amount of collagen, a connective tissue that can be tough and chewy if not fully cooked. Long, slow cooking works best for briskets.

• There is a meat tenderizer device that is a handle with 20 or so sharp little blades. It is pressed into the meat and pierces it. I like to use this tool on brisket, venison, and country-fried steak. But, the brisket can simply be pierced all over with a fork before marinating.

2 medium onions, cut into
    1-inch-thick rounds
1 (5- to 6- pound) piece flat
    end beef brisket, with fat
    cap intact, tenderized (see
    Notes)
2 tablespoons natural liquid
    smoke seasoning

1/4 cup Worcestershire sauce
2 teaspoons celery salt
1 teaspoon sweet paprika
1 teaspoon garlic powder
1 teaspoon freshly ground
    black pepper

Choose a glass baking dish or lidded casserole large enough to comfortably hold the meat. Arrange the onion rounds in the bottom of the dish, then place the brisket fat side up on top of the onions. Pour the smoke flavoring and Worcestershire sauce over the meat. Sprinkle the celery salt, paprika, garlic powder, and pepper over the surface. Cover tightly with plastic wrap and marinate in the refrigerator for 24 hours.

Preheat the oven to 200°F.

Remove the plastic wrap and cover the baking dish tightly with a lid or foil. Bake for 1 hour. Uncover and bake for an additional 5 hours.

Remove the brisket from the oven, and as hard as it seems, do not taste it. Allow to cool to room temperature. Cover and refrigerate for 5 hours.

Preheat the oven to 325°F.

Remove the cover and spoon off the fat that has solidified on the surface of the juices. Remove the brisket from the liquid and wrap it in foil. Pour the juices into a small saucepan. Place the foil-wrapped brisket in the baking dish in the oven and warm through, about 15 minutes.

Simmer the pan juices and reduce to a thin, saucelike consistency. Thinly slice the brisket diagonally across the grain. Serve with the sauce.

• Allowing the brisket to cool fully produces a better meat texture for slicing, whether the brisket is reheated or served cold on sandwiches. If you cannot stand not eating the brisket right away, go ahead and serve it, but the texture will be stringy and the slices will shred rather than slice nicely.

AFTER most restaurants have shut down for the night and the day world is sleeping, musicians do their creeping. At my first bakeshop, Bottletree Bakery, in the college town of Oxford, Mississippi, we were often startled in the wee hours by errant, hungry bands pounding on the big garage-style back door. About the time the first batches of bread and pastries were coming out of the oven, the musicians had just finished loading up. We never turned any of them away. The same thing occasionally happens at the Mockingbird, with most of them looking for a cup of coffee for the long drive through the big Delta night. This custom of feeding musicians has led to some strange visits. Late, late one night a friend from the aptly named band "The Night People" tapped on my window. "Baby!" he pleaded. "Some men might come here wanting sexual favors. Honey, I just want you to cook me some bacon and eggs!" I got up, put on my robe, and fried him some.

Cabbage Rolls
Tastes Change

• • •

My great-grandmother, Momee, used to say your tastes change every seven years. I could not stand cabbage rolls well into adulthood. Then one day, when I was twenty-eight years old, I loved them. Never knew why. If you haven't tried them in seven years or so, give them another chance.

Place a cored cabbage in the freezer for several hours, then soak it in warm water to thaw. The leaves will be pliable and ready to roll around the savory beef and rice filling. • SERVES 6

1 cup long-grain white rice
$^1/_4$ cup diced onion
$^1/_4$ cup chopped red bell pepper
$^1/_2$ cup chopped celery
$^1/_2$ cup chopped mushroom caps
4 tablespoons ($^1/_2$ stick) unsalted butter
2 cloves garlic, minced
1 (14.5-ounce) can diced tomatoes, drained
2 tablespoons tomato paste
$^1/_2$ teaspoon chili powder

$^1/_3$ cup packed light brown sugar
$^1/_2$ teaspoon ground ginger
$^1/_2$ teaspoon freshly grated nutmeg
1$^1/_2$ pounds ground beef sirloin
Salt and freshly ground black pepper
1 large head cabbage
1 (8-ounce) can tomato sauce
2 tablespoons cider vinegar
2 tablespoons olive oil
2 teaspoons ketchup
$^1/_2$ teaspoon caraway seeds

Simmer the rice with 2 cups water over low heat until it has absorbed nearly all of the water, about 20 minutes. Cover the pan and turn the heat to low. Cook until the rice is tender, 5 to 7 minutes. Uncover, fluff with a fork, and let cool.

Meanwhile, in a large skillet over medium heat, cook the onion, bell pepper, celery, and mushrooms in the butter for 4 to 6 minutes, until tender and beginning to brown. Add the garlic, tomatoes, tomato paste, chili powder, brown sugar, ginger, and nutmeg. Cook and stir for 2 minutes. Remove from the heat.

In another skillet, brown the beef over medium-high heat until no longer pink, about 6 minutes. Drain well.

NOTES

• If the cabbage leaves rip with handling, make a patch with a piece of another leaf.

• Leftover rice works pretty well in this recipe, too; you will need 1$^1/_2$ cups.

• If you wish to make stuffed peppers instead of cabbage rolls, prepare bell peppers for stuffing by removing the tops, cores, and seeds from the peppers. Drop in boiling water for 2 minutes to tenderize. Fill with rice and beef filling and carry on the same as for cabbage.

Combine the beef and tomato mixtures. Fold in the rice, season with salt and pepper, and set aside.

Heat the oven to 350°F. Butter a 9 x 13-inch baking dish.

Remove the largest cabbage leaves from the head; you will need about 12 leaves.

Lay each leaf flat. Center 1 to 2 tablespoons of filling on each leaf. Roll burrito-style, folding in the ends as you roll up each leaf. Place each roll seam side down in the baking dish. Repeat, fitting the rolls snugly beside each other.

In a small bowl, combine the tomato sauce, vinegar, and ketchup. Pour over the cabbage rolls and sprinkle with the caraway seeds. Bake for 1$\frac{1}{2}$ hours. Serve the rolls with a little of the sauce from the baking dish spooned over the top.

Venison Roast
With Root Vegetables

• • •

When this roast is served, a coating of gingersnap crumbs combined with melted butter and herbs tumbles into the rich sauce and caramelized root vegetables.

• SERVES 6 TO 8

1 ($3^1/_2$- to 4-pound) boneless venison roast or boned leg of venison, trimmed
2 tablespoons olive oil
Salt and freshly ground black pepper
3 garlic cloves, minced
2 rosemary sprigs, plus $^1/_2$ teaspoon finely chopped
1 cup beef broth
8 red pearl onions, peeled and halved
1 sweet potato, peeled and diced

1 rutabaga, peeled and diced
2 carrots, peeled and cut into thirds
2 parsnips, peeled and cut into thirds
1 celery root, peeled and chopped
1 teaspoon juniper berries, crushed
$1^1/_2$ cups gingersnap crumbs
2 tablespoons butter, melted
1 tablespoon cornstarch mixed with 2 tablespoons apple juice

Preheat the oven to 325°F.

Pat the roast dry with paper towels. Brush the roast with a little of the oil and season with salt, pepper, and the garlic. Tie the roast to create an even shape, tucking the rosemary sprigs under the string.

In a large skillet, heat the remaining oil over medium-high heat. Sear the roast on all sides and the ends until well browned, about 3 minutes per side. Transfer the roast to a roasting pan fitted with a rack. Add the broth to the pan and scatter the onions, sweet potato, rutabaga, carrots, parsnips, celery root, and juniper berries around the pan. Roast for $1^1/_2$ hours, or until an instant-read thermometer measures 125°F. in the center, basting with the pan juices occasionally.

In a small bowl, combine the crumbs, butter, and chopped rosemary. Remove the roast from the oven and pat the crumb mixture onto the surface of the roast. Return to the oven for 10 minutes, or until the crumb crust is slightly browned.

NOTES

• To peel pearl onions, cut the stem tip off and drop the onions in boiling water for a minute or two.

• Beets, either golden or red, may be added to the vegetables.

• Parsnips are sweeter in the winter. Look for small ones; large ones may need the woody centers removed.

• The vegetables can be peeled and cut up ahead and kept refrigerated in a storage bag for a day or two.

• Pork, beef, or lamb may be roasted in this manner with fine results. Cook to appropriate degree of doneness.

• The crumb topping is similar to *persillade,* a mixture of bread crumbs and parsley often used to coat roast lamb. Ginger Molasses Cookies (page 215) can be used for the crumbs.

• Never add cornstarch directly to a hot liquid; always make a slurry with a cool liquid first. The sauce must be returned to a simmer to reach its full thickening potential and remove the starchy taste before it is served.

Remove the roast from the rack. Spoon the vegetables from the pan onto a serving platter, tent with foil, and set aside. Place the roasting pan over high heat and whisk in the cornstarch–apple juice mixture. Simmer, scraping up any browned bits, until the sauce is translucent and thickened, about 3 minutes.

To serve, place the roast on a heated serving platter and surround it with the vegetables. Slice, and serve the sauce alongside.

• Muscadine grapes tend to
fall to the ground when
ripe in September and
early October, so they can
be harvested by spreading
an old bedsheet on the
ground and giving the vine
a hard shake; otherwise,
the fruits have to be picked
one by one, as they tend to
ripen at different times. A
mature vine can yield 20
or more pounds of fruit
each season.

"SHIM lay, half
dozing, in a ham-
mock swung under
the black-gum tree
in the front yard.
From the kitchen
the tart smell of
boiling muscadines
came to him, wrin-
kling his nose and
making the insides
of his cheeks draw.
Henry had brought
Miss Cherry a water
bucket full of mus-
cadines, and she
and Fanchie were
making jelly."

—RUBEN DAVIS, *SHIM*,
1953

Muscadine Lamb Chops
Grilled and Glazed

• • •

*Also called Southern fox grape, the muscadine is native to the southeastern United
States. Its burnished purple fruits grow in loose clusters. Scuppernongs are brassy
green-gold cousins to the muscadine, but the names are often used interchangeably
these days. Noted for their tart musky sweetness, muscadines are often boiled down, the
thick skins and numerous seeds strained, and the resulting juice used to make jelly. If
muscadine jelly is unavailable, a combination of black currant and plum jellies creates
a close approximation.* • SERVES 4

LAMB	GLAZE
8 (1-inch-thick) loin lamb chops	$1/3$ cup muscadine grape jelly
2 garlic cloves, halved	1 garlic clove, minced
2 tablespoons olive oil	1 teaspoon Worcestershire sauce
Salt and freshly ground black pepper	$1/2$ teaspoon finely chopped fresh rosemary
	1 tablespoon chopped fresh mint

Set a grill 6 to 8 inches above the coals or heat source and heat the
grill to medium.

PREPARE THE LAMB. Rub each lamb chop with the cut sides of the
garlic. Brush with the oil and season with salt and pepper.

MAKE THE SAUCE. In a small saucepan, combine the jelly,
minced garlic, Worcestershire, and rosemary. Heat over medium
heat until the jelly has melted. Remove from the heat.

When ready to grill, you should be able to hold your palm over
the coals for about 2 seconds and there should be a light ash coating
on the glowing coals. Put the chops on the hot grill rack and grill
the chops for 3 to 4 minutes per side. Brush with the glaze and grill
for 2 minutes more for medium-rare. Move the chops off the grill
onto a platter to rest for 5 minutes; tent with foil.

Add the mint to the glaze and also pour any juices from the
platter into the glaze. Return the glaze to a boil for 1 minute. Serve
the sauce over the chops.

Salmon Croquettes
Sunday Supper

• • •

Salmon don't live anywhere around here. And unless you caught the fish yourself, or your friend gave you some, fresh fish were just not available in our local inland markets during the 1960s and '70s. And really just until recently, you could not buy a piece of salmon or tuna right here in Greenwood, or for 100 miles in any direction. But the colorfully illustrated cans of salmon and jack mackerel were always way back in the pantry and ready on grocers' shelves, particularly at the end of the month when budgets were tight. Now there are even shelf-stable drainless pouches of salmon. They may not have nostalgic artist renditions of sporting fish on the labels, but they make better croquettes than I remember from childhood.

Croquettes are a good, fast dinner. When Sunday night becomes consumed with laundry to knock out before the week starts, having these ingredients in the pantry to make a quick dinner is a godsend. • **SERVES 4**

1 pound cooked salmon (two 8-ounce foil packages, or two 8-ounce cans, drained)
1 large egg
1 teaspoon fresh lemon juice
1 tablespoon minced onion or 1 green onion, white and green parts, finely chopped

1 teaspoon dill pickle relish
1 cup saltine cracker crumbs
1/4 teaspoon freshly ground black pepper
1 tablespoon vegetable oil

Combine the salmon, egg, lemon juice, onion, relish, crumbs, and pepper. Shape with a damp hand into oval cakes about 1/2-inch thick. Refrigerate for 20 minutes to firm up some.

When ready to cook, heat a large nonstick skillet over medium heat; add the oil. Cook the croquettes for 8 minutes, turning them over about halfway through, until lightly browned and crisp. Drain briefly on a paper towel–lined plate before serving.

NOTES

· If the salmon mixture seems too dry to shape, add a little milk or buttermilk.

· The cracker crumbs can be replaced with 1 cup left-over mashed potatoes.

· Patties made from this mixture can be served on buns, like a burger.

Paper Sack Catfish
En Papillote

• • •

This is a fine way to serve catfish for company, an easy take on a classic French technique, only using plain paper lunch sacks instead of parchment paper. The bags swell and steam the fish in the undiluted flavorings. When sliced open at the table, the puffed bags release a wonderfully aromatic steam. • SERVES 6

2 tablespoons unsalted butter
2 garlic cloves, minced
1 teaspoon sea salt
1 tablespoon olive oil
1 teaspoon grated lemon zest
1/3 cup fresh lemon juice

6 (6-ounce) U.S. farm-raised catfish fillets, rinsed and patted dry
1/2 teaspoon freshly ground black pepper
6 sprigs fresh dill
1 lemon, sliced into 6 thin rounds

With nonstick cooking spray, lightly spray all over the outside of six lunch-size paper sacks. The bags should be slightly translucent after spraying. Cut six 8-inch lengths of butcher's twine. Set aside.

Adjust the racks in the oven, placing one in the lowest slot and one in the middle position. Preheat the oven to 350°F.

In a small saucepan over low heat, melt the butter with the garlic, salt, oil, lemon zest, and lemon juice.

Place the catfish in a single layer in a dish. Pour the sauce evenly over the fish, and then sprinkle with the pepper. Place one dill sprig and one lemon slice on each fillet. Gently slide one fillet into each paper sack. Gather the mouth of the bag and give it a twist, then tie with twine.

Place three bags on a large rimmed baking sheet and the other three on another baking sheet. Bake for 10 minutes, halfway through reversing the pans. Serve at once, placing an inflated sack on each dinner plate. For maximum effect, slice open the bags at the table.

NOTES

• The sacks can be assembled and refrigerated 1 hour before baking. Add 5 minutes to the baking time if the sacks are coming right out of the fridge.

• For added flavor and to round out the meal, place a few blanched asparagus spears beneath the fish and a thin slice of prosciutto or country ham draped across the top of the fish in each bag before baking.

• This same dish can be prepared with fennel and oranges in place of the lemon and dill.

A famous New Orleans dish, pompano en papillote was created at Antoine's in 1890 to celebrate the triumphs of Brazilian hot-air balloonist Alberto Santos-Dumont. The same chef, Jules Alciatore, son of the restaurant's founder, presented Oysters Rockefeller to the world in 1899.

Fried Catfish and Hush Puppies
Saturday Night Fish Fry

• • •

Just as when Louis Jordan sang about it in the 1940s, the Saturday night fish fry is a hopping social event. It is sometimes held as a rent party where plates brimming with catfish, hush puppies, and coleslaw are sold to make the rent, sometimes as a charity fund raiser, and sometimes just for the fun of it. Most of the time these kick off in the late afternoon and have a way of drawing out for the whole night with batches of everything being fried up throughout the night. • SERVES 4 TO 6

HUSH PUPPY BATTER
2 cups self-rising cornmeal
1/2 cup self-rising flour
1/2 teaspoon salt
1/4 teaspoon sugar
1/2 cup grated onion
1/4 cup finely chopped bell
    pepper or jalapeño
1 cup buttermilk
1 large egg

CATFISH
8 (6-ounce) U.S. farm-raised
    catfish fillets, patted dry
2 cups corn flour
Salt and freshly ground black
    pepper
Vegetable oil, for frying

MAKE THE HUSH PUPPY BATTER. In a mixing bowl, whisk the cornmeal, flour, salt, and sugar to mix and remove any lumps. In a separate bowl, combine the onion, bell pepper, buttermilk, and egg. Mix the wet ingredients into the dry, stirring well to combine. Let the batter sit for 15 minutes or until after the fish has been fried.

COOK THE FISH. Season both the fish and the corn flour liberally with salt and pepper. Place the seasoned corn flour in a bag. Add the fish pieces one by one, and shake until completely covered. Set the coated fish on a wire rack to dry slightly while the oil heats.

Set a wire rack over a baking sheet lined with newspaper or paper towels. In a deep pot or fryer, heat at least 4 inches of oil to 375°F. Drop the fish fillets into the hot oil, being careful not to crowd the pot, and fry until ginger tan, slightly curled, and floating, about 4 minutes (8 to 10 minutes for whole fish). Remove with a skimmer or slotted spoon. Set the fish on the rack to drain while frying the hush puppies.

NOTES

• I am a strong proponent of cottonseed oil for fish frying. It is an excellent medium: It has a high smoke point of 450°F. and does not impart as strong a flavor as peanut oil. Dark cottonseed oil straight from the mill is termed "crude" and must be refined further for most culinary uses. Some cotton-land residents swear by it because of the nutty flavor it imparts. When driving by an oil mill, the smell filling the air makes me crazed with hunger.

• Never fill a vessel to be used for frying more than two-thirds full. The grease will rise and sputter violently. Many fires have happened because this rule was overlooked.

• Never, ever, throw water on a grease fire.

• Many an experienced fish-camp cook checks the oil temperature by flicking a Diamond Strike Anywhere Match across the surface of the hot oil. If it lights, the grease is ready.

Do not stir the hush puppy batter, which would deflate it. Dip two spoons in the hot oil. Then with one of the coated spoons, scoop up a spoonful of batter and carefully slide the batter into the hot oil, using the other spoon to help guide the hush puppy into the pot. Repeat, dipping the spoons again if the batter begins to stick, until all the batter has been used. Be careful not to overcrowd the pot. Fry the hush puppies until crisp, turning them as needed, until they turn deep reddish brown and begin to float. Remove from the pot and drain on the wire rack before serving.

• Look for corn flour sold boxed or bagged as fish fry, like Zatarain's. It is a very finely ground cornmeal.

• Hush puppies fried after the fish are much more flavorful than those fried before. Mixing the hush puppy batter and letting it rest while the fish is frying bestows them ethereal crispness.

• If desired, add $1/2$ cup of fresh, in-season corn kernels to the hush puppy batter.

IN reference to hush puppies, Nash Buckingham wrote in *The Sally Hole*, "They can be eaten until your mind changes."

Pecan-Smoked Catfish
Shell Game

• • •

Pecan and other nut shells produce a good smoke for flavoring fish. Finely crushed dry shells can be used in a stovetop smoker in the same manner as wood shavings. For use on an outdoor smoker or grill, the shells can be left in larger pieces and soaked for 30 minutes in strong tea. • SERVES 4

NOTES

• Shaping fish in this manner is called *en paupiette.*

• Smoked catfish is good served warm over Pecan Rice (page 159) or as a centerpiece for a composed salad.

• Homemade Mayonnaise (page 66) with a little added horseradish is also a nice accompaniment. Additionally, topping flaked smoked catfish with the mayonnaise makes a nice canapé on toasted bread. A topping of sea salt and horseradish whipped cream is delightful.

• Smoked catfish is a good addition to dips and very good in place of salmon in croquettes (see page 127).

4 (6-ounce) U.S. farm-raised catfish fillets, rinsed and patted dry
1 tablespoon Worcestershire sauce
1 lemon
Salt and freshly ground black pepper
1 teaspoon chopped marjoram
1 tablespoon unsalted butter, softened

Sprinkle the catfish fillets with the Worcestershire sauce. Grate the lemon zest over the fish and then squeeze the juice over the fish. Season with salt and pepper and the marjoram.

Roll the fillets lengthwise into a corkscrew shape with the nice rib side facing out. Place on a smoking rack seam side down. Dot each fillet with softened butter.

Heat a smoker or covered grill. Add crushed pecan shells suitable for your style of smoker, and follow the manufactuer's directions for preparing the smoker. Smoke the fish for 12 minutes at 200°F. or until the flesh is opaque and the surface slightly golden. Gently remove from the smoker. Serve warm or chilled.

Greenwood Pompano
Private Booth Dining

• • •

Lusco's Restaurant hangs on at the low end of Carrollton Avenue, amid boarded-up storefronts and next to an old out-of-business memorial garden office. The restaurant features curtained private dining booths, white linen—draped tables, and a buzzer to push for service. This uniquely Greenwood-style dining practice originated in the early 1900s with Prohibition, and then later the Brown Bag Liquor Policy prescribed a need for privacy, with servers providing any imaginable mixers for the liquor brought in, conspicuously enough, encased in brown paper bags.

Big deals being cut between planters and cotton factors and bankers before every planting season, as well as on-the-sly clandestine dalliances, benefited from Lusco's dining arrangement. However, the walls of these small, intimate dining rooms don't go from floor to ceiling and many, many conversations held under the influence of this illusion have been run through the gossip mill the next day.

Pompano is one of the most expensive fish per pound and was a much requested entrée of Delta travelers fresh from vacations on the Gulf Coast or New Orleans. The name comes from the Spanish word for "vine leaf" and aptly describes the shape of this fish. No fish cooked at home will be quite the same as the ones at Lusco's. After all, they have had 74 years of practice. This recipe is a pretty good substitute, though, if you can't get a booth reservation or you live too far away. • SERVES 2

2 (1½-pound) pompano, dressed
Salt and freshly ground black pepper
2 teaspoons canola oil
¼ cup Cottonseed Oil and Vinegar dressing (page 71)
2 tablespoons unsalted butter
Crusty bread, for serving

Put a rack in the oven so that it is 4 inches from the heat source. Put a large roasting pan on the rack and preheat the broiler.

Deeply score each fish diagonally in both directions, creating a diamond pattern on one side. Season with salt and pepper inside and out.

Brush the hot roasting pan with the oil. Place the fish in the pan. Drizzle the dressing over the fish and dot with the butter.

Broil for 10 minutes, or until the flesh is opaque. Serve in deep platters with the pan drippings poured over and crusty bread for sopping.

NOTES

• The eyes of fresh whole fish should not be cloudy or sunken. The flesh should be firm and will not hold an indention when pressed. Give the fish a good sniff; it should smell like seawater and not at all fishy.

• Keep pompano in the refrigerator in a plastic bag placed in a colander full of ice and the colander set inside a bowl. This is a very delicate fish and should be cooked the same day it is purchased for optimum freshness.

• Flounder also works well with this preparation and is sometimes easier to find.

• Check out more on Greenwood's tradition of private booth dining by visiting southernfood ways.com and clicking on the oral history link.

Seafood Pan Roast
The Four-Hour Lunch

• • •

Pascal's Manale, a place in uptown New Orleans right off the St. Charles Avenue streetcar line at Napoleon, inspired this dish. Since its founding by Frank Manale in 1913, this restaurant has been the place to hang out for a leisurely lunch. Most diners with the full intention of blowing off the afternoon of work kick off the approaching weekend at the big oyster bar cornered right inside the door. Later, once they've gathered around dining-room tables, dishes of barbecued shrimp, eggplant stuffed with crabmeat, and combination pan roasts are ordered and passed around to share.

Frank Manale transformed his grocery into a restaurant, as so many Italian entrepreneurs did in the early 1900s in most Mississippi river towns. His nephew Pascal Radosta, Sr., took it over when the old man retired decades later and named the place accordingly. • SERVES 6

3 cups half-and-half
2 tablespoons unsalted butter
1 tablespoon minced shallot
¼ cup chopped celery, leaves and all
½ teaspoon minced garlic
1½ cups dry French bread crumbs

Salt and freshly ground black pepper
3 dozen shucked oysters (1 pint), drained
1 pound jumbo lump crabmeat
8 ounces peeled, deveined medium shrimp

Preheat the oven to 450°F.

In a saucepan over low heat, bring the half-and-half, butter, shallot, celery, and garlic to a simmer. Pour into a 3-quart casserole dish. Add the bread crumbs and season with salt and pepper. Bake for 10 minutes, or until a brown crust begins to form.

With a large spoon, turn the thin crust over and under; return the dish to the oven and repeat the process. When the mixture has browned for the second time, fold in the oysters, crab, and shrimp. Return to the oven and bake until the shrimp are pink and slightly curled, the crust is deep brown, and the sauce is bubbly, about 5 minutes.

NOTES

• To check for cartilage in crabmeat, run it under a hot broiler for 2 minutes, the translucent cartilage will turn opaque or slightly pink. Work quickly, as it will fade. Do not leave under the broiler too long; we are not trying to cook the crabmeat.

• If the mixture begins to brown too much, reduce the oven temperature and crack the door a little. Do not cover the baking dish, or the crust will get mushy.

• Any combination of seafood can be used.

Shrimp Boats

Pirogue Pistolettes

• • •

The term étouffée *is used in French cooking for what we Southerners call "smoth-ered." That is just what this dish is—smothered shrimp. Crusty French rolls shaped like pirogues, the flat-bottomed boats poled through the brackish marshes of the Gulf wetlands, are toasted, sliced, then filled with savory shrimp étouffée.* • SERVES 6

$1/2$ cup (1 stick) unsalted
    butter
$1/2$ cup chili sauce
$1/4$ cup chopped onion
$1/4$ cup chopped celery
1 pound peeled and deveined
    shrimp

$1/4$ cup dry white wine
$1/4$ cup chopped fresh parsley
2 green onions, white and
    green parts, finely chopped
6 crusty French rolls, split
    down center of the tops,
    toasted

In a large skillet over medium heat, melt the butter. Add the chili sauce, onion, and celery. Cook and stir until the vegetables are tender, about 3 to 5 minutes.

Add the shrimp and wine. Cook and stir until the shrimp begin to turn slightly pink, about 4 minutes. Stir in the parsley and green onions.

Spoon into the toasted rolls and serve.

NOTES

• A green salad on the side makes this a perfect lunch or late-night dinner.

• The shrimp filling freezes well and may be doubled.

• A 1-pound package of crawfish may be used in place of the shrimp.

• Leftover ham or smoked sausages can be incorpo-rated nicely. Cooked, diced chicken can be used in place of or in addition to the shrimp.

FIELD PEAS, GREENS, SIDES, AND THE LIKE

Delta Peas and Rice
Where I Cook

• • •

I once did a presentation at a conference of the International Association of Culinary Professionals, entitled "The Rhythm of the Kitchen." Leonard "Doc" Gibbs of Emeril Live Band fame provided informative foot-tapping commentary on playing music to cooking. For my part, I tried to stump the audience by making my version of perhaps the most ubiquitous dish in the world, rice and beans, and seeing if people could place its origins just by tasting it. And sure enough, guesses ranged from the Caribbean and Africa to the Carolinas and Portugal. Then the audience got to sample the dish while riffs of classic blues music filled the air. That did it: they all knew and understood where the dish was from, and people were calling it Delta peas and rice all over the place. This dish tastes a little like all the places guessed first and it tastes a lot like the one named last. • SERVES 4 TO 6

$2^1/_2$ cups frozen black-eyed peas
Kosher salt
2 tablespoons soybean oil
1 medium white onion, peeled and diced
2 garlic cloves, minced
2 cups diced, peeled ripe tomatoes

1 teaspoon thyme leaves
1 tablespoon apple cider vinegar
1 teaspoon sugar
$^1/_4$ teaspoon red pepper flakes
3 cups cooked long-grain white rice
$^1/_4$ cup minced parsley
Freshly ground black pepper

In a large stockpot or Dutch oven, combine the peas, 1 teaspoon salt, and enough water to cover. Simmer the peas over medium-low heat until tender, about 20 minutes. Drain the peas and set aside.

Heat a Dutch oven over medium heat and add the oil and onion. Cook and stir the onion for 5 minutes or until tender. Add the garlic and continue to cook for 1 minute. Add the tomatoes, thyme, vinegar, sugar, and red pepper flakes. Cook, stirring occasionally, for 15 minutes. Add the black-eyed peas and simmer for 15 minutes.

Stir in the cooked rice and parsley. Season with salt and pepper to taste before serving.

Field Peas with Snaps
Sprinkle with Pepper Vinegar

• • •

Field peas cover many varieties of what are termed "Southern peas" (by horticulturists, not just me). Black-eyed peas, purple hull peas, pink-eye purple hull, crowders (bumpy peas that are crowded in the pods), and cow peas all fall in this category. The "snaps" are truly the underdeveloped pods cooked right along with the mature shelled peas. Most often, though, the snaps are young green beans cooked alone. After the peas make their way around a dinner table, pepper vinegar follows hot on their heels, to be sprinkled generously over the Southern peas. Most likely there's some cornbread not far behind. • SERVES 6

1 quart shelled fresh field peas with snaps, or 3 cups peas and 1 cup (1-inch) fresh green bean pieces
1 smoked ham hock

1 small onion, chopped
Salt and freshly ground black pepper
Pepper vinegar (see Notes)

Rinse and pick through the peas.

In a large saucepan over medium-high heat, bring 3 cups of water and the ham hock to a boil. Cook for 15 minutes, spooning off any scum that rises to the top.

Add the onion and the peas and snaps. Reduce the heat and simmer for 20 minutes.

Season with salt and pepper, and cook for 15 to 20 more minutes or until the peas are quite tender. Serve with pepper vinegar. (The cook gets the ham hock.)

NOTES

• If you salt field peas too early, the skins will be tough.

• For pepper vinegar, combine small bird's eye or Anaheim chiles in a bottle with white vinegar. Let steep, refrigerated, for a week or more. Sprinkle on peas and greens.

Crumb Cauliflower
Only If Donald Makes It

• • •

I thought I did not like cauliflower. Turns out, I did not like overcooked cauliflower. I was converted with this dish, a specialty of my husband, Donald. He gets the cauliflower just tender and showers it with a savory combination of crunchy bread crumbs, garlic, and cheese. Even our son, Joe, loves cauliflower this way. • SERVES 4

NOTES

• Cauliflower is a member of the cabbage family and a cousin to the mustard green. It is the sulfur properties it has in common with mustards that give it the pungent smell when cooking. The longer it cooks, the stronger these flavors become. I find it best cooked just until tender.

• The compact florets are called curds. Look for cauliflower that is creamy white, with tight curds, and that feels heavy for its size.

• A serving of cauliflower contains almost a full day's supply of vitamin C.

1 small head cauliflower, trimmed and separated into florets
1/2 cup olive oil
2 garlic cloves, minced
1/2 cup dry bread crumbs
2 tablespoons chopped parsley

1 tablespoon extra-virgin olive oil
1 tablespoon grated Parmesan cheese
Salt and freshly ground black pepper

In a Dutch oven over medium-high heat, cook the cauliflower in the olive oil for 2 minutes. Stir to coat with the olive oil, then cover and cook for 5 more minutes. Scatter the garlic and the bread crumbs over the florets. Cook uncovered, stirring, for 5 minutes or until the cauliflower is tender and the crumbs are nice and brown. Add the parsley.

Turn out onto a warm serving platter. Drizzle with the extra-virgin olive oil, sprinkle with the cheese, and season with salt and pepper. Serve hot.

Molasses Baked Beans
Slow Cooker

• • •

No backyard barbecue is complete without baked beans and coleslaw. These beans cook a long time—about the same amount of time it takes to make good barbecue. An electric roaster, Dutch oven, or slowcooker can be used to cook the beans. It is real hard to go back to the ones in a can after you have had the real deal. • SERVES 12

1 pound dried great northern
   beans
4 strips thick-cut bacon
1 large yellow onion, chopped
1 cup beer
$^1\!/_2$ cup molasses
2 tablespoons light brown
   sugar

1 tablespoon dry mustard
1 teaspoon sweet paprika
2 tablespoons sweet pickle
   relish
Salt

In a large stockpot over high heat, bring 2 quarts of water to a boil. Add the beans and let cook for 5 minutes. Spoon any scum from the surface. Remove from the heat and let soak for 1 to 2 hours. Drain the beans and discard the liquid.

In a large ovenproof skillet over low heat, render the fat from the bacon, cooking until the bacon is just beginning to brown, about 4 minutes. Remove the bacon to drain on paper towels, reserving the fat in the pan. When the bacon is cool, chop it and set aside.

Preheat the oven to 250°F.

Put the pan with the bacon drippings over medium-low heat and add the onion. Cook until golden, about 4 minutes. Add the beer and scrape up the browned bits from the pan. Add 2 cups water, the molasses, brown sugar, mustard, paprika, reserved bacon, and drained beans. Cover and bake for 3 hours, stirring every hour.

Add the relish and bake, uncovered, for 30 minutes or until the beans are tender and the sauce has thickened. Season to taste with salt.

NOTES

• One pound of canned beans can be substituted. Rinse and drain the beans thoroughly and reduce the baking time to $1^1\!/_2$ hours.

• The sweet pickle relish adds a tart, spicy element to the beans.

• If the cooking liquid seems a little low, add more beer, preferably a pale ale.

Greens and Cornbread Croutons
Pot Likker

• • •

I favor collards, though turnip and mustard greens find favor with a lot of folks and wild poke sallet is foraged in the cooler months. A combination of some of these greens is much appreciated on a cold winter's night.

Collards derive their name from the bastardization of the English colewort, *"a variety of cabbage that does not heart." Greens with cornbread is too soulful a dish to be thought of as heartless, I think. Thelonious Monk, the great jazz innovator from Rocky Mount, North Carolina, wore a collard green in his lapel and he knew soul.*

• **SERVES 8**

1 smoked ham hock or turkey neck or leg, or 1 (1-inch) piece of salt pork
4 large bunches greens, rinsed
3 tablespoons lard or bacon grease
Pinch of sugar

1 pecan, in its shell
8 slices Big Black Skillet Cornbread (page 174)
Softened butter
Creole seasoning blend
Salt and freshly ground black pepper

In a large covered stockpot, simmer the ham hock in 1 quart of water for 1 hour.

Meanwhile, with scissors or a paring knife, remove the thick stems and thick veins from the leaves of the greens. Cut into 1-inch strips.

Add the greens, lard, and sugar to the pot. Drop the pecan into the pot and cook for 4 hours on a low simmer, until the greens are very tender and the liquid has reduced by half.

When the greens are nearly ready, preheat the oven to 400°F. Split the cornbread slices. Butter the cut halves and sprinkle with Creole seasoning. Toast open-faced in the oven until slightly brown and crisp, about 4 minutes.

Season the greens with salt and pepper. Spoon them into a serving bowl and top with the toasted cornbread.

NOTES

• Greens are most tender in the colder months. In the market, pick greens with tender stems.

• A whole pecan in the pot is said to diminish the smell of cooking greens, which is quite powerful.

• Greens are about 80 percent water. One bunch may seem like a mountain of greens, but it cooks down to pot likker and enough greens for two people.

• Eat greens on New Year's Day to ensure a year's worth of financial prosperity. Or, for true believers, tack them to the ceiling or over the front door to keep bad luck from coming in your kitchen.

"THE North Carolinian who is not familiar with pot likker has suffered in his early education and needs to go back and begin it over again."

—J. P. CALDWELL, 1907

Green Chile Rice

Poblano and Farmer Cheese

• • •

Served with Chile Lime Skirt Steak (page 117) and fresh tortillas, this rice side dish makes a meal come together quite harmoniously.

The poblano is a dark green, spearhead-shaped, moderately hot pepper. To roast and seed it, broil the pepper on all sides until the skin is charred. Let cool, then peel, and remove the stem and seeds. • SERVES 4

1 teaspoon olive oil
1 small white onion, chopped
1 poblano chile, roasted, peeled, seeded, and chopped
2 cups cooked long-grain white rice
1 large egg white, lightly beaten

1 cup crumbled farmer cheese, queso blanco, or large-curd cottage cheese, drained
1 cup shredded Colby jack cheese
1 tablespoon chopped cilantro

Preheat the oven to 325°F.

In a large ovenproof skillet, heat the oil over medium heat. Add the onion and cook until tender and beginning to brown, 3 to 4 minutes.

Add the chopped chile. Remove from the heat. Stir in the cooked rice, egg white, and farmer cheese. Spread evenly in the skillet and bake, covered, for 10 minutes.

Remove the cover and top with the shredded cheese. Return to the oven and bake for 5 minutes, or until the cheese is bubbly. Sprinkle the cilantro over the top and serve.

NOTES

• One (12-ounce) can of golden hominy, rinsed and drained, can be added with the rice.

• Cook the rice in broth for extra flavor, or use saffron rice.

See photograph page 116.

Tallahatchie Tomatoes
Bright Spot on the Buffet

• • •

I have been to any number of brunches where most of the dishes were beige and contained cheese. This dish is a bright splash of color, and it complements egg dishes quite well. • SERVES 12

3 (28-ounce) cans whole
  peeled tomatoes, drained,
  or 24 ripe plum tomatoes,
  peeled
2 cups packed fresh baby
  spinach, stems trimmed
1½ teaspoons salt
1 teaspoon freshly ground
  black pepper
1 teaspoon grated lemon zest

¹/₈ teaspoon freshly grated
  nutmeg
¹/₄ cup chopped parsley
1 cup fresh bread crumbs or
  panko
¹/₃ cup packed light brown
  sugar
6 tablespoons (³/₄ stick)
  unsalted butter, melted

Preheat the oven to 350°F. Butter a 9 x 13-inch baking dish.

In a large bowl, combine the tomatoes, spinach, salt, pepper, lemon zest, nutmeg, and parsley. Pour the mixture into the buttered dish. Bake uncovered for 20 minutes.

Meanwhile, in a small bowl, combine the bread crumbs, brown sugar, and butter.

Remove the tomatoes from the oven and turn and stir. Sprinkle the crumb topping over the tomatoes and bake for 15 to 20 minutes, or until they are bubbly and the crust is brown and crisp. Serve hot.

NOTES

• If using canned tomatoes, I favor Red Gold brand. They always come out whole and are very deep red. If fresh plum tomatoes are truly ripe, I use them instead but only find it worth the trouble if they are very good tomatoes.

• Fresh basil or dill is also good in flavoring the tomatoes.

See photograph page 136.

BOBBY Gentry familiarized the nation with the Tallahatchie River in the darkly puzzling song she penned and performed, "Ode to Billy Joe." The song became a hit in 1967, reaching number 13 on the charts. The Tallahatchie and Yalobusha Rivers flow in opposite directions and come together to form the Yazoo River, which joins the Mississippi at Vicksburg.

Corn and Red Pepper Pudding

Covered-Dish Favorite

• • •

Warm corn pudding complements most entrées. This is a good choice to bring to a covered-dish supper when the main course is a mystery. • SERVES 4

1 cup whole milk
2 tablespoons unsalted butter, melted
2 large eggs yolks
2 teaspoons sugar
1 tablespoon cornstarch
1 (12-ounce) package frozen creamed corn

2 tablespoons finely chopped red bell pepper
2 tablespoons finely chopped onion
1 teaspoon chopped sage
Salt and freshly ground black pepper
2 large egg whites

NOTES

• The water bath may seem like a pain, but it really creates a much smoother pudding.

• Chopped pimientos or jarred roasted red peppers can be used here.

Preheat the oven to 300°F. Butter a 2-quart baking dish and set it inside a roasting pan.

In a large bowl, whisk together the milk, butter, egg yolks, sugar, and cornstarch. Add the corn, bell pepper, onion, and sage. Season with salt and pepper.

Whip the egg whites to soft peaks. Fold the beaten whites into the corn mixture. Scrape the mixture into the prepared baking dish. Put the roasting pan and baking dish in the oven. Pour hot water into the roasting pan to come halfway up the sides of the baking dish. Bake for 40 minutes, or until the pudding is light golden brown.

Succotash

So Long, Summer

• • •

When corn, beans, and tomatoes are at their peak, this combination of flavors and textures is stupefyingly good. A simple vegetarian dish, this freezes well and can be brought out as a promise of summer to come. Frozen vegetables can be substituted if you didn't plan ahead or it is just not that time of year yet. • SERVES 6

1 large red onion, chopped
2 teaspoons unsalted butter
1 cup vegetable broth
1 cup heavy cream
3 cups corn kernels

1^1/$_2$ cups fresh lima beans
2 teaspoons chopped thyme
1 pint cherry tomatoes, halved
Salt and freshly ground black
  pepper

In a large saucepan over medium-high heat, cook the onion in the butter until tender, about 3 minutes. Add the broth, cream, corn, lima beans, and thyme. Cook over low heat for 20 minutes, until the lima beans are tender. Add the tomatoes and cook for 10 minutes more, or until the liquid is reduced by half. Season with salt and pepper.

NOTES

• Do not salt the corn until it is tender. Salting too early will toughen the cases.

• If preparing this dish ahead of time, add the tomatoes when it is being reheated.

Jule's Carrots
Ginger and Caraway Seeds

• • •

Carrots are often relegated to salads—or to cloyingly sweet, candy-glazed treatments. My friend Jane Rule Burdine, called "Jule" by her nieces and nephews, turned me on to this preparation. The little flare of heat from ground ginger and dry mustard sets this dish apart. I enjoy these slightly sweet, shiny carrots served at home along with simple roast chicken and a nice green salad. • SERVES 6

6 medium carrots, peeled and $1/8$-inch thick sliced on the diagonal
4 tablespoons ($1/2$ stick) unsalted butter
$1/2$ teaspoon caraway seeds
$1/2$ teaspoon ground ginger
$1/4$ teaspoon dry mustard
$1/4$ teaspoon salt
$1/4$ cup packed light brown sugar

Bring a large saucepan of salted water to a boil. Add the carrots and cook until slightly tender, about 4 minutes. Drain well.

In a large skillet over medium heat, melt the butter. Add the carrots, caraway seeds, ginger, mustard, salt, and brown sugar.

Cook and stir for 6 to 8 minutes, until the carrots are fully cooked and glazed. Serve hot.

NOTES

• Just $1/2$ cup halved black seedless grapes are beautiful, added during the last few minutes of cooking.

• Caraway seeds are often associated with returning home. A sprinkle of seeds in a lover's dish was thought to prevent him or her from straying. The tiny crescent-shaped seeds were even baked into cakes fed to homing pigeons to encourage their return.

• Caraway plants are similar in looks to Queen Anne's Lace or the green tops of carrots. The dill-like fronds can be used in salads. Aquavit and gin are flavored with caraway. In any of its forms, the frilly greens of the caraway plant are a fine-looking addition to the table arrangement.

Baked Sweet Onions
Clove Studded

• • •

It is not that varieties of sweet onions, like Vidalia and Texas Supersweet, contain more sugars than other onions; their mild flavor is often a matter of where and how they are grown—generally in low-sulfur soil, which lends them their perceived sweetness. These onions are low in pyruvic acid, the compound that gives onion heat; with the heat at a minimum, the sweetness is allowed to shine through.

My figs begin to ripen as a new crop of sweet onions arrives, right toward the end of June. Baked together and topped with black walnuts and a drizzle of good balsamic, this dish matches up nicely with a roasted pork loin and showcases that inherent sweetness. • SERVES 4

4 small sweet onions, peeled
16 whole cloves
4 teaspoons unsalted butter
Salt and freshly ground black
    pepper
1 cup apple juice

2 cups diced small fresh figs
1 tablespoon black walnut
    pieces
1 tablespoon aged balsamic
    vinegar

Preheat the oven to 325°F.

Halve the onions crosswise (around the equator). Stud the sides of each onion half with two cloves. Place the onion halves in a shallow baking dish cut sides up. Dot each with butter and season with salt and pepper. Pour the apple juice into the dish. Cover and bake for 1 hour.

Remove the onions from the oven and uncover. Using a small spoon, scoop out the centers of the onions, forming a cup of several layers. Set aside the onion cups. Chop the onion centers and combine with the figs and a little of the cooking liquid. Spoon the fig mixture into the onion cups and top with the walnut pieces.

Bake until the center is warmed through, about 10 minutes. Drizzle with the balsamic vinegar before serving.

NOTES

• Small cipolline onions are also good studded with cloves, cooked in apple juice, and served whole.

• You can use 1 1/2 cups dried figs; leave them to soak in the apple juice mixture as the onions cook and they will plump up.

• Rub the cut side of an onion on a scar a couple of times a day to help it go away. Many popular scar treatments, like Maderma, are made of onion extract.

• The Eastern black walnut is prized by cooks and woodworkers alike. Cooks and ice-cream and fudge makers adore the flavor, which is often reminisced about. There are many stories of black-stained hands and the taste of these deeply flavored nuts. Visit www.nutsonline.com if you have a hard time finding them; common English walnuts may be substituted.

All for Okra and Okra for All

End Discrimination

• • •

Okra is often discriminated against because of its very nature. Soaking the okra and flash-frying thin strips produces a crisp, tender side dish that has none of the offending slime often associated with this delectable vegetable. • SERVES 6

1 pound small, tender okra
    pods
1 cup cider vinegar
$1/4$ cup vegetable oil
$1/2$ yellow onion, thinly sliced

$1/4$ teaspoon red pepper flakes
3 garlic cloves, minced
1 medium ripe tomato, seeded
    and diced

Soak the okra in 1 quart water mixed with the vinegar for 1 hour. Drain and pat the okra dry. Using a v-slicer, mandoline, or sharp knife, cut the okra lengthwise into very thin slices.

In a large skillet, heat the oil over high heat. Add the onion and red pepper flakes, and cook and stir for 2 minutes. Add the garlic and cook for 1 minute or less; do not let it darken. Using a slotted spoon, scrape the onion mixture from the skillet onto a plate and set aside. Add the okra to the skillet and stir-fry for 3 to 5 minutes, or until tender. Add the tomato and cooked onion. Cook and stir for 2 minutes. Serve immediately.

NOTES

• Cook okra in a stainless steel or enameled pot. Cast iron will darken it to an unpleasant grayish green.

• Okra is a cousin to the mallow plant and to cotton.

"PARIS would be the greatest city in the world if I could just find some okra."

—BEST LINE FROM *ROUND MIDNIGHT*, THE 1986 MOVIE
DIRECTED BY BERTRAND TAVERNIER

Hot Fruit

Funcle Jon's Christmas Carols

• • •

Funky Uncle Jon Foose loves a celebration. He has a seasonal ritual of reworking "low on the radio dial" Christmas carols. To the holiday blues standard "Bells Will Be Ringing," he has penned "Belzoni Women," which celebrates the attributes of the local gals. "Good King Wenceslas," in Jon's verse, "gets lost on his way to Eden, where soybeans grow round about, rich and thick and even." To the classic "Let It Snow," he has created the family classic that sums up the holidays with ". . . And the cousins are getting indignant, And the Hot Fruit's about to Blow, I think I'll motor in to Jackson to the show."

This hot fruit favorite is made with an array of canned fruits. Fresh fruit is wonderful in this, too, and if you have the time and the season is right (somewhere in the world), substitute as many as you can. • SERVES 6 TO 8

1 (29-ounce) can pear halves in pear juice
1 (29-ounce) can peaches in light syrup
1 (17-ounce) can pitted tart cherries or Bing cherries (or frozen)
1 (20-ounce) can pineapple chunks in juice

1 (17-ounce) can peeled apricots in light syrup
2 bananas, peeled and diced
$\frac{1}{4}$ teaspoon salt
3 tablespoons unsalted butter
3 tablespoons unbleached all-purpose flour
1 teaspoon mild curry powder

Preheat the oven to 350°F. Butter a large baking dish.

Drain the fruits, reserving the juices all together. Combine the fruits in the buttered dish.

In a small saucepan, combine $\frac{3}{4}$ cup of the juice mixture, the salt, butter, and flour. Cook and stir over medium-low heat until thick. Add the curry powder.

Pour the mixture over the fruit and bake for 30 minutes or until bubbly.

NOTES

• This can be assembled a day or two ahead, and refrigerated and baked when needed. It is wonderful served for brunch or a dinner with roast chicken or lamb.

• Lychees, which give fruit cocktail syrup its unique flavor, are a pleasant addition to this fruit dish.

• Make punch for the children with the leftover juices mixed with lemon-lime soda.

• Spanish moss, the silver ambience-enhancing tangle seen draped from live oak trees, is a member of the pineapple family, a bromeliad.

JON FOOSE is co-author of *Up From the Cradle of Jazz: New Orleans Music Since World War II.*

Sunflower Squash
Anonymous Gifts on Doorsteps

• • •

Jamie and Kelly Kornegay turned me on to this dish: spoonfuls of grated squash in cornmeal batter that blossom like sunflowers as they sizzle to a crisp brown. When it is not possible to eat all the squash that comes out of the backyard garden quickly enough, the Kornegays have admitted to leaving anonymous gifts on neighbors' doorsteps under the cover of darkness. They, too, have been on the receiving end of this generous gesture. Kelly tried the recipe she got from a neighbor one particularly prolific summer, when she had exhausted her many uses for crooknecked squash. • SERVES 8

2 cups self-rising cornmeal
$^1/_2$ cup self-rising flour
$^1/_2$ teaspoon salt
$^1/_4$ teaspoon sugar
$^1/_2$ cup grated onion

1 cup grated yellow summer squash
1 cup buttermilk
1 large egg
Vegetable oil, for frying (1 to 2 cups)

In a large mixing bowl, whisk the cornmeal, flour, salt, and sugar to get out any lumps. In a separate bowl, combine the onion, squash, buttermilk, and egg. Mix the wet ingredients into the dry and stir well to combine. Let sit for 15 minutes.

Meanwhile, heat about 4 inches of oil in a deep pot or deep-fryer to 375°F. Set a wire rack over newspaper or paper towels to cool and drain the squash after frying.

Do not stir the batter. Dip two spoons in the hot oil, then scoop up one spoonful of batter and slide it into the hot oil using the other spoon. Repeat to make more fritters, dipping the spoons again into the hot oil if the batter begins to stick. Fry the squash for 2 minutes, turning as needed until crisp and deep golden brown.

Drain on the rack set over newspaper. Serve hot.

NOTES

• If the squash is very large, halve it and scoop out the seeds before grating.

• A spider works well for gently lifting the sunflower squash from the oil.

• These are terrific with a grating of pecorino cheese over the top while warm. They're also good served as an alterative to hush puppies at a fish fry.

Baked Macaroni and Cheese
A Vegetable in Some States

• • •

"What vegetables you want, hun?"

"I'll have greens, butter peas, and macaroni and cheese, please."

Macaroni and cheese is considered a vegetable, not just a side dish, in many places. The kind from a box, however, does not fall into the same category. Baked homemade macaroni and cheese is the only type that qualifies for this amended food pyramid.

• SERVES 8

1 pound fusilli pasta
2 teaspoons unsalted butter
1 cup fresh bread crumbs
8 ounces extra-sharp Cheddar cheese, grated (2 cups)
1/4 cup freshly grated Parmesan cheese
3 1/2 cups whole milk

1/4 cup unbleached all-purpose flour
1/2 teaspoon minced garlic
1 teaspoon whole-grain mustard
1/2 teaspoon salt
1/4 teaspoon freshly ground black pepper

Preheat the oven to 350°F. Butter a shallow 3-quart baking dish.

Cook the pasta in boiling salted water according to the package directions until al dente. Drain well. Set aside.

In a large saucepan over medium heat, melt the butter. Add the bread crumbs and cook and stir until browned and crisp, about 3 minutes. Transfer to a small bowl and add 2 tablespoons of the Cheddar and half of the Parmesan cheese.

Return the saucepan to medium-high heat and add the milk, flour, and garlic; whisk to combine. Bring to a boil, then reduce the heat and simmer for 2 minutes. Remove from the heat and stir in the remaining Cheddar and Parmesan and the mustard, then season with the salt and pepper. Add the cooked pasta and turn the mixture into the prepared baking dish.

Sprinkle the crumb topping over the pasta. Bake for 30 minutes or until bubbly around the sides and the crumbs are deep golden brown.

NOTES

• To make fresh bread crumbs, crumble the heels of bread loaves in a food processor and keep them stored in a bag in the freezer to have on hand. That odd hot-dog or hamburger bun can end up in there, too.

• Two 8-inch square baking dishes can be used instead of one big one.

• Additions can round out mac and cheese to a one-dish meal. Chopped ham and well-drained sautéed spinach, diced cooked chicken, and mixed vegetables are all good choices.

• Smoked Gouda or just about any other cheese can be used. Grown-ups like a little goat cheese and roasted red pepper. Add your favorite fresh herbs to the cheese sauce.

• If you are pressed for time, alternate the cheeses and a sprinkling of the flour and spices and layers of noodles. Pour the milk over the top and bake for 40 minutes. Top with the crumb combination and bake until browned, about 7 minutes.

Pecan Rice

Pilau with Spice

• • •

I like cooking this pilaf in the oven. You don't have to worry about boilovers, or somebody coming through the kitchen and taking the top off your rice and getting it all sticky.

The name "Pilau" comes from the Persian word for "rice." Dishes of these types are thought to have been spread throughout India and West Africa by Arab traders. The name has become interchangeable in the Southeast with pilaf, particularly in the coastal regions. • SERVES 6 TO 8

1 quart vegetable broth
5 tablespoons unsalted butter
2 cups long-grain white rice, rinsed
¼ cup grated peeled carrot
¼ cup chopped celery
1 teaspoon fresh thyme

½ cup chopped green onion, white and green parts
1 cup pecans, toasted (see Notes, page 15)
Salt and freshly ground black pepper
Pinch of ground allspice

Preheat the oven to 350°F.

In a saucepan, bring the broth to a boil over medium heat.

In a large ovenproof skillet with a lid, melt the butter over medium heat. Add the rice and cook and stir for 3 to 4 minutes, until the rice is slightly browned. Add the hot broth to the skillet, cover, and bake for 20 minutes.

Remove the rice from the oven and stir in the carrot, celery, and thyme. Return to the oven and bake uncovered for 15 minutes, or until the liquid is absorbed.

Add the onion and pecans, and toss lightly with a fork to combine. Season with the salt and pepper and sprinkle with the allspice. Serve hot or at room temperature.

• In spring, tender young peas are a nice addition to this dish. They should be added during the last 10 minutes so as not to overcook.

• Dried cranberries are a seasonal addition for the holidays.

• Allspice, sometimes referred to as pimento in island cookery, is a dried berry from a tropical evergreen tree. The wood is traditionally used for walking sticks, often carved with totems and faces, some in lascivious poses. This folk art was carried on in New Orleans with strong influences of the Haitian, Maltanagran, and Afro-Caribbean culture. The practice was outlawed in the nineteenth century, for fear of devastating the valuable spice trade, but like many illegal trades, the practice endured. One walking-stick man from New Orleans, Hugh "Daddy Boy" Williams, whom I met as a child, is such an adept carver that he carved a replacement for his nose, which had been shot off in a disagreement. He attached it to some glasses. And at no farther away than you are from this book, you would never know it wasn't his real nose.

Cheese Grits

All Around the World

• • •

Grits—they're not just for breakfast anymore. In the past few years, Southern cooks have taken a cue from Italians with their polenta, and we now see grits served with all sorts of savory additions and at any time of day.

This is the classic brunch rendition of grits, open for personal interpretation.

• SERVES 12

3^1/$_2$ cups whole milk
2 tablespoons unsalted butter
1 garlic clove, minced
1 teaspoon salt
1^1/$_4$ cups quick-cooking grits
8 ounces sharp Cheddar
   cheese, grated (2 cups)

1 teaspoon hot pepper sauce
^{1}/$_4$ teaspoon freshly ground
   black pepper
5 large eggs
^{1}/$_8$ teaspoon hot paprika

Preheat the oven to 325°F. Butter a shallow 2^1/$_2$-quart baking dish.

In a large saucepan over medium-high heat, combine 1^1/$_2$ cups of the milk, 2 cups water, the butter, garlic, and salt. Bring to a rolling boil. Slowly whisk in the grits. Whisk continuously for a minute, until no lumps remain. Reduce the heat, cover, and simmer for 5 minutes. Remove from the heat and stir in the cheese.

In a large bowl, whisk together the remaining 2 cups milk, the hot sauce, pepper, and eggs. Gradually add the hot grits, stirring to combine. Pour the grits into the prepared dish and sprinkle with paprika.

Bake for 45 minutes, until puffy around the edges and a knife inserted into the center comes out clean.

NOTES

• Grits are ground dried hominy. For this recipe, quick grits are used, *not* instant grits. Old-fashioned slow-cooking grits can be used, but they require longer cooking time. There are several good stone-ground artisanal grits available; they have superior flavor and it is always good to help the little guy. I like Anson Mills.

• This casserole can be assembled the day before, refrigerated, and baked the next day. Add 20 minutes onto the baking time.

WHEN I left for cooking school in France, the plan was to meet up with a fellow pastry chef I used to work with in Los Angeles. When I got to the Gare de l'Est train station, he was nowhere to be found. I called and his French girlfriend answered. "He is not here. He is a rat. He has gone to Italy. I hope I never see him again." Click. Apparently my plans had changed.

Armed with my feeble language skills and paperback guidebook, I hailed a taxi and made my way to Place St.-Michel, the student area. Bumping my preposterously large duffle bag along the stone streets, I found a room in a cheap hotel. The desk clerk led me up the stairs, peering back as I hoisted my belongings up countless flights. He opened the door at the top of the stairs and left me in my Camille-like dormer room.

Not the reception I had imagined, but I gathered myself with a combined That Girl/Mary Tyler Moore aplomb. I had gotten all the way from Yazoo City to Paris. And, Paris here I came. With that, I tromped down the stairs and swung open the door to the streets of Paris, knocking over a very tall West African man carrying a cello. The case slid across the damp cobblestones. The cello's irate owner picked me up by my shoulders and shook me with all his might. I apologized in my broken French, and in broken English he rightfully demanded "What is wrong with you!" And though I am not the crybaby sort, I tearfully shouted, "I'm from Mississippi!" With that he set me down and a look came over his face that seemed, well, like he felt sorry for me—really close to pity. He picked up his instrument and stared at me. "Where are you going?"

"I don't know, my friend was supposed to meet me and he stood me up, and I don't know anybody and my French is really bad and I don't know my way around. . . ." I blubbered.

"Calm down, calm down. Here, I have some time before my rehearsal. I will take you where there are more Americans."

Thinking that I could outrun a guy with a cello, and as no other options seemed to be presenting themselves, away we went.

We walked across Pont Neuf and I saw the City of Lights for the first time that night. We walked all the way to St. Denis. There, he led me into a bar, the walls covered with black-and-white photos of boxers, and sat me down. He bought me a whisky and said that the people here were nice, and I would find one of them to help me. Then he just up and left, without my even getting his name.

So, there I was, still in the same boat, but at least a whisky in hand. Now, I was wondering if I could find my way back to the hotel and what the name of the hotel was. The guy sitting next to me kept looking at me, like, you look familiar. And he did look familiar, but what were the chances?

"Where are you from?" he asked.

"Mississippi."

"Well, I know I don't know you from there!"

"I did just move from L.A."

"Wait—did you cook at Georgia over on Melrose?"

"Yes, yes I did. I made the desserts."

"I worked at the salon upstairs. I knew I had seen you before." With that we became fast friends. His mother was from the South and he had grown up with her cooking. I told him I had brought grits in my suitcase in case I got really broke, or homesick. Shelly alerted his companions that I had grits in my suitcase. He told me to go back and get my grits, and meet him at the address he wrote on a napkin. After a little searching for the hotel, I retrieved my grits and went on over. I made a big batch of cheese grits and some good friends. Leila, Shelly, and E.J. offered me a place to stay. I would have never met them without bumping into my cello-toting guardian angel. I would have never lived at 7 Avenue Carnot if it weren't for grits.

• • •

Crisp Baby Reds
With Parsley Salt

• • •

I like to use size B new potatoes, not just little potatoes—which are just little potatoes—but new potatoes that, just as the name says, are small, young potatoes with tender flesh harvested when the plant is still green. For best results, pick potatoes close to the same size or cut larger ones so they cook in the same amount of time. Although tedious to peel, fingerling potatoes work well in this dish.

Served as a side dish or as an hors d'oeuvre, these uniquely textured potatoes are always popular. Adding your favorite herb to complement the meal means endless variations. • SERVES 6

2 tablespoons olive oil
1 quart chicken broth
2 pounds small red potatoes, peeled (about 1½ inches in diameter)

1 tablespoon finely chopped fresh parsley
2 teaspoons coarse sea salt or kosher salt

Preheat the oven to 425°F.

Pour the oil into a shallow baking dish or roasting pan and put it in the oven to heat.

In a large pot, bring the broth to a boil over medium-high heat. Add the potatoes to the boiling broth and cook for 6 minutes, or until the surface of the potatoes is very tender. Drain the potatoes well and reserve the cooking liquid for another use (see Notes).

Return the potatoes to the pot over medium heat and cover. Shake the pot briskly for 1 minute to dry the surface of the potatoes. The potatoes will look a little velvety.

Remove the baking dish of hot oil from the oven. With a slotted spoon, add the potatoes a couple at a time, stirring to coat with the oil with every addition. When all of the potatoes are added, return the pan to the oven and bake for 45 minutes, or until crunchy golden brown.

Combine the parsley and salt and sprinkle over the potatoes. Serve immediately.

NOTES

• Most potatoes are stored a couple of weeks before shipping. This gives any scrapes time to heal and allows the skin to dry for prolonged storage.

• Don't store potatoes under the kitchen sink. Solvents and cleaners can penetrate the porous skin.

• The broth used to boil the potatoes can be used as a soup base or in sauces and gravies. The starch left behind from cooking the potatoes will thicken the mixture a little as well as add nice flavor.

• Fresh dill added to the salt mixture creates a perfect accompaniment to baked salmon.

Sweet Potato Soufflé
No Cinnamon in Sight

• • •

Like carrots, sweet potatoes rarely get out from under a syrupy glaze. Here,
they are presented in an elevated savory dish that pairs nicely with roast pork or game.

• SERVES 6

1¹/₂ **pounds sweet potatoes**
¹/₂ **cup freshly grated dry**
    Monterey jack cheese
2 tablespoons unsalted butter
1 cup finely chopped onion
1 garlic clove, minced
¹/₂ **teaspoon chopped fresh**
    rosemary
¹/₂ **teaspoon ground ginger**

¹/₄ **teaspoon cracked black**
    peppercorns
2 tablespoons unbleached
    all-purpose flour
1 cup whole milk
1 cup grated Edam cheese
4 large egg yolks
4 large egg whites
Pinch of salt
Caraway seeds

Preheat the oven to 375°F.

Place the sweet potatoes on a baking sheet and bake for 45 minutes, or until very tender when pierced with a knife. Set aside to cool.

Butter a 2-quart mold or six individual soufflé dishes and coat with some of the jack cheese.

When the sweet potatoes are cool enough to handle, scoop out the flesh and mash or push it through a ricer or food mill.

In a large saucepan over medium heat, melt the butter and cook the onion, garlic, and rosemary until softened, about 3 minutes. Add the ginger, pepper, and flour, and stir to combine. Cook and stir for 3 minutes before adding the milk. Cook, whisking, until thickened, about 4 minutes. Remove from the heat. Add the Edam cheese and stir until melted. Add the sweet potatoes and stir to combine. Add the egg yolks one at a time, whisking after each addition.

In an electric mixer, whip the egg whites with the salt until the whites hold a soft peak. Fold the whites into the sweet potato mixture in four additions. Spoon the mixture into the soufflé dish, filling it to the top. Sprinkle with the remaining jack cheese and the caraway seeds. Run a damp fingertip around the rim of the dish.

Bake for 45 minutes, or until puffed and golden. Serve immediately.

NOTES

• Mississippi produces 238 million pounds of sweet potatoes a year. Vardaman, Mississippi, bills itself as the "Sweet Potato Capital of the State."

• The soufflé can be prepared up to 4 hours ahead of time, refrigerated, and baked when needed. Let the soufflé sit at room temperature for 30 minutes before baking.

Inside-out Sweet Potatoes
Sure, It Is for the Kids

• • •

Irresistible to children once they find out there is a marshmallow inside, and a guilty pleasure for adults once they become privy to the same secret, these surprising potatoes are always a hit at the holidays. • SERVES 8

1 cup crushed cornflakes
1 large egg
6 sweet potatoes, baked and
    mashed (see Notes)
4 tablespoons ($^1/_2$ stick)
    unsalted butter, melted
$^1/_3$ cup packed dark brown
    sugar
$^1/_2$ teaspoon ground cinnamon
$^1/_4$ teaspoon freshly grated
    nutmeg

Pinch of ground cloves
$^1/_4$ teaspoon baking powder
1 tablespoon unbleached
    all-purpose flour
1 tablespoon orange juice
1 tablespoon sherry, Bourbon,
    or vanilla extract
8 large marshmallows
Canola oil, for frying
    (1$^1/_2$ cups)

Put the cornflake crumbs in a shallow dish or pie pan. Beat the egg with 1 teaspoon water in a small bowl. Set aside.

Combine the mashed sweet potatoes with the butter, brown sugar, cinnamon, nutmeg, cloves, baking powder, flour, orange juice, and sherry. Working with your hands, use the mixture to encase each marshmallow, forming a ball. Dip each ball in the egg wash and then roll in the crumbs. Refrigerate while preparing to fry.

Preheat the oven to 200°F. Set a wire rack over newspaper or paper towels to cool and drain the balls after frying.

In a 2-quart saucepan, heat the oil over medium-high heat to 375°F.

Fry the balls one or two at a time for 3 to 4 minutes, turning as needed, until lightly browned. Remove with a spider or slotted spoon, and place the drained balls on the prepared rack and in the oven to keep warm while frying the remaining batches. Serve warm.

NOTES

• To make mashed sweet potatoes, preheat the oven to 375°F. Place the sweet potatoes on a baking sheet and bake for 40 minutes, or until tender and easily pierced with the tip of a sharp knife. Allow to cool in their jackets. When cool enough to handle, halve them, scoop out the flesh, and mash it with a fork or potato masher.

• If the sweet potato mixture seems too soft to hold its shape, stir in some of the crumbs to thicken it.

• You can form these ahead of time and roll them in the crumbs right before frying. They can be baked if you really want to, but are better fried, like most things. Bake on a baking mat or parchment, if you do.

• Marshmallows are named for the wild plant that lent its roots to the first marshmallow confections. Most marshmallows today are made with gelatin or gum arabic.

HOT FROM THE OVEN

Apron String Biscuits
Red-Eye Gravy or Tomato Gravy

• • •

There are so many types of biscuits—buttermilk, sweet milk, beaten, dropped, cat head, and fist, just to name a few. I have grown accustomed to square biscuits. When cutting round biscuits, you have to take much care to produce as few scraps as possible because the next batch, made from the rolled trimmings, won't be nearly as nice as the first. So, I just started cutting them in squares so they would all be nice, and started calling them "apron string biscuits," because if you don't have a knife handy a taut apron string will do the trick to cut them. Plus, my child is constantly tugging at my apron strings, wanting to know if they are still too hot to eat. The square shape also holds a slice of country ham better, for it is never round. While the biscuits are in the oven, Red-Eye Gravy or Tomato Gravy can be warming on the stove to serve, spooned in the middle of a split biscuit or two. • MAKES 2 DOZEN BISCUITS*

2 cups Southern all-purpose
   flour (low-protein, like
   White Lily or Martha White)
1 tablespoon baking powder
¼ teaspoon baking soda
1 teaspoon salt
6 tablespoons vegetable
   shortening or lard, cold

¼ cup buttermilk, cold
2 tablespoons unsalted butter,
   melted
Red-Eye Gravy with Ham
   or Tomato Gravy (see page
   173)

In the bowl of a food processor fitted with the metal blade, combine the flour, baking powder, baking soda, and salt. Pulse several times. Add the shortening and pulse several times more, until the shortening is in pieces the size of baby English peas. Dump the mixture into a mixing bowl. Using a fork, stir in the buttermilk until all of the flour is moistened. On a floured surface, knead the dough for just 1 minute, then pat into a ½-inch-thick square. Wrap in plastic and chill for at least 20 minutes or overnight.

Preheat the oven to 450°F.

With a sharp knife or taut string, cut 2-inch squares. Place 2 inches apart on a baking sheet. Bake for 10 to 12 minutes, or until golden brown. Remove from the oven and then brush the tops with the melted butter. Serve warm or place on a rack to cool. Serve with Red-Eye Gravy or Tomato Gravy.

NOTES

• Southern flours are milled from soft wheat, which has less protein than the hard wheat used for most all-purpose flours, and therefore does not develop as much gluten when kneaded.

• If you prefer to make biscuits with self-rising flour, remember to shape them with all-purpose flour. The leavening in self-rising flour can leave a bitter chalky film.

• Lard yields a crispier biscuit than shortening. Look for trans fat–free shortenings in the baking aisle.

• I may be stoned for saying this, but I like to cut in the fat quickly with a food processor so my fingers do not warm the mixture. Of course, purists can cut it in with fingertips, or a pastry blender, or iced-tea spoons. Do not, however, ever add the buttermilk to the food processor. The resulting biscuits will be tough.

• If you do cut your biscuits in rounds, make sure to use a sharp cutter; a juice glass will compress the sides and they will not rise so fine.

RED-EYE GRAVY WITH HAM

MAKES 1 CUP

1 teaspoon unsalted butter
8 biscuit-size slices of country
   ham

1 cup strong black coffee with
   $1/4$ teaspoon sugar, or 1 cup
   cola soda pop

In a heavy stainless steel or enameled skillet over medium heat, melt the butter. Fry the ham slices for 2 minutes on each side, or until browned and slightly crisp. Set aside in a warm place. Increase the heat under the skillet and add the coffee. Scrape up the browned bits and then reduce the heat. Simmer for 2 minutes.

TOMATO GRAVY

MAKES $1 1/2$ CUPS

2 tablespoons bacon drippings
   or unsalted butter
2 tablespoons all-purpose
   flour

1 (14.5-ounce) can stewed
   tomatoes, with juice, or
   2 large ripe tomatoes,
   peeled and seeded
$1/2$ cup tomato-vegetable juice
   blend or tomato-and-clam
   juice

In a heavy stainless steel or enameled skillet, heat the drippings over medium heat. Add the flour and stir with a fork. Cook for 2 minutes, or until the flour begins to brown. Add the tomatoes and the juice. Simmer for 5 minutes, or until thickened and bubbly.

- For tender biscuits, bake biscuits with sides barely touching in a cake pan.

- For a shiny top on biscuits, brush with a little egg wash before baking.

- Owing to the buttermilk, these biscuits should be baked first if any are going to be frozen.

Big Black Skillet Cornbread
Codicil to the Will

• • •

A well-seasoned cast-iron skillet is essential for a good Southern-style, crisp-crusted cornbread. Make sure in your final will and testament that it is clearly stated who inherits your cast-iron skillet. You can prevent a rift after you have departed.

• MAKES ONE 8-INCH CAKE OR 6 TO 8 INDIVIDUAL SERVINGS

2 cups self-rising white cornmeal (not cornmeal mix)
$^1/_2$ cup unbleached all-purpose
  flour
$^1/_2$ cup bacon drippings (from
  8 slices cooked bacon) or
  corn oil

$^3/_4$ cup whole milk
$^3/_4$ cup buttermilk
1 large egg, lightly beaten
1 teaspoon cornmeal

Preheat the oven to 450°F.

In a large bowl, combine the self-rising cornmeal and flour; set aside.

Heat an 8-inch cast-iron skillet in the hot oven for 6 to 8 minutes. Add the bacon drippings to the hot skillet and return to the oven to heat the drippings, 2 minutes.

Meanwhile, add the milk and buttermilk to the flour mixture and stir with a wire whisk to combine.

Working very carefully, remove the hot skillet of drippings from the oven. Pour almost all of the hot drippings (reserve about 1 tablespoon of drippings in the skillet) into the batter and stir to combine. Add the beaten egg and stir until well blended.

Sprinkle the surface of the reserved hot drippings in the skillet with the teaspoon of cornmeal. Pour the cornbread batter into the prepared skillet. Bake for 18 to 20 minutes, until a deep golden brown. Remove from the oven and turn out onto a serving plate.

NOTES

• If self-rising cornmeal is unavailable, substitute 2 cups regular cornmeal combined with 1 teaspoon baking powder, 1 teaspoon baking soda, and $^3/_4$ teaspoon salt.

• The additional cornmeal sprinkled in the skillet right before baking crisps the crust and helps prevent sticking.

• Try a slice of warmed leftover cornbread with honey for breakfast the next day, or save leftovers in the freezer to use in stuffings for chicken, pork, or bell peppers.

• The Big Black River skirts the eastern boundary of the Delta and joins the Mississippi River just above Port Gibson.

• Whenever there is a big golden full moon, and in my busy life I notice it, I always say aloud, if even to myself, "Look at that corn-bread moon."

I overheard two great-aunts of a local boy at his wedding to a New Hampshire girl say, "This marriage is never going to last; she doesn't even save her bacon grease." Sure enough, that marriage didn't last even two years. You can save up your bacon drippings and keep them in the refrigerator for a couple of weeks.

Good Sandwich Loaf
Slicing Bread

• • •

This is a plain loaf, nothing spicy or seeded or whole grained, just a nice bread to slice for sandwiches or toast. • MAKES ONE 9-INCH LOAF

1 tablespoon active dry yeast
Pinch of sugar
1/3 cup warm water (110°F)

3 1/2 cups unbleached bread flour
2 1/2 teaspoons salt
1/4 teaspoon unsalted butter

NOTES

• After adding the salt, mix until the dough clings to the hook and is smooth and elastic.

• The slow, repeated risings and slow fermentation give this loaf a chewy texture and depth of flavor.

• For a shiny, crisp crust, brush the dough with a little egg wash before slashing it.

• Slashing the loaf gives it room to expand.

• A pie pan full of ice cubes can be added to the oven just before the bread goes in to create a steamy atmosphere, like commercial bread ovens. It will release steam as the bread bakes.

See photograph page 46.

In a small bowl, sprinkle the yeast and the sugar over the warm water. Let sit for 5 minutes or until foamy.

Put the flour into the bowl of an electric stand mixer fitted with the dough hook. Add 1 cup cold water to the yeast mixture. Slowly pour this into the flour, mixing on low speed. Gradually increase the speed to medium and mix until the dough begins to grab onto the hook, about 7 minutes. Turn off the mixer and let the dough rest, covered with plastic, for 10 minutes.

Sprinkle the salt over the dough and mix on low speed for 5 minutes. Place the dough in a lightly oiled large bowl, turn over to coat, cover with plastic, and let rise for 1 hour or until doubled in size.

Tip the dough out onto a floured work surface. Pat the dough into a rectangle and fold in thirds like a business letter. Place the dough back in the bowl and flip again to coat with oil. Cover and let rise again for 1 1/2 to 2 hours, or until more than doubled in size.

Butter a 9 x 5 x 3-inch (2-quart) loaf pan.

On a floured work surface, gently pat the dough into an 8-inch-long rectangle. Fold the dough in thirds and place seam side down in the loaf pan. Let rise for 1 hour, or until doubled in size.

Place the oven rack on the bottom shelf of the oven and heat the oven to 400°F.

With a serrated knife, slash the surface of the loaf down the center. Bake for 20 to 30 minutes, or until a deep golden crust has formed and the loaf sounds hollow when tapped. Remove from the oven and turn out of the pan. Return the loaf to the oven directly on the oven rack and bake for 5 minutes. Remove and cool completely on a wire rack.

Sweet Potato Biscuits
Pass the Ham

• • •

I made these biscuits the other day for a Biscuit Clinic at a gathering of food-crazed anthropologists, ethnologists, restaurateurs, chefs, good home cooks, and culinary aficionados of all sorts, with a few musicians thrown in for good measure. They lapped them up. Everyone from Paula Deen to Drew Nieporent has fallen for these biscuits.

I have made them fancy, with warm pear chutney and smoked duck dividing the crisp bottom from the tender top. And I have made them not so fancy, day-old with smoked ham and Jezebel Sauce (page 68) sandwiched inside. If you manage to hide any away, heat them the next day with a little salty country ham and a drizzle of cane syrup. • MAKES 12 BISCUITS

1 cup mashed baked sweet
   potato (about 2 medium;
   see Notes, page 167)
^{2}/$_3$ cup whole milk
4 tablespoons (^{1}/$_2$ stick)
   unsalted butter, melted

1^1/$_4$ cups unbleached
   all-purpose flour
3^1/$_2$ teaspoons baking powder
2 tablespoons sugar
^{1}/$_2$ teaspoon salt

Preheat the oven to 450°F. Grease a baking sheet and set aside.

In a medium bowl, mix the sweet potato, milk, and butter. Sift together the four, baking powder, sugar, and salt. Add to the potato mixture. Gently mix the dry ingredients into the sweet potato mixture to form a soft dough. Drop the dough by tablespoonfuls onto the prepared baking sheet.

Bake for 12 to 15 minutes, or until a deep golden orange tinged with brown. Serve warm or let cool on a wire rack.

NOTE

• Sweet potatoes should be stored in a dark place at around 50°F. for 16 to 24 days.

Overnight Dinner Rolls
Rise and Shine

• • •

The simple dough for these rolls is made and then left to rest for the night. The next day it is rolled, dipped in butter, and folded over into little half-moon pillows that rise and bake to a shiny golden brown.

Serve these at a large gathering or freeze the whole batch, taking a handful of rolls out and browning them at dinnertime (see Notes). • MAKES 30 ROLLS

NOTES

• The rolls can be baked until they just take on color, then cooled and frozen in zipper-top freezer bags for up to three months. Finish the baking to golden brown in a 350°F. oven for 6 minutes.

• Think about dividing this batch into several "flavors": Place a small cocktail smoked sausage in the fold when you shape them; sprinkle inside and out with cinnamon sugar; dip some in garlic butter and sprinkle with black pepper; or add a dab of marmalade to the center before folding.

1 cup whole milk
$^1/_4$ cup sugar
$^1/_4$ cup vegetable shortening or lard
$1^1/_2$ teaspoons active dry yeast
3 cups unbleached all-purpose flour

$^1/_2$ teaspoon salt
$^3/_4$ teaspoon baking powder
$^1/_4$ teaspoon baking soda
4 tablespoons ($^1/_2$ stick) unsalted butter, melted

Heat the milk, sugar, and shortening in a saucepan over medium heat just until the mixture begins to simmer. Pour into a large bowl. Stir to melt the shortening; set aside to cool to 110°F. Add the yeast and 1 cup of the flour to the milk mixture. Stir until no lumps remain and the mixture looks like pancake batter. Cover with plastic wrap and let stand in a warm place for 2 hours.

Remove the cover and add the salt, baking powder, baking soda, and $^1/_2$ cup of the remaining flour. Stir well and add the remaining $1^1/_2$ cups flour $^1/_2$ cup at a time, stirring well after each addition.

Tip the dough out onto a lightly floured work surface and knead for a couple of minutes to form a smooth, elastic dough. Oil a large bowl lightly, add the dough, and turn to coat with oil. Cover and refrigerate overnight or for at least 12 hours.

Roll the dough out on a lightly floured surface to $^1/_4$-inch thick. Cut out 2-inch rounds of dough with a sharp biscuit cutter. Dip each round in melted butter to coat and then fold in half like a pocketbook. Place 2 inches apart on a baking sheet. Loosely cover with plastic wrap and let rise for $2^1/_2$ hours, or until almost doubled in size.

Preheat the oven to 400°F.

Uncover the rolls and bake for 8 to 10 minutes or until golden. Cool on racks or serve immediately.

Cornbread Sticks
For Sopping and Dunking

• • •

I like tender, moist cornbread sticks that hold together when sopping up stew. If you do not have a cast-iron cornstick pan, an 8- to 10-inch skillet or a 12-cup muffin tin will work. • MAKES 11 TO 15 CORNBREAD STICKS

6 to 7 tablespoons clarified
   butter (see Notes), melted
1 cup yellow cornmeal
1 cup unbleached all-purpose
   flour
$1^1/_2$ teaspoons baking powder
1 teaspoon light brown sugar

1 teaspoon salt
$^1/_2$ teaspoon cracked black
   peppercorns
2 large eggs
$^1/_2$ cup sour cream
1 cup half-and-half

Preheat the oven to 400°F. Generously brush a cornbread stick pan with 1 tablespoon of the clarified butter.

In a large bowl, combine the cornmeal, flour, baking powder, brown sugar, salt, and pepper. In a separate bowl, whisk together the eggs, sour cream, half-and-half, and 4 tablespoons of the clarified butter. Add the wet ingredients to the dry ingredients and stir until moistened, being careful not to overmix.

Place the buttered cornstick pan in the oven to heat for 5 minutes. Spoon the batter into the hot cornstick molds, filling them two-thirds full. Return the pan to the oven and bake for 10 to 12 minutes, or until the cornbread sticks are golden brown. Turn the sticks out onto a rack and repeat, using more clarified butter for the molds, until all of the batter is used. Serve warm.

NOTES

• I prefer a fine-milled cornmeal for sticks and a coarser meal for cornbread.

• Blue cornmeal can be used instead of yellow; a little chili powder changes it a bit, too.

• Do not allow the pan to get too hot in the oven. If for some reason the butter gets too dark or begins to smoke, allow the pan to cool, wipe clean, and start again.

• Clarified butter is great for cast-iron baking. To clarify butter, melt the butter over medium-low heat until it begins to foam. Reduce the heat to low and cook until the foaming has subsided. Pour into a fat separator pitcher or liquid measuring cup. Let cool until slightly warm. Pour the pure golden butterfat into a storage bowl. Discard the white milk solids. (If you use a gravy separator, the milk solids are easy to pour out first.) When I make clarified butter, I use 2 sticks of unsalted butter at a time. This gives me plenty to have on hand whenever I make pancakes, or any time I want to have a buttery flavor when I cook over high heat. It will keep for a month refrigerated in an airtight container.

See photograph page 168.

Blue Cheese Pecan Bread

For the Hostess

• • •

Whether serving this at your next gathering or presenting it as a gift, you will enjoy the ease in preparing this plump, savory round. I love this bread sliced thin and toasted, served with a glass of white wine. Ring the doorbell with your elbow and present the hostess with a bottle of wine and this bread, and you will most likely be invited back.

• MAKES ONE 8-INCH ROUND LOAF

4 cups unbleached all-purpose
    flour
$1/2$ cup sugar
$1^1/2$ teaspoons baking soda
$1^1/2$ teaspoons baking powder
1 teaspoon salt
4 tablespoons ($1/2$ stick)
    unsalted butter, cut in
    $1/2$-inch pieces, chilled

2 ounces blue cheese,
    crumbled ($1/2$ cup)
$1/4$ cup chopped pecans
$1^1/2$ cups plus 1 tablespoon
    buttermilk
1 large egg, beaten
Freshly ground black pepper

NOTES

• If the loaf begins to brown too much, tent it with foil.

• To crumble blue cheese, put a wedge or block of cheese in a sandwich bag and break it up with your fingers. This keeps the pungent smell off your hands.

• Sliced Granny Smith apples and red grapes are appealing served with this bread.

Preheat the oven to 400°F.

In a large bowl, sift together the flour, sugar, baking soda, baking powder, and salt. Cut in the butter until the mixture looks like oatmeal. Add the cheese and nuts, and toss to distribute in the flour. Make a well in the center and add $1^1/2$ cups of the buttermilk and the egg. Stir with a sturdy spoon until you have a shaggy dough.

Tip the dough out onto a lightly floured work surface and knead gently to bring together. Form into a slightly flattened 6-inch round. Place on a parchment-lined baking sheet. Brush with the remaining 1 tablespoon buttermilk and sprinkle with pepper. With a serrated knife, cut a shallow *X* in the top of the loaf.

Bake for 10 minutes. Reduce the oven temperature to 375°F. and bake for 35 minutes, or until the loaf is deep golden brown and sounds hollow when thumped on the bottom. Cool on a wire rack.

Gingerbread
Ride Around and See the Lights

• • •

My mother is a Christmas lights enthusiast. She barely puts up any kind of display herself, mind you, but she is the most fervent supporter of folks who do. She has been known to drive 210 miles, up to Jackson, Tennessee, to that stretch of highway leading into town just to drive really slow and wonder, "Who put that up? How long did that take them?" and, "What their power bill must be!"

She loves as much as anything when my son accompanies her, peering out the window from his booster seat in the back. He judges displays by squealing with approval at houses Santa would particularly like, with little slices of gingerbread clutched in his dimpled fingers. • MAKES ONE 10-INCH TUBE CAKE

<table>
<tr><td>

$1/2$ cup (1 stick) unsalted butter, melted and cooled
$1/4$ cup vegetable oil
$3/4$ cup molasses
$3/4$ cup packed dark brown sugar
2 large eggs
$2^1/2$ cups unbleached all-purpose flour

</td><td>

2 teaspoons baking soda
$1/2$ teaspoon baking powder
1 tablespoon ground ginger
$1^1/2$ teaspoons ground cinnamon
$1/2$ teaspoon ground cloves
$1/2$ teaspoon freshly grated nutmeg
1 cup boiling water

</td></tr>
</table>

Preheat the oven to 350°F. Spray a 10-inch tube pan with nonstick spray.

In a medium bowl, combine the butter, oil, molasses, brown sugar, and eggs. In a separate large bowl, combine the flour, baking soda, baking powder, ginger, cinnamon, cloves, and nutmeg. Combine the molasses mixture with the dry ingredients. Stir well to combine. Pour in the boiling water and stir very well. Pour into the prepared tube pan.

Bake for 40 minutes, or until the top springs back slightly when touched. Cool in the pan for 10 minutes and then turn out onto a serving platter. Serve now or later. Wrap up the gingerbread if you'll be waiting more than 2 hours to serve it.

NOTES

• Set the water to boil while you measure the other ingredients. You can add one or two of your favorite herbal tea bags to the pot, adding another set of unique flavors.

• This batter can be baked in just about any shape you want. If using a large loaf pan, check the center of the top crevice with a toothpick for doneness; a few moist crumbs should be hanging on it when slowly removed.

• I think the flavor improves when this cake is wrapped in plastic once cooled and let sit overnight. It will keep well in an airtight tin for five days and also freezes well. The recipe can be doubled or tripled for gift giving.

• Grown-ups enjoy $1/4$ cup finely diced candied ginger stirred into the batter. Kids may find that a little too strong.

Pain Perdu
Lost Bread from Louisiana

• • •

Alois Binder Bakery in New Orleans is known for the cheerful slogan "The Happy Baker with the Light Brings You Hot French Bread." My mother followed the delivery truck back to the bakery on the corner of Frenchman and Rampart Streets the first time she recognized the logo. There was an offshore-oil guy in front of her at the counter picking up 600 royal sticks, the short snub-nosed loaves. I guess she was overcome by the heady smell of all that bread, and in a classic case of impulse buying, she came home with 100 loaves herself. She had to pull over and put the bread in the trunk because she kept getting into it. When she got home the entire car was filled with crumbs.

Co-owned by seven brothers and sisters, this New Orleans institution bakes the kind of bread that po' boys are built on. This bread has a freshness window of one day. After that it shatters into shards when crunched. When rehydrated with brown sugar custard, and baked until golden and puffed, however, it takes on a whole new perspective. Set the bread to soaking before you go to bed and bake the dish of French toast first thing in the morning. Serve with a side of spicy Cajun smoked sausage. • **SERVES 6 TO 8**

2/3 **cup firmly packed brown sugar**
1/2 **cup cane syrup or maple syrup**
1 **tablespoon unsalted butter**

10 **(1-inch-thick) slices French bread**
4 **large eggs**
1 1/2 **cups whole milk**
1 **teaspoon vanilla extract**
1/4 **teaspoon salt**

Spray a 9 x 13-inch baking dish with nonstick cooking spray.

In a medium saucepan, combine the brown sugar, syrup, and butter. Bring to a boil over medium heat, stirring constantly for 1 minute.

Pour the syrup evenly over the bottom of the prepared dish. Arrange the bread slices in the dish on top of the syrup mixture. Set aside.

In a large bowl, whisk together the eggs, milk, vanilla, and salt. Pour the mixture over the bread slices. Cover and refrigerate overnight.

When ready to bake, preheat the oven to 350°F.

Uncover the dish and bake for 30 minutes, or until the French toast is lightly browned and slightly puffed. Serve hot.

NOTES

• If you want to give a little flavor of the New Orleans classic Bananas Foster to this dish, add 2 sliced medium bananas to the syrup in the bottom of the dish before you add the custard.

• Your favorite raisin bread can be substituted for the French bread.

• Sliced fresh peaches are terrific piled up on servings of this caramelized French toast.

Delta Cream Doughnuts

Baptism by Fire

• • •

John T. Edge, noted Southern food writer and connoisseur of all things fried, wrote the book on doughnuts—literally. When queried on the subject of flatland doughnuts, he shared these thoughts: "Just as Southerners dote on hot breads—biscuits, cornbread, hushpuppies—we're keen on hot doughnuts. Yeast-raised doughnuts, if you want to get technical about it, best appreciated not long after their baptism in oil. And Delta Kream is the fryer of choice in the Delta." I concur.

I've tried to make a close approximation to those newly immersed sweet converts found at Delta Kream Doughnuts. • MAKES 12 DOUGHNUTS

2 packages active dry yeast
1/2 cup warm water (110°F.)
1/2 cup whole milk
1/3 cup vegetable shortening or lard
1/3 cup granulated sugar
1 teaspoon salt

3 1/2 to 4 cups unbleached all-purpose flour
2 large eggs
2 cups confectioners' sugar, sifted
1/2 teaspoon vanilla extract
Vegetable oil, for frying

In a small bowl, sprinkle the yeast over the warm water and let it sit for 3 minutes. Stir with a fork and set aside.

Meanwhile, in a medium saucepan, combine the milk, shortening, sugar, and salt, and bring to a simmer over medium heat. Pour into the bowl of an electric mixer and allow to cool until as warm as a baby bottle. Add 1 cup of the flour and beat well. Beat in the softened yeast and the eggs. Add enough of the remaining 2 1/2 to 3 cups flour to form a soft dough that pulls away from the sides of the bowl. Mix well.

Oil a large mixing bowl, put the dough in, and flip it to grease all sides. Cover and chill for 3 hours or overnight.

Turn the dough out onto a lightly floured surface or nonstick silicone baking mat and pat or roll to a 1/3-inch thickness. Cut with a floured doughnut cutter or make 3-inch squares with a pizza cutter. A hole in the center will allow the doughnuts to cook more evenly. Place on a lightly floured baking pan. Allow to rise undisturbed for 30 to 40 minutes, or until very light and more than doubled in size.

NOTES

• Freshly grated nutmeg or ground cardamom makes a great addition to the dough, or can be combined with cinnamon sugar for plunking hot unglazed doughnuts.

• The large end of a decorating or pastry tip works well for cutting holes.

• A long wooden dowel or handle of a wooden spoon is great for sticking through the hole in the doughnut and lifting it out of the hot oil.

• These are a major hit with the pre-teen spend-the-night party set. Make them when the party starts up, and when they come out of the oil all warm and sweet, about midnight, you will become a teen idol.

While the dough is rising, in a medium bowl, combine the confectioners' sugar with 3 tablespoons water and the vanilla using a wire whisk. Set this glaze aside until the doughnuts are fried.

Heat at least 2 inches of oil to 375°F. in a deep heavy-bottomed pot or deep-fryer. Set a cooling rack over a newspaper-lined baking sheet to drain the doughnuts after they come out of the fryer.

Gently lift the doughnuts and place a few at a time in the hot oil. Fry for 2 minutes or until brown, turning once. Lift out of the oil and allow to drain over the pot a few seconds and then drain on the cooling rack. While still warm, dip them into the glaze and place back on the rack to allow the glaze to set, or eat while warm.

Blueberry Muffins
From Old Mr. Ashcraft

• • •

A week or so before we opened Mockingbird Bakery, an older gentleman in a straw hat came through the back kitchen door, walking with a cane in one hand and the support of his mannerly young grandson on the other. He introduced himself, tipping his hat. Next, his grandson slowly loosened his grip on the man's hand long enough for Mr. Ashcraft to extend it for a handshake. "Wanted to come by and see if y'all were going to need blueberries," drawled Mr. Ashcraft.

"Why, yes!" I exclaimed. "All you've got!"

"Well, honey, I got about 200 acres of them."

"Oh, guess I just mean a bunch of them, then." Every season we stocked the freezer with hundreds of pounds of his berries to keep us going year-round, folding the plump—almost black they're so blue—berries into this tangy buttermilk-moistened batter. • MAKES 18 MUFFINS

2 cups unbleached all-purpose flour
²/₃ cup packed light brown sugar
1 tablespoon baking powder
¹/₂ teaspoon baking soda
¹/₂ teaspoon salt
Grating of nutmeg
1¹/₂ cups fresh or frozen blueberries (do not thaw)

2 large eggs
1 cup buttermilk
¹/₂ cup (1 stick) unsalted butter, melted
1 teaspoon grated lemon or orange zest
¹/₄ teaspoon almond extract
¹/₂ teaspoon vanilla extract

Preheat the oven to 475°F. Spray 18 muffin cups or line with paper baking cups.

In a large bowl with a whisk, combine the flour, brown sugar, baking powder, baking soda, salt, and nutmeg. Toss the blueberries to coat with the flour and evenly distribute. In a separate bowl, whisk together the eggs, buttermilk, butter, zest, and almond and vanilla extracts.

Using a rubber spatula, combine the wet ingredients into the dry ingredients. Stir just until everything is moistened. Divide the batter among the muffin cups, filling each two-thirds full. Bake for 15 minutes, or until the tops spring back lightly when touched. Allow to cool for 5 minutes and then turn out of the pan onto a rack.

NOTES

• Mr. Ashcraft says not to wash fresh berries before you freeze them or they will get tough. Wash them in cold water after you remove them from the freezer. Do not thaw frozen berries before using. Toss them in the dry ingredients and then fold in the liquids.

• Yogurt, sour cream, or heavy cream can be used in place of the buttermilk.

• Measure and mix the dry ingredients and measure and combine the eggs, buttermilk, zest, and extracts. Refrigerate the wet ingredients before you go to bed. Then you can just add the melted butter and stir them together without a thought before the coffee kicks in the next morning.

• Don't let the muffins cool completely in the pan. The bottoms will get soggy.

• I like to fill every other cup in the muffin pan. You get larger tops (the best part) and the muffins seem to bake more evenly.

• If you wish to add a streusel topping, combine 1 cup sugar with ³/₄ cup all-purpose flour. Make a well in center and add 4 tablespoons melted butter. Toss with your fingertips to form a crumbly topping to sprinkle over the muffins before baking. Add some sliced almonds in there, too, if you like.

Plucking Bread

Pull Apart with Sugary Little Fingers

• • •

This recipe can keep a passel of children entertained for an entire rainy day. Making the dough will take a while, and dipping the pieces in the butter and cinnamon sugar is better than play dough. The smell of cinnamon will fill the house when naptime is over.

• MAKES ONE 10-INCH RING

DOUGH
1 package active dry yeast
1/4 cup warm water (110°F.)
1/2 cup warm milk (110°F.)
1/4 cup sugar
1 teaspoon salt
4 tablespoons (1/2 stick)
   unsalted butter, softened
2 large eggs
2 1/2 cups unbleached
   all-purpose flour

TOPPING
1/3 cup granulated sugar
1/3 cup packed light brown
   sugar
1 teaspoon ground cinnamon
5 tablespoons unsalted butter,
   melted

NOTES

• Start this kitchen project early in the day. It will not be ready for at least 3 1/2 hours and somebody might need a nap while the dough is rising.

• Try grinding your own cinnamon in a spice mill or with a Microplane zester. The superior flavor of the freshly ground may spoil you from that old store-bought.

MAKE THE DOUGH. In a small mixing bowl, sprinkle the yeast over the warm water and let stand for 5 minutes. Whisk to combine.

In the bowl of an electric mixer, combine the milk, sugar, salt, butter, and eggs. Add the yeast mixture and beat thoroughly. Add the flour and mix until well combined and a soft dough is formed.

Knead the dough on a floured work surface for 5 minutes, until smooth and elastic. Form into a ball, place in a lightly oiled bowl, and turn to coat. Cover with plastic wrap and let it rise for 2 hours, or until doubled in size.

MAKE THE TOPPING. In a small bowl, combine the granulated sugar, brown sugar, and cinnamon.

Divide the dough into 30 equal pieces. Dip each piece of dough in the melted butter and then in the cinnamon sugar. Stack the pieces in a 12-cup nonstick tube cake pan or Bundt pan. Cover and let it rise for 1 hour.

Center a rack in the oven and preheat the oven to 450°F.

Uncover the bread and bake for 25 to 30 minutes, or until deep golden brown. Immediately turn out onto a serving platter. Allow to cool for at least 10 minutes before serving.

Holiday Fruit and Nut Bread

Jewel Studded

• • •

This loaf is studded with glacé fruits, citrus peel, and nuts. It should not be mistaken for fruitcake. I do not believe there are any bad gift-giving jokes about this loaf; it is seriously good. • MAKES ONE 9-INCH LOAF

$1/2$ cup dried zante currants

$1/2$ cup chopped candied red cherries

$1/2$ cup chopped candied pineapple

$1/2$ cup chopped dried apricots

$1/2$ cup chopped walnut pieces

1 cup natural applesauce

2 cups sugar

2 large eggs

$1/2$ cup vegetable oil

$1/2$ teaspoon almond extract

1 teaspoon grated lemon zest

1 teaspoon grated orange zest

$2^1/4$ cups unbleached all-purpose flour

$1^1/2$ teaspoons baking powder

$1/2$ teaspoon baking soda

$1/2$ teaspoon fine sea salt

Preheat the oven to 325°F. Spray a 9 x 5 x 3-inch loaf pan with nonstick spray or line with parchment paper.

In a medium bowl, combine the currants, cherries, pineapple, apricots, and nuts. Set aside $1/2$ cup of the fruit and nut mixture to top the loaf.

In a large bowl, whisk together the applesauce and sugar until the sugar dissolves. Add the eggs, oil, almond extract, and lemon and orange zests. In a separate bowl, combine the flour, baking powder, baking soda, and salt. Stir the dry ingredients into the applesauce mixture. Fold in the fruits and nuts. Fill the prepared loaf pan with the batter. Sprinkle the reserved $1/2$ cup fruit and nuts over the top.

Bake for 1 hour, or until a toothpick inserted in the center comes out clean. If the fruits on top begin to darken, tent the loaf with foil as it bakes. Cool in the pan for 10 minutes. Run a sharp knife around the edge of the loaf, tip out onto a wire rack, and set upright to cool.

NOTES

• Use high-quality glacé fruits for this loaf. They are a little more expensive, but are not as cloyingly sweet as the cheaper ones.

• Dried pears are also a nice addition. Substitute as you wish, aiming for a total of 2 cups of assorted candied or dried fruits and nuts.

• If you like, plump the dried fruits in a bit of warm brandy before draining them and adding them to the bread.

Biloxi Banana Bread

The Great Banana Train Wreck

· · ·

I don't know how the decision was made, in an area with no people for 3 miles in any direction, to place East Highway 49 South at a sloping curve as it crosses a dogleg in the railroad track, with the gravel Hillside Wildlife Refuge Road and Bee Lake Road both coming into the highway at the top of the curve. This feat of engineering has led to countless wrecks, and the area has come to be called Billfold Bend.

Train cars regularly flip off the tracks, eighteen-wheelers lose their loads, and a couple of fishing-boat trailers take a spill each year. Once a trainload of patio furniture flipped in the late '50s and provided the seating around Aunt Mary's swimming pool. A glider and a few chairs are still hanging in there. One twilight derailment left a boxcar of corn and a boxcar load of sugar flipped, and their contents were hauled away by moonshiners by sunrise.

Way down on the Mississippi Gulf Coast, where this railroad originates, is the second busiest tropical fruit port in North America. Just about all the bananas sold in the United States come through there—more than 8,000 pounds a week. Many of the train cars full of the fruit clatter this treacherous stretch of North Delta Railway. Once, several boxcars chock-a-block with bananas took Billfold Bend a little too fast. Lots of people showed up to help carry off the 200-pound bunches of bright green bananas. Cars with bananas sticking out of rolled-down windows and trunks with the lids tied down bulged with fruit as they sped on down the highway. No telling how many loaves of banana bread were baked that week. • MAKES ONE 9-INCH LOAF

NOTES

· Use ripe brownish bananas. Mash, do not puree, for this bread.

· I think this bread improves when wrapped in foil and eaten the next day.

· Cloves are the dried flower buds from a tall tropical evergreen. *Clove* is from the Latin for "nail" and they are named in several languages for their shape. Cloves should be used sparingly; oil of clove is used to numb toothaches.

· Sliced thin, this makes the bread for the ultimate peanut butter and banana sandwich.

2½ cups unbleached all-purpose flour	¼ cup buttermilk
1¼ teaspoons baking powder	1 teaspoon vanilla extract
¼ teaspoon baking soda	½ teaspoon grated lemon zest
1 teaspoon ground cinnamon	½ cup (1 stick) unsalted butter, melted
¼ teaspoon salt	¼ cup packed dark brown sugar
¼ teaspoon freshly grated nutmeg	½ cup granulated sugar
Pinch of ground cloves	3 large eggs
1½ cups mashed ripe bananas	1 cup pecan pieces, if desired

Preheat the oven to 350°F. Spray a 9 x 5-inch loaf pan with non-stick cooking spray.

In a medium bowl, combine the flour, baking powder, baking soda, cinnamon, salt, nutmeg, and cloves with a whisk to break up any lumps. In a separate bowl, combine the bananas, buttermilk, vanilla, and lemon zest.

In an electric mixer at medium speed, beat the butter, brown sugar, and granulated sugar for 5 minutes. Add the eggs one at a time. Reduce the speed to low and add half of the flour mixture. Add half of the banana mixture, beating just long enough to combine. Repeat with the remaining mixtures. Add the pecan pieces, if desired, and mix until just incorporated.

Pour the batter into the prepared loaf pan. Bake for 1 hour and 10 minutes, or until a toothpick comes out with moist crumbs attached when poked in the center. Let cool for 5 minutes in the pan. Remove to a wire rack to continue cooling.

THE summer before I was born, a train came off the tracks at Billfold Bend and disinterred several boxcars of floor tiles. My father and his buddies loaded them up and set off selling them. They made a good bit of money, and with it my father bought a watch, a 1967 Rolex Oyster Perpetual with a smoky black face. This year he gave it to me for my birthday.

Versatile Pie Crust Dough
All Encasing

・・・

There are some things people feel they will just never make as good as their mothers'. I find this to be particularly true with pie crusts. My friend Corleigha is convinced she will never make a pie crust as good as her mother's. She lives in Mississippi, and her mother is over in Blytheville, Arkansas. Corleigha gets her momma to FedEx frozen homemade pie crusts to her.

This pie crust freezes beautifully and will keep for several months in the freezer. I always figure if you are going to go to the trouble of making a little something, make a lot. You never know when you might need a pie crust. So double the recipe if the spirit moves you. • MAKES ONE 9-INCH PIE CRUST

$1^1/_2$ **cups unbleached all-purpose flour**
$^1/_2$ **cup cake flour**
1 teaspoon salt
1 teaspoon sugar

$^3/_4$ **cup (1$^1/_2$ sticks) unsalted butter, cold, cut into small pieces**
$^1/_4$ **cup vegetable shortening or lard, cold, pinched into small pieces**

Fill a small pitcher with ice water and set aside.

In a large bowl, combine the flours, salt, and sugar. Add the chilled butter and shortening pieces and toss with flour to coat. Using your fingertips, work the shortening and butter into the flour until there are no pieces of fat larger than a black-eyed pea. Sprinkle $^1/_4$ cup ice water over the mixture and mix with a fork to combine and form a shaggy dough.

Gather the dough into a ball. Break off pieces of dough about the size of an egg. Using the heel of your hand, smear dough on your work surface with a pushing motion away from you. Repeat until all of the dough has been smeared. Gather the dough again and pat into a ball and press down to form a disk. Wrap and chill for 30 minutes in the refrigerator.

Place the disk between two pieces of plastic wrap. Roll the dough in one direction, rotating the disk one-eighth turn before each roll to help keep the crust in the shape of a circle. Peel and replace the piece of plastic wrap on the surface of the dough as

NOTES

• This smearing method of mixing the dough yields a remarkably flaky crust; in French baking the technique is called *frissage*.

• I like to freeze these crusts in disposable aluminum pans inside zipper-top freezer bags. To conserve space, dough rolled between pieces of plastic wrap can be rolled into a cylinder, placed in a freezer bag, and frozen just like that. Allow the dough to come to room temperature before placing in a pie pan. Chill again before baking.

• To blind bake or pre-bake a crust before filling, dock the bottom crust by piercing it several times with a fork. Line the crust in the pie pan with parchment paper or coffee filters sprayed with nonstick cooking spray, and fill with rice, beans, a small chain, or pie weights. Bake at 400°F. for 12 minutes, remove the paper and weights, and bake for 5 more minutes or until the desired degree of doneness.

needed as the circle gets larger. Roll the dough into an 11-inch circle. Remove one sheet of plastic wrap and press the naked side of the dough into a 9-inch pie pan. Carefully press out any air bubbles. Remove the remaining plastic wrap from the top. Fold the edge of the dough under to create a smooth edge and crimp with your fingers or the tines of a fork. Return to the refrigerator to chill for 30 minutes before baking, or wrap well and freeze.

THE SWEETEST THINGS

Baked Cup Custard

Comfort in a Cup

• • •

Where I'm from, soothingly smooth custard is a treasure brought to the home of the sick and infirm by little old ladies. There is just something about it that makes you feel better. If you are ever feeling blue, this little cup of custard can console you. • SERVES 6

2 cups whole milk
¹/₂ vanilla bean, split, or
   ¹/₂ teaspoon vanilla extract
2 large eggs

1 large egg yolk
¹/₄ cup sugar
¹/₄ teaspoon salt
Freshly grated nutmeg

Center a rack in the oven and preheat the oven to 325°F. Place six 4-ounce custard cups or ramekins in a large roasting pan or baking dish, allowing at least 1 inch of space between the cups. Set aside.

In a small saucepan, heat the milk and split vanilla bean, if using, until small bubbles begin to form around the edges of the pan. Remove the vanilla bean, rinse, and reserve for another use.

In a large bowl (or large measuring cup with a spout), whisk the eggs and yolk together. Add the sugar and salt, and whisk to combine. Slowly add the scalded milk, whisking constantly. If using vanilla extract, add it now. Ladle or pour the custard evenly into the cups in the roasting pan. Grate a little fresh nutmeg across the surface of each custard.

Place the pan in the oven and pour enough hot water to come halfway up the sides of the cups. Bake for 30 to 35 minutes, or until the custards are slightly firm around the edges. The centers of the custards will set as they cool. Remove the cups from the water bath and place on a wire rack to cool for 30 minutes before refrigerating. Serve chilled.

NOTES

• Take the eggs out of refrigerator and place under warm running water for a minute or two to warm them slightly. The warm eggs will incorporate easier and cook to a smoother consistency in the custard.

• For an added flavor dimension, add 1 cinnamon stick to the milk when heating.

• Those expectant mothers who long for the days of decaf to be over can add a few drops of coffee extract for an afternoon pick-me-up. Bake in ovenproof mugs for a cute presentation.

• Fill the roasting pan with water after it is in the oven to keep the sloshing down to a minimum. When removing the custards from the oven, use extra caution to avoid splashing water on the custards or yourself. Tongs are useful for this task.

Banana Pudding
Single Servings

• • •

I made this meringue-topped banana pudding for Oprah and her best friend, Gayle. Gayle likes hers warm (both Oprah and I find that strange), and she ate two helpings. The demure Miss Winfrey had a single serving. • SERVES 8

NOTES

• Use nice, ripe bananas. Green ones will make the pudding bitter.

• Rinse and dry the vanilla bean and reserve it for another use.

• Don't use the cheap vanilla wafer cookies; banana pudding is no time to be a skinflint.

• If the meringue looks dry or broken, add an additional egg white and whip briefly. For more about egg whites, check out the recipe notes for Brown Sugar Angel Food Cake (page 221).

• If you are concerned about undercooked eggs, bake the pudding until the meringue reaches 160°F.

• The band Southern Culture On the Skids has an ode to day-old banana pudding: "nice and funky with a skin on top . . ."

PUDDING
3/4 cup sugar
1/3 cup cake flour
1/4 teaspoon salt
4 large egg yolks
2 cups whole milk
1/2 vanilla bean, split, or
   1/2 teaspoon vanilla extract
Freshly grated nutmeg
1/2-inch piece of cinnamon
   stick

Quality vanilla wafer cookies
   or Cordelia's Mother
   Gwen's Tea Cakes (page 217)
4 medium bananas, peeled
   and sliced

TOPPING
4 large egg whites
1/4 teaspoon cream of tartar
5 tablespoons sugar
1/2 teaspoon vanilla extract

MAKE THE PUDDING. In a heavy-bottomed saucepan over medium heat, bring 2 inches of water to a boil. In a large stainless steel bowl, whisk together the sugar, flour, and salt. Whisk in the egg yolks, and then the milk, vanilla bean, nutmeg, and cinnamon. Place the bowl over the pan of water and cook, stirring until the mixture is thick and coats the back of a spoon, 12 to 15 minutes. Remove from the heat. Remove the cinnamon and vanilla bean. If using vanilla extract, stir it in now.

While the pudding is still warm, layer the cookies, bananas, and pudding in 1/2-pint canning jars or ramekins.

Preheat the oven to 425°F.

MAKE THE TOPPING. Whip the egg whites in an electric mixer on medium speed until frothy. Add the cream of tartar and slowly increase the speed as the egg whites become opaque. Add the sugar 1 tablespoon at a time. Add the vanilla extract. Whip until the whites form a soft peak. Spoon the meringue over the warm puddings, sealing it to the sides of the jars.

Bake the puddings for 4 minutes, or until the meringue is puffed and brown. Cool on a rack for 20 minutes, and then refrigerate for 2 hours, or until you can't stand it anymore.

Bread Pudding with Whisky Sauce

Bakes During Dinner

• • •

Having worked in bakeries for years, I have encountered hundreds of things to do with leftover bread. By far, bread pudding is the best thing to do with it. And as ashamed as I am to say this, my favorite bread to use for bread pudding at home is the big, fat Texas Toast from the grocery store. It swells with the custard as it sits soaking, puffs up so nicely when baked, and has a tender texture very different from the one achieved with a crisp-crust bread. Don't get me wrong; this recipe is great with leftover baguettes or biscuits, or croissants even, if you must, but the Texas Toast is the secret. • SERVES 8

NOTES

• If using crisp-crust bread, allow the custard and bread mixture to soak for about an hour.

• Add a thin layer of strawberry preserves to the bottom of the baking dish before filling, if desired.

• Golden raisins soaked in whisky are nice baked in, too.

• The sauce will keep refrigerated for a week. Reheat the sauce in a small saucepan over low heat or microwave on high for 45 seconds or until warm. Pour over ice cream, pound cake, or fresh sliced nectarines, peaches, and plums.

4 large eggs
1 large egg yolk
$2^1/_2$ cups whole milk
$2^1/_2$ cups heavy cream
$3/_4$ cup plus 2 tablespoons sugar
$3/_4$ teaspoon freshly grated nutmeg

3 tablespoons whisky
1 tablespoon vanilla extract
$1/_4$ teaspoon salt
8 cups cubed bread, in $1/_2$-inch pieces
2 tablespoons unsalted butter, melted
Whisky Sauce (recipe follows)

In a large bowl, beat the eggs and egg yolk. Whisk in the milk, cream, $3/_4$ cup sugar, the nutmeg, whisky, vanilla, and salt. Add the bread cubes; press them into the custard and allow to soak for at least 20 minutes.

Preheat the oven to 350°F. Butter a 13 x 9-inch baking dish.

Pour the bread mixture into the prepared dish. Drizzle the butter over the top, and sprinkle with the remaining 2 tablespoons sugar.

Bake until the top is light golden brown and the pudding begins to rise around edges of the baking dish, 45 to 50 minutes. The center will still be quite soft. Set aside on a wire rack and let cool for at least 45 minutes before serving. Serve warm, at room temperature, or even chilled, topped with Whisky Sauce.

WHISKY SAUCE

1 cup evaporated milk
1 cup whole milk
1 cup packed light brown
   sugar

3 tablespoons unsalted butter
$1\frac{1}{2}$ tablespoons cornstarch
2 tablespoons good whisky

In a large saucepan, combine the milks, brown sugar, and butter. Cook and stir over medium heat until the sugar is dissolved and the sauce is warm.

In a small dish, combine the cornstarch and whisky. Stir to remove any lumps, and then put the mixture into the saucepan. Cook and stir the sauce until it boils. Boil for 1 minute, stirring constantly, then remove from the heat. Serve hot.

Lemon Icebox Pie

The Wonder of Sweetened Condensed Milk

• • •

Sweetened condensed milk has saved lives and may have won a war. Prior to refrigeration, there was no way to safely keep milk for more than a few hours. Gail Borden used vacuum pans to condense fresh milk by evaporating over 60 percent of the water and sweetening the residue. After several failed attempts, he was granted a patent in 1854 for his new product, shelf-stable milk. It fueled the Union troops during the War Between the States. Borden's plants in New York, Connecticut, and Maine were commandeered to supply milk for the troops.

While it has an astounding history, it also has a wondrous effect on eggs and citrus juice. Without Mr. Borden the world would not have dulce de leche, pastel de tres leches, *Key lime pie, or, the one I am most thankful for, Lemon Icebox Pie.*

• MAKES ONE 9-INCH PIE

Note references to Banana Pudding (page 198).

1^1/$_2$ cups graham cracker crumbs
^{1}/$_4$ cup granulated sugar
^{1}/$_2$ teaspoon ground cinnamon
^{1}/$_2$ cup (1 stick) unsalted butter, melted

2 (14-ounce) cans sweetened condensed milk
4 large egg yolks
1 teaspoon grated lemon zest
^{1}/$_2$ cup fresh lemon juice
2 cups heavy cream
6 tablespoons confectioners' sugar

Preheat the oven to 350°F.

In a medium bowl, combine the crumbs, granulated sugar, cinnamon, and melted butter. Pat into a 9-inch deep-dish pie pan and bake for 6 to 8 minutes, or until slightly browned. Remove to a wire rack to cool.

Meanwhile, in a large bowl, whisk together the milk, yolks, lemon zest, and lemon juice. Pour the lemon filling into the cooled crust. Bake for 10 minutes, until set. Cool on a rack. Chill the pie for 30 minutes.

When the pie is completely cooled, whip the cream with the confectioners' sugar until stiff peaks form. Mound the whipped cream on top of the pie and chill for 1 hour.

NOTES

• If making the pie to serve the next day, 1 teaspoon of gelatin may be dissolved in 2 tablespoons water and added to the whipped cream just before it reaches a stiff peak.

• To help the cream whip, have the cream, bowl, and beaters or whisk very cold. Set the beaters and bowl in the freezer for 10 minutes before you need them.

• For those who prefer a meringue topping, follow the steps for the meringue topping on Banana Pudding (page 198).

• Mr. Gail Borden lived in Liberty, Mississippi. His patented method of preserving milk brought a safe source of nutrition to many infants and children.

Sweet Tea Pie

With Candied Lemon and Mint

• • •

This recipe began as my entry in the Crisco State Fair Pie Baking Contest in 1987, the summer after I got out of high school. It was one of my first forays into baking. I didn't win, didn't even place. I did get my picture in the paper and a souvenir apron.

Over the years this recipe has evolved into the pie it is today—a pie that has appeared in just about every story about me. Anne Willan, John T. Edge, and Fred Thompson are a few who have ballyhooed this pie.

The flavor tastes a little like state fair saltwater taffy, and the texture is like pecan pie without the pecans. I think you will enjoy it. • MAKES ONE 9-INCH PIE

NOTES

• Any strongly steeped tea you like can be used here; try herbal blends.

• The filling mixture will look curdled when it is finished mixing; do not worry—it will bake just fine.

• Garnish with candied lemon peel, sweetened whipped cream, and mint leaves.

• To candy lemon peel, boil strips of lemon peel in $1/2$ cup light corn syrup combined with $1/4$ cup sugar and 1 cup water until translucent, about 8 minutes. Remove from the syrup and rinse in warm water. Toss in granulated sugar and let dry on a rack or waxed paper.

CRUST

6 ounces cream cheese, softened

1 cup (2 sticks) unsalted butter, softened

2$1/2$ cups unbleached all-purpose flour

FILLING

1 cup (2 sticks) unsalted butter, softened

2 cups sugar

8 large egg yolks

$3/4$ cup strong steeped orange pekoe tea, cooled

1 teaspoon grated lemon zest

1 tablespoon fresh lemon juice

2 tablespoons unbleached all-purpose flour

1$1/2$ teaspoons cornmeal

$1/2$ teaspoon salt

MAKE THE CRUST. In an electric mixer, beat the cream cheese and butter until well combined. Add the flour and mix until the dough forms a ball. Pat the dough into a 9-inch pie pan. Chill until ready to use.

Preheat the oven to 350°F.

MAKE THE FILLING. In an electric mixer, beat the butter and sugar at medium speed until light. Add the yolks one at a time, beating at low speed until well incorporated. Slowly add the tea, lemon zest, and lemon juice. Scrape down the sides of the bowl with a rubber spatula. Add the flour, cornmeal, and salt and mix well.

Pour the mixture into the prepared crust. Bake for 45 minutes or until set. Cool completely on a wire rack, and then chill for 2 hours before serving.

Black Bottom Pie
Gingersnap Crust and Brandy

• • •

This pie is more requested for birthdays than cake in my family. A ginger crumb crust with strata of dark chocolate and rum layers topped with whipped cream and chocolate shavings is an ideal way to say "Happy Birthday" to the men in your life.

- MAKES ONE 9-INCH PIE, SERVES 8

NOTES

· This pie creates a lot of dirty dishes but is worth it, I promise.

· Crumbs from Ginger Molasses Cookies (page 215) are very good in the crust. Just crush them and add the butter. Omit the sugar, as they are already sweet enough with their sugary coating.

· If you are a novice custard maker, cook the milk and egg yolk mixture in a double boiler for insurance against curdling. If your custard seems lumpy, run it through a sieve or give it a couple of zaps with an immersion blender.

· Pasteurized egg whites are available in the dairy case if you are concerned about consuming raw eggs. I'm not.

· Chill your bowl, whip, and cream in the freezer for 10 minutes before you whip the cream. It will stay fluffy longer and have a better texture.

CRUST
1^1/$_2$ cups gingersnap crumbs
^{1}/$_4$ cup granulated sugar
6 tablespoons (^{3}/$_4$ stick) unsalted butter, melted

FILLING
2 cups whole milk
^{1}/$_2$ vanilla bean, split
1 cup granulated sugar
4^1/$_2$ teaspoons cornstarch
4 large egg yolks, beaten
1^1/$_2$ ounces unsweetened chocolate

1^1/$_2$ teaspoons vanilla extract
1^1/$_2$ teaspoons brandy
1 tablespoon unflavored gelatin, sprinkled over ^{1}/$_4$ cup cold water
4 large egg whites
^{1}/$_2$ teaspoon cream of tartar
^{1}/$_8$ teaspoon salt
^{1}/$_2$ cup heavy cream
1 tablespoon confectioners' sugar
^{1}/$_2$ ounce semisweet chocolate

MAKE THE CRUST. Preheat the oven to 325°F.

Combine the crumbs, granulated sugar, and butter in a bowl. Pat the mixture into a 9-inch pie pan. Bake for 10 minutes, until the crust bubbles slightly and is puffed. Set aside to cool.

MAKE THE FILLING. In a medium heavy-bottomed saucepan over medium heat, bring the milk and vanilla bean just to a simmer. Remove from the heat.

In a mixing bowl, whisk together ^{1}/$_2$ cup of the granulated sugar and the cornstarch. Add the egg yolks and whisk until there are no lumps. Remove the vanilla bean from the milk, rinse, and reserve for another use. Slowly whisk the hot milk into the yolk mixture. Return the entire mixture to the saucepan and cook over very low heat, stirring constantly with a spatula, until the mixture boils for 1 minute. Remove from the heat.

Remove 1 cup of the custard to a small bowl. Add the unsweetened chocolate and vanilla extract to the small bowl of custard.

Pour this chocolate custard into the cooled baked pie crust. Mix the brandy and softened gelatin into the remaining custard. Cool the saucepan of brandy custard in an ice bath.

In an electric mixer, whip the egg whites at low speed until frothy. Add the cream of tartar. With the mixer running, add the remaining $1/2$ cup granulated sugar, 1 tablespoon at a time, and the salt. Once all of the sugar has been added, increase the speed and whip the whites until they hold soft peaks. Fold the egg whites into the cooled brandy custard. Smooth the mixture over the chocolate layer in the pie.

Whip the cream and confectioners' sugar until the cream holds soft peaks. Spoon it in big dollops over the brandy layer. Shave, or grate, the semisweet chocolate over the top. Refrigerate for 3 hours, or until set.

If I make only one of these pies, when it is time to give it away, sudden possessive feelings come over me and I want to keep it for myself. This recipe doubles nicely.

Peach Fried Pie

I Will Only Eat Two

• • •

There are two words, each beautiful on its own but, when combined, heart-stoppingly lovely: fried pie. *The word* indulgent *has become a popular catchphrase for dishes we should not eat for health's sake. I never use it to describe food, only poor parenting.* • MAKES TEN 3-INCH PIES

PASTRY

2 cups unbleached all-purpose
   flour
2 teaspoons baking powder
$3/4$ teaspoon salt
6 tablespoons vegetable
   shortening or lard
$3/4$ cups whole milk

FILLING

2 cups chopped fresh or
   frozen peaches
$1/2$ cup packed light brown
   sugar

$1/2$ teaspoon ground allspice
2 tablespoons cider vinegar
1 teaspoon cornstarch
1 teaspoon fresh lemon juice

2 tablespoons granulated
   sugar
$1/2$ teaspoon ground
   cinnamon
1 large egg
Canola oil, for frying

MAKE THE PASTRY. In a large bowl, combine the flour, baking powder, and salt. Cut in the shortening until no pieces are larger than a pea. Add the milk and combine, using a fork. Gather the dough and knead lightly for 1 minute. Wrap in plastic and refrigerate while preparing the filling.

MAKE THE FILLING. In a medium heavy-bottomed saucepan, combine the peaches, brown sugar, and allspice. Cook and stir over medium heat for 5 minutes, or until the sugar is dissolved and the peaches are juicy. In a small bowl, combine the vinegar and cornstarch. Add to the peaches and cook and stir for 10 minutes, or until the mixture is thick and glossy. Stir in the lemon juice. Transfer the mixture to a shallow dish to cool.

In a small shallow dish, combine the granulated sugar and cinnamon. Set aside.

MAKE THE PIES. Roll the dough $1/8$-inch thick on a lightly floured surface.

NOTES

• For a twist grown-ups enjoy, omit the allspice and add $1^{1}/2$ teaspoons curry powder. After frying, toss the pies in a mixture of curry powder and sugar.

• If in a hurry, whole fruit spread can be used as a filling.

• If you are of the indulgent mindset, fry these in clarified butter and top with ice cream.

With a sharp knife or cutter, cut ten 6-inch circles. Place 2 tablespoons of peach filling in the center of each circle. Beat the egg with 1 teaspoon water. Brush a thin line of egg wash around the edges of the circles. Fold to form a half-moon shape. Lightly press out any air pockets. Press the edges with the tines of a fork to seal. Pierce one time on top of each pie with a fork to let steam escape while frying.

Heat 1 inch of canola oil in a large skillet to 375°F. Set a wire rack over a baking sheet lined with newspaper or paper towels.

Gently place the pies, two at a time, pierced side up, in the skillet. Fry to golden brown, turning once, 2 minutes per side. Remove from the oil and let drain briefly on the wire rack. Toss in the cinnamon sugar and allow to cool for 5 minutes.

Silent Shade Cobbler
Reflected in Blues

• • •

Silent Shade Bridge was a beautiful decorative little bridge over the Yazoo River. The name sounded much more melodic than any of the memorial-named bridges. The small bridge was raised and lowered with a tractor and cable, and a mule before that. Eventually the bridge was turned sideways, the run of the river, and taken out of commission.

I get the blues when I think of that lovely, peaceful river-crossing now all but forgotten. I guess this sweet deep-blue cobbler is a fitting memorial. • SERVES 8

5 cups fresh or frozen
   blueberries
2 tablespoons fresh lemon
   juice
2 cups unbleached all-purpose
   flour
2 teaspoons baking powder
1 teaspoon salt
$^{1}/_{4}$ teaspoon freshly grated
   nutmeg

$^{1}/_{4}$ teaspoon ground mace
3 cups sugar
1 cup whole milk
5 tablespoons unsalted butter,
   softened
$^{1}/_{2}$ teaspoon vanilla extract
2 tablespoons cornstarch
$1^{1}/_{2}$ cups boiling water

NOTES

• Mace is the thin rust-colored veins that encase the nutmeg seed, ground to a powder.

• Nectarines and plums are delightful additions to this lustrous cobbler.

• The sugary topping cooks down into the crust to form a tender, glossy glazed top.

Preheat the oven to 350°F.

Spread the blueberries in a 9 x 13-inch baking dish. Drizzle the lemon juice over the berries and set aside.

In a medium bowl, combine the flour, baking powder, $^{1}/_{2}$ teaspoon of the salt, the nutmeg, mace, $1^{1}/_{2}$ cups of the sugar, the milk, butter, and vanilla. Spoon over the berries and spread in an even layer.

In a small bowl, combine the remaining $1^{1}/_{2}$ cups sugar, the remaining $^{1}/_{2}$ teaspoon salt, and the cornstarch. Sprinkle this mixture over the batter. Pour the boiling water evenly over the top of the cobbler. Poke a few holes down in the batter with the handle of a wooden spoon. Bake for 1 hour or until the top is golden brown, frosted, and shiny. Serve warm or at room temperature.

Dewberry Dumplings
Worth the Scratches

• • •

All along fence posts in the Mississippi countryside, brambles droop with dark fruits in the height of summer. Dewberries, a member of the rose family, are low–bush black-berries that grow wild and are some of the first blackberries of the season. A bowl of sweet warm dumplings and purple preserves with a little cream poured over the top is worth the scrapes you may get from jumping into the briar patch to pick the berries.

•   SERVES 12

6 cups fresh dewberries or
    frozen blackberries, thawed
2 cups sugar, or more to taste
4 tablespoons (^{1}/2 stick)
    unsalted butter
^{1}/4 teaspoon freshly grated
    nutmeg
^{1}/4 teaspoon ground cinnamon

Pinch of salt
1 tablespoon cornstarch
2 tablespoons orange juice
2 cups Baking Mix (opposite),
    Bisquick, or Pioneer
    baking mix
^{2}/3 cup whole milk
Heavy cream, for serving

In a Dutch oven, combine 4 cups of the berries, the sugar, butter, nutmeg, cinnamon, and salt. Cook over medium heat, stirring occasionally, until boiling. In a small bowl, combine the cornstarch and juice. Add to the blackberries and cook and stir for 1 minute, until the mixture is translucent.

In a medium bowl, using a fork, combine the baking mix and milk. Drop the mixture by tablespoonfuls into the simmering berries. Cook over low heat, covered, turning the dumplings occa-sionally, for 12 to 15 minutes, or until the dumplings are cooked through. Add the remaining 2 cups berries.

Serve warm in bowls with a little cream if you like.

NOTE

• Be sure to taste the berries once they have cooked down a bit and adjust the sweetness if necessary by adding a little more sugar. A few under-ripe berries will help thicken the sauce, as they have more pectin in them, but they are best when fully ripe. Some say they should be picked in the morning when still wet with dew.

BAKING MIX

This baking mix can be used in recipes in place of commercial baking mixes and makes a nice drop biscuit. • MAKES ABOUT 4 CUPS

2 cups unbleached all-purpose flour
1 cup cake flour
6 tablespoons nonfat powdered milk

2 tablespoons baking powder
1/2 teaspoon salt
1/2 cup vegetable shortening, cold

In a large bowl, combine the all-purpose and cake flours, the powdered milk, baking powder, and salt with a whisk. Using a pastry blender or your fingertips, work the shortening into the dry ingredients until no lumps remain. Store in an airtight canister for up to 1 month.

To make drop biscuits with this mix, combine 2¼ cups biscuit mix with ⅔ cup milk in a large bowl using a fork. Drop by tablespoons on a baking sheet. Bake at 375°F. for 8 minutes or until golden.

Summer Pudding
Too Hot to Cook

• • •

In the summer of 1953, my then elementary-school-age mother, Cindy Vaughan, and great-aunt, Carrye Vaughan Heard, attended the dedication of a memorial to Casey Jones. The wreck of the #382, a coal-fired freight train, has become an American folk tale from the Industrial Age. John Luther "Casey" Jones made his famous final run on April 29, 1900, and we all know it ended badly. My family members were attending the ceremony to represent the Vaughan family. My great, great, great-grandfather, Major Henry Vaughan, granted a right-of-way for a railway through the area in the 1830s in exchange for the promise of a depot.

The tale of the hot summer day has been told for years. That day my mother met the former Jane Brady, Mrs. Casey Jones. The eighty-one-year-old red-headed widow was overheard by just about everyone, saying about the master of ceremonies, "Tell him to sit down and shut his damn mouth! It's hot as hell out here!"

This refreshing, cool dessert doesn't require any baking so it is great if you can't stand the heat. • **SERVES 6**

3 cups raspberries
2 cups blueberries
1 cup hulled strawberries
1 cup sugar

1 (2-pound) loaf good white bread, crusts removed, sliced 1/2-inch thick
2 tablespoons raspberry liqueur

In a medium saucepan over medium heat, combine the raspberries, blueberries, strawberries, and sugar. Cook and stir for 5 to 7 minutes, or until the berries are juicy but still recognizable.

Line a 2-quart bowl with plastic wrap. Line the bottom and sides of the bowl with slightly overlapping slices of bread. Then repeat the overlapping in the opposite direction.

With a slotted spoon, layer the berries and bread in the lined bowl, making three layers. Top with a layer of bread. Stir the liqueur into the remaining juice from the berries. Pour over the final bread layer. Press plastic wrap over the surface of the pudding. Place a dish or pan directly on the pudding to weight it down. Set two 1-pound cans on top of the dish. Refrigerate for 24 hours.

When ready to serve, invert the pudding onto a platter with a rim to catch the juices.

NOTES

• Just about any combination of stone fruits and berries works here. Do watch the amount of strawberries, which can make the pudding too watery.

• The berries can be cooked in the microwave if it is too hot to even turn on the stove.

• Challah or egg bread can be used in place of the white bread here. Good Sandwich Loaf (page 175) can be used here.

• This old-fashioned dessert can be served with sweetened whipped cream or sherbet on top to add a creamy element.

Leontynes

Priceless Sweet Arias

• • •

Leontyne Price's voice has been described as able to soar to radiant high notes and plunge luxuriously into a vat of chocolate. Australians honored a favorite ballerina with the light meringue dessert Pavlova. I honor Laurel, Mississippi, born Ms. Price with these airy chocolate meringues.

Her debut performance with the Metropolitan Opera was met with a 42-minute standing ovation. Her career there, over the course of 21 seasons, included 201 performances, with 44 of them in Verdi's Aida. *I fell in love with her voice when I heard her sing "This Little Light of Mine."* • MAKES 12 SANDWICH COOKIES

³/₄ cup ground pecans	3 tablespoons granulated sugar
1¹/₄ cups confectioners' sugar	12 pecan halves
1¹/₂ tablespoons unsweetened cocoa powder	6 ounces semisweet chocolate, chopped
2 large egg whites	1 tablespoon unsalted butter

Preheat the oven to 325°F.

In a food processor fitted with the metal blade, combine the ground pecans and confectioners' sugar. Pulse until the mixture is a fine powder. Add the cocoa powder and pulse briefly to incorporate.

In an electric mixer, whip the egg whites at medium speed until frothy. Add the granulated sugar 1 tablespoon at a time, increasing the speed to high. Whip to form soft glossy peaks. With a large, flat spatula, fold the dry ingredients into the egg whites one-third at a time.

Drop by tablespoons onto parchment-lined baking sheets, spacing them 3 inches apart (about 24 cookies). Press a pecan half gently into the top of 12 of the meringues. Bake for 20 to 25 minutes, until set. Remove from the oven and transfer the parchment papers with the cookies onto a slightly damp counter, and let cool for 5 minutes. Peel the cookies off the paper and let cool on a rack while preparing the filling.

In a bowl set over simmering water, stir together the chocolate and butter until melted and smooth.

Spread the underside of one pecan-topped cookie with the chocolate mixture and press onto the flat side of a cookie with no pecan to form a sandwich. Repeat for the remaining cookies.

NOTES

• These cookies should not be refrigerated. They will keep for three or so days in an airtight container.

• Always outspoken, Ms. Price personified the name *diva*. She is credited with quite a few bons mots:

"We should not have a tin cup out for something as important as the arts in this country, the richest in the world. Creative artists are always begging, but always being used when it's time to show us at our best."

"The ultimate of being successful is the luxury of giving yourself the time to do what you want to do."

Ginger Molasses Cookies
Rolled in Sugar

• • •

We used to sell bags and bags of these cookies every day at Mockingbird Bakery. The key to getting them at their chewy best is keeping a close watch on them while they are in the oven and removing them from the hot pans straightaway to a cooling rack. Store them in an airtight container to keep them fresh. • MAKES 24 COOKIES

2³/4 cups unbleached
   all-purpose flour
1 teaspoon baking soda
¹/2 teaspoon salt
1¹/2 teaspoons ground ginger
1 teaspoon ground cinnamon
¹/2 teaspoon ground allspice
¹/4 teaspoon ground cloves

³/4 cup packed dark brown
   sugar
³/4 cup (1¹/2 sticks) unsalted
   butter, softened
1 large egg
³/4 cup molasses
1 cup granulated sugar

Preheat the oven to 350°F.

In a medium bowl, whisk together the flour, baking soda, salt, ginger, cinnamon, allspice, and cloves. In an electric mixer fitted with the paddle attachment, beat the brown sugar and butter at medium speed until light in color. Add the egg and molasses, and beat until well combined, scraping the bowl as necessary. Reduce the speed to low and slowly add the flour mixture. Scrape the bowl and mix for 1 minute at medium speed.

Form the dough into tablespoon-size balls. Roll each ball in granulated sugar and place 2 inches apart on a parchment-lined baking sheet. Bake for 10 to 12 minutes, until slightly brown and puffed. Transfer to a rack to cool.

NOTES

• Spray the measuring cup with a little nonstick spray before adding the molasses and the molasses will slip right out.

• A little bit of diced crystallized ginger pushed into the center of the cookies before they go in the oven dresses them up and adds a little zing.

• These cookies can be rolled in sugar, then frozen, and baked a few at a time right from the freezer for an afternoon coffee break pick-me-up. Increase the baking time to 15 minutes.

Dark Secrets

Fudge Squares

• • •

Deeply fudgy, these are beyond brownies. A thin undercoating of sugar adds a sweet sandy contrast to the moist bars. • MAKES 24 BARS

$^1/_2$ **cup (1 stick) unsalted butter**

6 ounces unsweetened chocolate

4 large eggs

$^1/_2$ **teaspoon fine sea salt**

2 cups sugar, plus extra for sprinkling

1 teaspoon vanilla extract

1 cup unbleached all-purpose flour, sifted

Preheat the oven to 325°F. Line a 9 x 13 x 2-inch pan with foil, extending the foil 4 inches past the edges of the pan to help remove the bars after baking.

Melt the butter and chocolate together in a double boiler or microwave. Stir well to combine, and then set aside to cool.

In a medium bowl, whisk together the eggs and salt. Gradually whisk in the 2 cups sugar and the vanilla until the mixture is light and smooth. Fold in the cooled chocolate mixture. Fold in the flour until no white streaks remain. Pour into the prepared pan. Bake for 30 minutes or until the smell catches your nose and the batter is set and does not move when pan is gently shaken.

Cool on a wire rack for 10 minutes. Run a knife around the edge of the pan. Gently lift the fudge squares out by the foil handles. Invert onto a baking sheet and peel off the foil. Sprinkle with a little granulated sugar and cut into 1$^1/_2$-inch squares. Place the squares sugar side down on a serving platter.

NOTES

• One cup of chopped nuts may be folded into the batter.

• At Christmas, coat the underside of the squares with crushed peppermint candy.

• These freeze very well, boxed with waxed paper between the layers.

• I know it's not nice, but my mother did it to me. When the kids want some of the baking chocolate and you tell them they won't like it and yet they still persist, go ahead and give them a nibble. Lesson learned—and they do make horribly funny faces.

Cordelia's Mother Gwen's Tea Cakes
Warm on Radiator

• • •

Miss Cordelia, my father's great-grandmother, was very old when I was little. The oldest person I knew, she made these cookies for me when I would come to visit. My father taught me to balance them on the radiator of her dimly lit living room to get them warm and soft. I have the letters she wrote me while I was away at summer camp, when I was eight. The writing was so shaky, barely legible. I felt shy around her, and I was never a shy child. I guess I felt a kind of reverence for her. I knew she had seen and known things that were long gone—like why these cookies were called "cakes."

• MAKES 48 COOKIES

1 teaspoon baking soda
2 teaspoons cream of tartar
2 teaspoons freshly grated
  nutmeg
About 3 cups unbleached
  all-purpose flour

1 cup (2 sticks) unsalted
  butter
2 cups sugar
3 large eggs

Preheat the oven to 375°F. Line a baking sheet with parchment paper or aluminum foil.

Sift the baking soda, cream of tartar, nutmeg, and 2 cups of the flour together.

In an electric mixer, beat the butter and sugar together until light and fluffy, about 4 minutes. Add the eggs one at a time, beating after each addition.

Slowly mix in the flour mixture. Continue to add additional flour until a soft dough is formed. Wrap the dough in plastic and chill for 30 minutes.

Roll out the dough to a thickness of about ¼ inch on a floured board, between pieces of parchment paper, or on a silicone rolling mat. Cut out 48 cookies with a 3-inch round biscuit cutter, gathering the scraps and rerolling as needed.

Place the dough rounds 2 inches apart on the prepared baking sheet and bake for 8 to 10 minutes, or until slightly brown around the edges. Be careful not to bake them too long as the cookies will harden when cooled.

NOTES

• For a softer, chewier cookie, substitute light brown sugar for the granulated sugar.

• Two teaspoons of poppy seeds and 1 teaspoon of grated lemon zest can be beaten into the dough with the butter and sugar.

• This recipe was originally written with no exact measurements. The ones given above were "calculated" in the 1920s by Mother Gwen's granddaughter, my great-grandmother "Momee," Susie Peaster Thompson.

Polka Dot Shortbread
All Butter

• • •

The secret to the sandy texture of this adorable shortbread is rice flour. Little dots of fruit jam and lemon curd dress up the tops and melt right into the buttery cookie.

- **MAKES 16 COOKIE WEDGES**

1³/₄ cups unbleached all-purpose flour
¹/₄ cup rice flour
¹/₂ cup sugar
¹/₂ teaspoon salt
1 cup (2 sticks) unsalted butter, cold, cut into small pieces

¹/₂ teaspoon vanilla extract
2 tablespoons seedless raspberry jam
2 tablespoons lemon curd

Preheat the oven to 325°F.

In a food processor fitted with the metal blade, blend the flours, sugar, and salt. Add the butter and vanilla and pulse several times to form a dough. Press the dough into an 8-inch tart pan with a removable bottom or into a ¹/₄-inch-thick round on a parchment-lined baking sheet. Score the dough to mark 16 wedges. Bake for 10 minutes.

Meanwhile, fill two small piping bags or sandwich bags with the jam and lemon curd.

Remove the shortbread from the oven. With a wooden dowel or spoon handle, make small divots around the surface of the dough, pressing about halfway through the dough. Fill some dots with a small squirt of jam and some with a small squirt of lemon curd. Return to the oven and bake for 10 more minutes, or until golden around the edges. Be careful not to let them get too dark; just the edges should begin to brown. Cool in the pan on a rack.

Remove from the pan and cut along the scored marks.

NOTES

- Use a top-quality butter or European-style or organic cultured butter for the freshest butter flavor.

- This basic dough is wonderful baked without the dots, but can also be flavored many ways. Try adding ¹/₄ teaspoon lemon, orange, or mint extract in place of the vanilla.

- Look for lemon and lime curd in the jam section at the market. Apricot jam and seedless blackberry jam are also a good combination.

- If making these on a baking sheet, press the outer edge with the tines of a fork to decorate.

- This shortbread keeps well in a tin and ships well, too.

Simply Cake
Basic Pound Cake

• • •

She simply lost her mind. I had simply had enough. It was a simply beautiful wedding. These are a few examples of how my mother can use the word "simply" in a variety of ways. My mother uses the word more than any person I know. This is what she makes when she simply wants some cake.

Mrs. Mildred Nicholas gave my mother this recipe. Mrs. Nicholas had made one for my father just about every time she came to his office for a doctor's visit. When her illness seemed to be worsening, she brought my mother the recipe and told her how she knew Michael loved that pound cake, and she would hate for him not to have any once she was gone. It is simply a wonderful pound cake and Mrs. Nicholas was simply a lovely lady. • MAKES ONE 10-INCH CAKE

NOTES

• To make chocolate pound cake, add $1/4$ cup unsweetened cocoa powder to the flour before sifting.

• Do not mix at a high speed after the eggs are added. The cake will have tunnels and be tough, if you do.

• If the cake begins to brown too much, tent with foil.

3 cups unbleached all-purpose flour
$1/2$ teaspoon salt
$1/2$ teaspoon baking powder
1 cup (2 sticks) unsalted butter, softened
$1/2$ cup vegetable shortening

3 cups sugar
1 teaspoon vanilla extract
1 teaspoon lemon extract
1 teaspoon almond extract
5 large eggs
1 cup whole milk

Preheat the oven to 325°F. Grease and flour a 12-cup (10-inch) tube pan.

Sift together the flour, salt, and baking powder.

In an electric mixer, beat the butter, shortening, and sugar at medium speed until fluffy. Add the vanilla, lemon, and almond extracts. Reduce the speed and add the eggs one at a time, beating well between additions; do not overmix. Add the flour mixture alternately with the milk, ending with the milk.

Spoon the batter into the prepared pan and tap lightly on the counter to level. Bake for 1 hour and 20 minutes, until a skewer inserted comes out clean. Cool in the pan on a rack for 10 minutes. Tip the cake out of the pan and continue to cool completely on the rack.

Brown Sugar Angel Food Cake
The Bride Wore Ecru

• • •

My grandmother Elsie was very ill when I returned from cooking school in France. Her dear friends Tot, Virginia, and Dicey wrote and called every day, as she slowly succumbed out at my parents' farmhouse, Gumgrove. She was not really up to visitors.

A call each day at eleven o'clock went like this: "Martha? Virginia. How's Elsie?" Reports would follow, met always with many "best of wishes" and "keep us posted." As Elsie was quite tired of our hovering and lack of gossip, a tea party was planned.

The "girls" (Tot, Virginia, and Dicey, all in their seventies) came out, and with Elsie propped on pillows with a lap robe and turban, we all took high tea, with silver service polished on the sideboard. I made this cake, and the conversation was light and breezy. We were admiring some of my mother's needlework when Virginia chimed in, "Next time I marry, Cindy, I want you to make my wedding dress. Something with a high yoke." "Oh, Virginia!" exclaimed Tot. "Not a high yoke! Why, everyone will think you **had** *to get married!"*

This cake has a lovely ecru color and is perfect for tea parties, served with lemon curd and fresh berries. • MAKES ONE 10-INCH CAKE

1^1/$_2$ cups cake flour	14 large egg whites
1^1/$_4$ cups packed light brown sugar	1 teaspoon cream of tartar
	1^1/$_2$ teaspoons vanilla extract
1^1/$_2$ teaspoons salt	^{1}/$_4$ teaspoon almond extract

Preheat the oven to 350°F. Sift together the flour, brown sugar, and salt twice onto a piece of waxed paper or parchment.

In an electric mixer, whip the egg whites on low speed until frothy. Add the cream of tartar, increase the speed, and whip until the whites hold soft peaks. Whip in the vanilla and almond extracts.

Transfer the whites to a large mixing bowl. Sift the flour and brown sugar mixture over the whites in three additions, folding them in with a large, flat rubber spatula.

Turn the batter into an ungreased 12-cup angel food cake pan. Bake for 20 minutes, or until the cake springs back when touched. Remove from the oven, invert the mold, and let cool in the pan. Run a thin knife around the sides of the pan. Unmold the cake and transfer to a cake stand or serving platter.

NOTES

• If you know you are going to make this cake ahead of time, separate the eggs the day before and you will have a higher cake.

• Allow the whites to come to room temperature before whipping and they will whip up nicer.

• Do not overwhip the whites. Whip them only to a soft peak stage. If the whites are too stiff, the cake will not rise and the texture will be crumbly instead of tender and nice. Carefully fold in the dry ingredients. Turning the bowl as you fold makes incorporating them easier.

• Cooling this cake upside down keeps it from falling in and getting squishy in the center. Angel food cake should cling to the sides of the pan to help it keep its shape.

• If your tube pan has legs on the top rim, just turn it upside down. If it does not, hang it over the neck of a full bottle.

• Use leftovers for bread pudding or make a trifle with them.

Darkness on the Delta
Cool Bittersweet Dessert

• • •

The lyrics to "Darkness on the Delta" are painted on the risers of the stairs that come down into my home kitchen. The wall next to the old barrel-house piano off the living room is papered with faded copies of sheet music for the song by Mildred Bailey; Author Tracy, "Street Singer of the Air"; Paul Whiteman's Rhythm Boys (No, I did not make that name up); Ambrose and his Mayfair Orchestra; and Yazoo City's own Herbie Holmes and his Orchestra. If this flood plain had an anthem, this song would be it. As the song drifts to a conclusion, it trails off with the aspiration "When it's darkness on the delta, let me linger 'neath the shelter of the night."

This deep, dark-as-night fudgy dessert is a cool ending to a dinner party on a starry evening. • SERVES 8

NOTES

• I like to stencil sugar stars across this cake, using a piece of cardboard with a cutout in it as a guide.

• Be aware that egg yolks should not sit in sugar too long. The sugar will sort of "cook" the yolk and make it grainy.

• This dessert can be frozen, well wrapped, for a month.

7 ounces bittersweet chocolate, chopped
²/₃ cup whole milk
¹/₃ cup plus 1 tablespoon granulated sugar
Freshly grated nutmeg
1 large egg yolk

1 cup (2 sticks) unsalted butter, softened
1 teaspoon vanilla extract
1 teaspoon Bourbon
Unsweetened cocoa powder, for serving
Confectioners' sugar, for serving

Put the chocolate in a large bowl and set aside.

In a saucepan over medium heat, bring the milk, ¹/₃ cup granulated sugar, and a little nutmeg to a simmer. In a small bowl, whisk together the egg yolk and remaining 1 tablespoon granulated sugar. Slowly whisk in half of the milk mixture. Return the entire mixture to the saucepan and cook over low heat, stirring constantly, until the mixture thickens; about 5 minutes. Do not boil.

Pour the hot mixture over the chopped chocolate. Let sit for 2 minutes. Slowly whisk in the butter a little at a time, and then add the vanilla and Bourbon. Whisk until the mixture is very smooth.

Spray a 6-inch cake pan with nonstick cooking spray, and line with plastic wrap. Scrape the mixture into the pan and smooth with a spatula. Cover with plastic wrap and freeze for at least 6 hours.

When ready to serve, invert the cake onto a serving plate and remove the plastic wrap. Dust with cocoa and confectioners' sugar.

THE LANGUID MELODY of "Darkness on the Delta" was used as the theme song for a young Willie Morris's radio show in Yazoo City. Willie wrote two coming-of-age stories that were adapted for the big screen—*Good Ole Boy* and *My Dog Skip*. My friend Willie loved his hometown, and many late nights he would recount tales of boyhood adventures to me. His eyes would always get a little full—not teary, more like puddled up with memories. Although a sentimental fool, Willie was wise to the ways of the world. He studied at Oxford University and went on to become editor of the *Texas Observer*. During his tenure as senior editor at *Harper's* magazine in the turbulent late 1960s, Willie challenged the nation and the region to take a look at his homeland, in a special supplement, "The South Today."

In 1971, the *New York Times Book Review*'s Dan Wakefield wrote, "In the deepest sense we all live in Yazoo. Mr. Morris' triumph is that he has made us understand that."

"Darkness on the Delta" was written by Marty Symes and Al J. Neiburg, with music by Jerry Levirson. Cassandra Wilson has an amazing arrangement of the song.

Fresh Coconut Layer Cake
For Mr. Joseph

• • •

My son is the namesake of a fine man, Mr. Joseph Newton. He was a caring man who lived to see all the children he raised raise their children, who in turn had children of their own. He passed at 96 this year. He had sapphire eyes and a lined face the color of a walnut shell. He taught me most of what I know about the difference between right and wrong. He also taught me how to crack a coconut.

When I was little, I would spend a lot of time with Joseph during the Christmas break from school. Every year, he would take the life-size, bulbous, light-up, plastic nativity-scene figures out of their burlap sacks down from the rafters in the back house behind my great-grandmother's home. I enjoyed this holiday ritual immensely. Our other duty at Christmastime was to crack coconuts for ambrosia and coconut cake.

Every time I make this cake I think of Mr. Joseph. • MAKES ONE 8-INCH LAYER CAKE

1 coconut, cracked, half shaved and half grated, with the liquid strained and reserved
2 1/4 cups sugar
3 cups cake flour
2 teaspoons baking powder
3/4 teaspoon salt
1 large egg

1/2 cup whole milk
1 cup (2 sticks) unsalted butter, softened
1 teaspoon vanilla extract
1 teaspoon coconut extract
5 large egg whites
Seven-Minute Frosting (see page 226)

In a small saucepan over medium-high heat, combine the coconut liquid with 1/2 cup water and 1/2 cup of the sugar. Bring the mixture to a boil, stirring occasionally, and reduce to a thin syrup, about 6 minutes. Remove from the heat and set aside to cool.

Preheat the oven to 350°F. Grease and flour three 8-inch round cake pans and set aside.

Toast the shaved coconut on a baking sheet in the oven for 5 minutes, or until the edges begin to brown ever so slightly.

Sift together the flour, baking powder, and salt. In a small bowl, whisk together the egg and milk.

In an electric mixer fitted with the paddle attachment, beat the butter, remaining 1 3/4 cups sugar, and the extracts until fluffy. Add

NOTES

• This is how Joseph taught me to crack and prepare a coconut. First, hold the coconut with a rag. Take an ice pick or a large nail and with a hammer, tap a hole in the center of each black eye. Shake the water out into a bowl. Now, wrap the coconut in the rag. Set it on the concrete and knock it with the hammer several times sharply. Take the broken pieces of coconut and put them in a hot oven for 15 minutes. Remove from the oven, wrap in a clean dish towel, and tap several times with the hammer. Using a flat-head screwdriver, pop the coconut meat out of the shell. With a sharp vegetable peeler, remove the brown skin and shave half of the meat into thin strips and grate the rest.

• Two cups shredded sweetened coconut and a 15-ounce can of sweetened cream of coconut (like Coco Lopez) can be substituted for the fresh coconut in this recipe.

• The cake can be baked, wrapped in plastic, and frosted the next day.

• This cake keeps well for several days, covered with a cake dome.

See photograph page 194.

the flour mixture alternately with the egg mixture and mix until combined.

In a clean bowl, whip the egg whites until they hold soft peaks. Fold the whipped egg whites by thirds into the batter. Divide the batter among the prepared pans. Bake for 25 to 30 minutes, or until a toothpick inserted in the center comes out with a few moist crumbs attached. Set on a rack to cool in the pans for 10 minutes. Tip the cakes out of the pans and cool completely.

Place one cake layer on a serving platter. With the handle of a wooden spoon, poke several holes around the cake. Pour one-third of the coconut syrup over cake. Spread with some of the frosting and sprinkle with some of the grated coconut. Repeat with the second and third cake layers. Frost the sides with the remaining frosting and press the toasted coconut into the sides of the cake.

The Devil's Own
Red Velvet

• • •

Most red velvet cakes involve at least $^1/_4$ cup of red food coloring and have a cake-mix-ishness about them. This red-tinged cake gets its color naturally. I love the contrasts of textures in this updated version of chewy cake and fluffy, crisp seven-minute frosting.

The frosting recipe requires a hand-held electric mixer or a partner to trade off with during the whisking. • MAKES ONE 9-INCH CAKE

CAKE

Unsweetened cocoa powder, for dusting
1 cup buttermilk
1³/4 cups packed dark brown sugar
5 ounces bittersweet chocolate, chopped
3 large egg yolks
1/2 cup (1 stick) unsalted butter, softened
1³/4 cups unbleached all-purpose flour
1 teaspoon baking soda
3 large egg whites

SEVEN-MINUTE FROSTING

2 large egg whites
1¹/2 cups sugar
1/4 teaspoon cream of tartar
1¹/2 teaspoons light corn syrup
1 teaspoon vanilla extract

NOTES

• If you do not have an electric hand-held mixer, you may want to frost the cake with your favorite cream cheese icing instead of making the seven-minute frosting.

• This is also a tasty snack cake without the frosting, and it keeps for almost a week in an airtight tin. Frosted, the cake will keep for two days if it is not too humid.

MAKE THE CAKE. Preheat the oven to 350°F. Butter a 9-inch springform pan and dust it lightly with cocoa powder; set aside.

In a medium saucepan over very low heat, combine 1/2 cup of the buttermilk, 3/4 cup of the brown sugar, and the chocolate. Cook and stir until the chocolate is melted and the mixture is smooth. Add one of the egg yolks and cook and stir until the mixture thickens, about 2 minutes. Transfer the mixture to a mixing bowl.

In an electric mixer fitted with the paddle attachment, beat the butter and remaining 1 cup brown sugar until light and fluffy, about 4 minutes.

In a small bowl, whisk together the remaining 2 egg yolks and remaining 1/2 cup buttermilk.

Add the flour alternating with the buttermilk mixture, beating at low speed. Mix until just combined. Stir in the cooled chocolate mixture. Dissolve the baking soda in 1 tablespoon of warm water and fold into the mixture.

Whip the egg whites to soft peaks. Fold the whites into the chocolate batter. Pour into the prepared pan and bake for 50 minutes, or until a toothpick inserted in the center comes out clean.

Run a thin knife around the sides of the pan. Cool on a wire rack for 20 minutes. Remove the sides of the pan and cool completely.

MAKE THE FROSTING. In a large bowl set over a saucepan filled with 2 inches of simmering water, combine the egg whites, sugar, 5 tablespoons water, the cream of tartar, and corn syrup. Whip with a hand-held electric mixer, scraping the sides often with a rubber spatula, for 7 minutes or until the frosting is a nice spreading consistency. Stir in the vanilla.

When the cake has cooled completely, frost it all around with the warm frosting. Allow to cool for 30 minutes before serving.

Commitment Caramel Cake
For Committing Someone to the Church,
Marriage, or the Ground

• • •

I know a guy who has one suit. He calls it his commitment suit. It is for all occasions that call for sincere solemnity. The caramel layer cake is the worsted-wool suit of cakes: it is appropriate for any and all occasions.

Some fine cooks shy away from making caramel cake owing to the intimidation factor of caramel icing. Although this is not the most traditional method, it uses marshmallows to keep the mixture spreadable and produces good results for beginners. Use a thermometer and work with a sense of urgency with the icing, and you will be fine. • MAKES ONE 9-INCH LAYER CAKE

NOTES

• You can set the frosting bowl on a heating pad, or in a bowl of hot water, to keep it at a nice spreading consistency.

• Caramel icing can sense fear. Do not psych yourself out and it will be perfect.

• Tuck pieces of waxed paper under the edge of the cake to protect the serving plate. Remove them before presenting the cake.

CAKE
8 large eggs
1 cup whole milk
1 tablespoon vanilla extract
$^1/_2$ teaspoon almond extract
$2^1/_2$ cups cake flour
3 cups sugar
4 teaspoons baking powder
1 teaspoon salt
2 cups (4 sticks) unsalted
  butter, softened

CARAMEL FROSTING
1 cup (2 sticks) unsalted
  butter
$^3/_4$ cup buttermilk
$2^1/_2$ cups sugar
1 tablespoon plus 1 teaspoon
  corn syrup
$^1/_2$ teaspoon salt
$1^1/_4$ teaspoons baking soda
15 marshmallows
1 tablespoon vanilla extract

MAKE THE CAKE. Preheat the oven to 350°F. Spray two 9-inch round cake pans with nonstick spray and line the bottoms with parchment paper. Lightly spray the parchment paper. Set aside.

In a small bowl, combine the eggs, milk, and vanilla and almond extracts; set aside.

In an electric mixer fitted with the paddle attachment, sift together the flour, sugar, baking powder, and salt. With the mixer on low speed, add the butter a tablespoon at a time and blend until a shaggy mass is formed. Slowly add half of the egg mixture. Mix on low speed until smooth. Increase the speed to medium and slowly add the remaining egg mixture, scraping the bowl as needed. Mix until well blended.

Divide the batter between the prepared pans. Tap lightly on the counter to level. Bake for 20 to 25 minutes, or until the cakes spring back lightly when touched in the center. Remove to wire racks for 10 minutes to cool. Tip the cakes out of the pans and let cool completely right side up.

Slice each cake layer in half horizontally to form two layers of cake.

MAKE THE FROSTING. In a heavy-bottomed pot over low heat, combine the butter, buttermilk, sugar, corn syrup, salt, and baking soda. Stir constantly until the sugar is dissolved. Add the marshmallows. Cook and stir until the mixture reaches 238°F. on a candy thermometer. Remove from the heat and stir in the vanilla.

With an electric mixer, beat the caramel until it begins to get cloudy and opaque, about 4 minutes. Working quickly, spread the frosting between the cake layers and then ice the surface of the cake. Let stand for at least 1 hour before serving.

Ponchatoula Strawberry Cupcakes
Really Pink

• • •

The scent from a flat of Louisiana strawberries will fill a room. And I do think the small, deep red berries are profoundly the sweetest around. California ones seem too big and watery, and can be almost hollow when you bite into them. Florida's are pretty good and have a nice color, but can be a little insipid. They must keep the good ones for themselves.

These little cakes draped with pink, red-specked frosting are full of the springtime taste of ripe strawberries. • MAKES 24 CUPCAKES

CUPCAKES

2¹/₂ cups cake flour
1 teaspoon baking soda
¹/₄ teaspoon salt
¹/₃ cup buttermilk
¹/₄ cup canola oil
¹/₂ teaspoon almond extract
1 teaspoon vanilla extract
¹/₂ cup (1 stick) unsalted
  butter
1¹/₂ cups granulated sugar
2 large eggs
1 cup mashed fresh or frozen
  strawberries
1 teaspoon grated orange zest

FROSTING

¹/₂ cup chopped fresh or
  frozen strawberries
2 tablespoons strawberry jam
1 teaspoon fresh lemon juice
1 (8-ounce) package cream
  cheese, softened
1¹/₂ cups (3 sticks) unsalted
  butter, softened
4 cups confectioners' sugar,
  sifted

MAKE THE CUPCAKES. Preheat the oven to 350°F. Spray a muffin tin with nonstick cooking spray or line with foil baking cups.

In a medium bowl, sift together the flour, baking soda, and salt. In another medium bowl, combine the buttermilk, oil, and almond and vanilla extracts; set aside.

In an electric mixer, beat the butter and granulated sugar until light and fluffy. Add the eggs one at a time, beating well after each addition. Gradually add the buttermilk mixture. Beat for 1 minute at medium speed.

Recipe continues.

NOTES

• Strawberries are an aggregate fruit, meaning the seeds are on the outside.

• Like many other fruits, strawberries do not ripen any more once picked.

• Wash strawberries right before you eat them. If damp when stored, they will mold and their skin will toughen.

• If the strawberry jam mixture seems runny, cook for 5 more minutes.

• Frosting beaten at too high a speed will be full of air bubbles and not have a smooth finish when spread.

• These may be baked in paper, foil, or silicone liners, if desired.

• Strawberry seedlings are planted in September in Louisiana for an early spring harvest. The 2005 Louisiana strawberry crop was almost decimated by flocks of cedar waxwings. In some areas the birds ate 50 percent of the crop, getting so fat some could not fly more than 50 feet.

• Tangipahoa Parish in Louisiana is home to a wonderful Strawberry Festival each April.

Reduce the speed to low and add the flour mixture. Mix until just combined. Stir in the strawberries and orange zest. Spoon into the prepared muffin tins, filling them two-thirds full. Bake for 18 to 20 minutes, or until the cupcakes spring back when touched lightly in the center. Cool in the pans for 10 minutes, then unmold the cupcakes and cool on racks.

MAKE THE FROSTING. In a small saucepan over medium heat, combine the strawberries, jam, and lemon juice. Cook and stir for 5 minutes, or until the jam is melted and the strawberries are soft. Press any big pieces with the back of the spoon to mash.

In an electric mixer fitted with the paddle attachment, mix the cream cheese and butter at medium speed until creamy. At low speed, slowly add the confectioners' sugar and mix until combined. Add the strawberries and mix at low speed until blended.

When the cupcakes are completely cool, spread with the frosting.

Father's Divinity

Confections with a Priest

• • •

The Southern Christmas season does not pass without these crisp, divine, white snow-drift mounds of whipped sugar candy.

The best advice I can give for making divinity is to pray. Even if you're not the praying type, and you are alone when you make this candy, you will most likely say under your breath, "Please, let this turn out" to some higher power.

I have a friend who is a priest and a hell of a cook, a funny kind of guy. He has a touch of Ignatius J. Reilly about him, although he recognizes his eccentricities. I dial him up over the holidays, when I make this recipe, to ask him to put in a good word for a low-humidity day, which is asking a lot in the South. • MAKES ABOUT 36 PIECES

3 cups sugar
1/2 cup light corn syrup
1/3 cup hot water
3 large egg whites

1/2 teaspoon salt
1/2 teaspoon vanilla extract
1/4 teaspoon almond extract

In a heavy-bottomed 3-quart saucepan over medium heat, bring the sugar, corn syrup, and water to a boil. Stir constantly until the sugar is dissolved. Cover and reduce the heat to low. Cook for 5 minutes.

Uncover and cook without stirring until the mixture reaches 270°F. on a candy thermometer. While the sugar is cooking, whip the egg whites, salt, and vanilla and almond extracts in an electric mixer at medium speed until they hold soft peaks.

With the mixer running, slowly pour the hot syrup into the whites. When the syrup is almost all incorporated, increase the speed to high. Do not scrape the bowl. Whip until the whites are glossy and hold their shape well. Using a couple of spoons, drop the fluffy candy mixture onto waxed paper, forming small round mounds. Leave alone to cool and dry for at least 1 hour.

NOTES

• Do not attempt this recipe on a rainy day.

• The candy can be divided after whipping, with part getting some nuts, some a little coloring to tint it pink and candied cherries folded in, some crushed lemon drops or peppermint sticks, and some left plain.

• If the candy begins to harden and is hard to shape, stir in a little hot water until it is soft enough to form.

Cream Puffs

Tap Dancing at Hattie B's

• • •

From her little Water Street café in Yazoo City, Miss Hattie B. kept the town supplied with light-as-a-cloud cream puffs. They were her specialty. Little girls would delight in receiving one if they tap danced on the counter to delight her. • MAKES 12 CREAM PUFFS

NOTES

• The water and butter must be at a full rolling boil before adding the flour or the paste will be greasy.

• If baking on parchment paper instead of a greased sheet, dab a little paste under the corners of the paper to hold it down.

• Dip your finger in water and press down any peaks in the dough before baking.

• For éclairs, pipe 5-inch-long $^1/_2$-inch-wide strips.

• For a chocolate filling, stir $^1/_2$ cup semisweet chocolate chips into the hot custard until melted.

• Rub a little cold butter across the surface of the hot custard to prevent a skin from forming.

• The empty puffs can be stored in an airtight container for a day.

• The filling custard base can be made a day ahead and refrigerated, and the whipped cream folded in right before filling.

PUFFS

1 cup unbleached all-purpose flour
$^1/_4$ teaspoon salt
6 tablespoons ($^3/_4$ stick) unsalted butter
4 large eggs

FILLING

2 cups whole milk
1 cup granulated sugar
$^1/_2$ cup unbleached all-purpose flour
2 large eggs
$^1/_2$ teaspoon vanilla extract
$^1/_2$ cup heavy cream
Confectioners' sugar, for dusting

MAKE THE PUFFS. Preheat the oven to 400°F. Lightly grease a baking sheet.

Sift together the flour and salt in a bowl.

In a medium saucepan, bring 1 cup water and the butter to a boil over medium-high heat. Add the flour all at once. Beat with a wooden spoon for 1 minute. The mixture will form a ball and leave a thin film in the bottom of the pan.

Remove from the heat and transfer to an electric mixer fitted with the paddle attachment. Beat the paste until it is no longer steaming, about 6 minutes. Add the eggs one at a time, beating after each addition.

Drop by tablespoonfuls onto the prepared baking sheet. Bake for 15 minutes.

Reduce the oven temperature to 325°F. and bake for 20 minutes, or until no beads of sweat are on the surface. Remove from the oven and cut a small slit in each puff for steam to escape. Let cool completely.

MAKE THE FILLING. Fill a large bowl halfway with ice water.

In a small saucepan, bring $1^{1}/_{2}$ cups of the milk to a boil over medium heat.

Meanwhile, in a small bowl, combine the sugar and flour. Slowly whisk in the remaining $^{1}/_{2}$ cup milk until smooth. Whisk in the eggs.

Reduce the heat under the milk so that the milk simmers and then slowly whisk in the egg mixture. Cook and stir until the mixture is very thick and boils for 1 minute. Remove from the heat and stir in the vanilla. Cool the mixture in the ice bath, whisking frequently. When cool, remove from the ice bath and refrigerate for 1 hour.

Whip the cream and then fold it into the custard. Fill the puffs and dust the tops with confectioners' sugar.

• To put the filling in the cream puffs, either slice in half and spoon filling onto the bottom half, then replace the top half; or fill a piping bag with the filling, fit with an open tip, and pipe into the slits in the puffs.

Swimming Pool Orange Sherbet
Kids Turn the Crank

• • •

I have a plug-in ice cream machine now, but I am on the lookout for one with a crank, just like the one we had when I was a kid. There are 15 first cousins on my mother's side of the family, so there were always plenty of kids to share the cranking. The miraculous transformation from a clotty-looking juice mixture to smooth sherbet thrills me still. I just love the whole process and accoutrements.

The smell of suntan oil (before the knowledge of SPF), chlorine, and oranges with a hint of salt air like the beach is how cold smells in summer. • MAKES 1 QUART

1½ cups sugar
2 cups water
Pinch of salt
2 cups fresh orange juice

2 tablespoons fresh lemon
 juice
2 cups whole milk, cold

Boil the sugar, 2 cups water, and the salt until you have 2 cups of syrup. Remove from the heat and let cool to room temperature.

Add the orange juice and the lemon juice to the syrup mixture.

Pour the chilled milk into an ice cream freezer container and then add the juice mixture. If the milk curdles slightly when the juice mixture is added, don't worry. It freezes smooth.

Freeze using the manufacturer's instructions. When firm, transfer the sherbet to the freezer. Allow it to harden for at least 30 minutes.

Buttermilk Peach Ice Cream
Chilton and Smith County Bounties

• • •

Chilton County, Alabama, produces some good peaches; I will pull over for the guy on the side of the road with the sign on his truck that says "Alabama peaches." Georgia is mighty proud of theirs, but I will brake for Alabama peaches. Closer to home, Smith County, Mississippi, makes a fine showing every year, whose fruits I enjoy in this ice cream at the height of summer. • MAKES 1 QUART

$1^1/_2$ teaspoons unflavored
   gelatin
1 cup buttermilk
$1/_2$ cup sugar
2 cups heavy cream

1 large egg yolk
Pinch of salt
$1^1/_2$ teaspoons vanilla extract
1 cup pureed ripe peaches,
   cold

Fill a large mixing bowl half full of ice. Set aside.

In a large saucepan, sprinkle the gelatin over the buttermilk. Whisk in the sugar. Over low heat, cook and stir until the gelatin and sugar are dissolved. Add the cream and whisk well. Whisk in the egg yolk, salt, and vanilla. Cook over low heat, stirring constantly, until the mixture reaches 160°F. Transfer the mixture to a metal bowl and nestle it down in the ice water. Cool the mixture in this ice bath until completely cooled, stirring often.

When ready to freeze, add the peaches and follow the ice cream maker's instructions.

NOTES

• Peaches will soften but not gain sweetness after being picked. Ripe peaches should yield softly to pressure and smell very sweet and peachy.

• Three-quarters of a cup of chopped strawberries can be used in place of the peaches.

• Add a couple of fresh peach leaves to the custard as it warms to give a perfume to the ice cream. Discard them before churning.

Southern Comfort Caramel
Dress Up Store-Bought Cake

• • •

I adore this sauce paired with perfumey Gala apples. Sauté the apples in a little butter and get them situated on top of pound cake with a pour of this sauce. Simply Cake (page 220) soaks this sauce up comfortably. • MAKES 3 CUPS

• Use a heavy-bottomed skillet such as a cast-iron pan to caramelize the sugar. It provides even heat and reduces hot spots.

• Be careful! Caramel is very hot. If caramel gets on your skin, do not try to brush it off; run cold water over it immediately.

• Remove the pan from the heat and turn off the burner when adding the liquor. The fumes can ignite and shoot back into the bottle.

• The sauce can be stored in the fridge. If it gets grainy, heat and stir over low heat.

• Southern Comfort really gained recognition beyond the French Quarter in New Orleans, where it was concocted by M. W. Heron, when it was served at the New Orleans Cotton and Industrial Exposition in 1885. That popularity spread to Europe, when his liqueur was awarded a Gold Medal at the World Exposition in Paris in 1900.

• The makers of Southern Comfort say that today fewer than 10 people know the secret recipe, which contains peach, orange, and cinnamon flavors.

$2^1/2$ cups sugar
1 large egg
$^1/2$ cup (1 stick) unsalted butter

$^3/4$ cup half-and-half
1 teaspoon vanilla extract
$^1/2$ cup Southern Comfort

In a small skillet over medium heat, cook $^1/2$ cup of the sugar until caramelized and dark brown. Do not stir; instead, swirl the pan once the sugar stars to color to produce even browning.

Meanwhile, in a deep saucepan, combine the remaining 2 cups sugar, the egg, butter, half-and-half, and vanilla. Bring to a boil over medium heat.

Add the caramelized sugar to the boiling mixture. Stir rapidly and cook until the caramel dissolves. Remove from the heat, add the Southern Comfort, and stir. Be careful, as the mixture will sputter and spit when the caramel and Southern Comfort are added. Serve warm.

THE Southern Comfort Music Fund was established after Hurricane Katrina to help New Orleans musicians get back on their feet. To contribute to this charity, visit socomusicfund.org.

Vinegar Hot Fudge
Better Than Hasty Tasty

• • •

The Hasty Tasty is always hopping. It is a busy drive-in with burgers, corn dogs, ice cream floats, malts, and banana splits. It has been the site of thousands of softball-league victory celebrations and teenage flirtations.

This hot fudge sauce is better than most found at dairy bars, drive-ins, and soda fountains. The vinegar balances out the sweetness and using real good semisweet chocolate bumps up the flavor quite a bit. • MAKES 2 CUPS

½ cup packed dark brown
   sugar
¼ cup Dutch-process cocoa
   powder
¼ teaspoon salt
1 cup heavy cream
½ cup whole milk
1 cup dark corn syrup

3 ounces semisweet chocolate,
   finely chopped
2 tablespoons apple cider
   vinegar
1 teaspoon vanilla extract
2 tablespoons unsalted butter,
   cold

In a deep, heavy-bottomed saucepan, combine the brown sugar, cocoa, and salt. Whisk in the cream and milk. Over medium-high heat, bring the mixture to a simmer. Add the corn syrup, half of the chocolate, and the vinegar. Bring to a boil, stirring constantly with a heatproof silicone spatula, making sure to scrape the bottom and sides of the pot, until the temperature reaches 225°F. as measured on a candy thermometer. This will take 8 to 9 minutes that seem like forever.

Remove from the heat and stir in the remaining chocolate and the vanilla. Stir until the chocolate is completely melted and incorporated. Add the cold butter, whisking to combine. Cool slightly before serving.

NOTES

• The temperature will seem to stall out at around 175°F. Be patient and continue to boil until the temperature reaches 225°F. on the thermometer, or until the sauce forms a thin thread when drizzled across a cool plate.

• The sauce can be reheated in the microwave on high at 30-second intervals, stirring to heat evenly.

• Add your favorite liquor to the sauce for a sophisticated flavor; 2 tablespoons should do the trick.

Acknowledgments

THE SUPPORT OF SO MANY PEOPLE HAS MADE MY DREAM—A BOOK OF MY OWN—A REALITY.

I give my deep love, respect, and thanks to my cousin Louis Stigler Thompson. He is, as my grandmother Elsie said, "completely without guile." Louis and his brother William's fine stewardship of the land on Pluto Plantation has ensured that their children, along with my son and all the cousins coming up, will see the seasons change and admire their beauty out here. I thank them and their talented families. I'd like to thank their brother Robert L. Thompson—Bobby T.—for showing me what it is to take up a craft and commit to it. I give my humble appreciation to their mother, Mary Stigler Thompson, my unwavering great-aunt, for teaching me by example the true meaning of the word "endure."

My mother, Cynthia Yandell Vaughan Foose, has given of herself with unyielding love and understanding every day of my life, and I admire her intellect and grace.

For more than a decade I have shared my life with Donald Bender. He has stood behind me, beside me, and cleared paths before me. He is a fine baker and a fine father.

I am lucky to count as my friends and family some remarkable people. They have put up with me, and I cannot thank them enough: Jane Rule Burdine; Darby Ricketts; Taylor Bowen Ricketts; Fred Thompson; Ari Weinzweig; the Howorths; Cody Morrison; Ron Shapiro; Jamie and Kelly Kornegay; Shawn McCoy; Yolande Van Heerden; Solveig Tofte; Ernestine Williams; Duff Dorrough; the Jacobs Family; the Anderson Women; Mr. Richard Sanders; Lucy Neal; the Joseph Newton Family; Miguel and Olga Henderson and family; Cousin LeAnne Gault; Aunt Caroline and Uncle Jon Foose; my brother, Robert Foose; and my father, Michael Foose.

In my professional life I have been fortunate enough to work for and with some generous people: Sumi Chang, Malcolm and Hal White, Susan Spicer, Andi Bidwell, Nancy Silverton, Jackie Sheehan, Brian McCarthy, Cindy Ojyczk, and Felipe Flores. I learned a lot from y'all.

I would also like to acknowledge the support and work of the Center for the Study of Southern Culture, the Southern Foodways Alliance, and the Delta Center for Culture and Learning.

Fred and Margaret Carl, Carol Puckett, and my friends and colleagues at Viking Range Corporation have been quite patient. Thank you for your good works.

Thank you to Sharon Bowers, my agent, and Angela Miller for plucking me out of the Delta and believing I had at least one book in me.

Rica Allannic, my editor, thank you for teaching me how to write a book. Even after you figured out what you had gotten yourself into. And to Kathleen Fleury for tolerating my poor phone skills.

Without the informed photography of gentleman Ben Fink, the guidance of creative director Marysarah Quinn, and thoughtful design of Maggie Hinders, this would be a list of ingredients. Thank you for the thousands of words your colorful work added to this book.

I am beholden to all y'all.

Index

FREE PUBLIC LIBRARY UNION, NEW JERSEY

3 9549 00409 6450